Project:
# Happily
# Ever After

# Project:
# Happily
# Ever After

Saving Your Marriage
When the Fairytale Falters

Alisa Bowman

RUNNING PRESS
PHILADELPHIA · LONDON

9   8   7   6   5   4   3   2

Digit on the right indicates the number of this printing

Library of Congress Control Number: 2010935160

ISBN 978-0-7624-3901-0

Cover & Interior design by Joshua McDonnell
Cover illustration by Marc Burckhardt
Edited by Jennifer Kasius
Typography: Archer, Bembo, and Cheltenham

Running Press Book Publishers
2300 Chestnut Street
Philadelphia, PA 19103-4371

Visit us on the web!
www.runningpress.com

For Kaarina

# Introduction

You are okay. Really, you are.

You are even if you have not one ounce of desire to ever bed down with your spouse in this lifetime or the next.

You are even if several times a week, day, or hour you fantasize about your spouse conveniently dropping dead.

You are even if you have a long mental list of the people you will definitely date (or possibly marry) once your current spouse becomes your late spouse.

You are even if you dread the moment your spouse arrives home from work.

You are even if you can't think of a single thing to say to your spouse over dinner.

You are even if you can't for the life of you remember what possessed you to marry that dolt in the first place.

You are even if you've ranted about your spouse so often that your friends, siblings, and coworkers are taking bets regarding how long your marriage will last.

You are okay. You're exceptionally normal. In fact, you and your marriage are downright typical.

You, of course, worry that you are not okay. Indeed, you are probably worried that such thoughts, feelings, and experiences are a sign that you deserve the Worst Spouse of the Year Award.

And you worry about this because you think that you are alone. You assume that none of your friends, family members, coworkers, or acquaintances has ever planned their very healthy spouse's funeral. You assume that they are all just as attracted to their spouses now—after many years of marriage—as they were when they met.

You assume that they still believe that they married their soulmates.

You assume all of these things because no one talks about being stuck in a bad marriage. People don't talk about that dread of having one's spouse move into the spoon position, and of thinking, "Oh for the love of my sanity, please don't let him want to have sex tonight, or tomorrow night, or ever, really! Why can't I be the woman whose husband is in dire need of Viagra?"

And because people don't talk about it, it makes you feel so very alone, as if you are the only screwup on the planet who accidentally married the wrong person.

But you're not.

No, you're definitely not. For one, there's me. I've thought and felt and done all of those above-mentioned things, and so have pa-*lenty* of others.

For instance, there are the thousands of unhappily married folks who read my blog. I can't tell you how many of them have emailed me and thanked me for outing the death fantasy. I also can't tell you how many friends and acquaintances fessed up to similar thoughts, feelings, and experiences once I finally started talking about mine.

What I can tell you is this. It doesn't matter how bad your marriage is. You can probably make it better. It doesn't matter just how strongly you believe that you married the wrong person. You probably didn't. It doesn't matter if your mother-in-law has already declared your marriage hopeless and has asked for you to return that heirloom silver service. You can probably prove her wrong.

That's why I wrote this book—because I've been where you are right now. In 2007 I planned every detail of my divorce. I planned every detail of my very healthy husband's funeral, too. But then a friend told me that I needed to try harder—that I needed to try everything before giving up.

So I did. I read 12 marital improvement books, I interviewed happily married friends (all three of them), and I studied the research.

Within just four months my marriage went from a 2 on the Happily Married Scale to an 8 and I was renewing my wedding vows.

Now, I feel closer to my husband than I ever have, and not a day goes by that I don't mentally thank the friend who told me to try everything.

That's how I know there's hope for you. Heck, if my abysmally bad marriage could be saved, there is hope for nearly everyone's marriage.

But you want more than hope, don't you? You want a 100 percent guarantee. When I embarked on my marriage project, I wanted one of those, too. I wish I could give you one, but I can't. No one—not me, not your parents, not your marriage therapist, and not your spouse—can know for sure whether your personal project will lead you to Happily Ever After.

No, you have to take a leap of faith. But I can guarantee this. If you take that leap, your life will improve. You will become stronger, happier, more assertive, and more confident. You will not regret your project. Even if, in the end, it does not save your marriage, your project will save *you*.

Take the leap.

Try everything.

Start your Project: Happily Ever After.

# 1

## Once Upon a Time

### MAY 2007

**"I dreamt my lady came and found me dead"**

—William Shakespeare, *Romeo and Juliet*

I knew something was terribly wrong with my marriage when I planned my husband's funeral. I did it in late 2006 and early 2007, between Mark's fortieth and forty-first birthdays. At least 210 times that year, I fantasized about the day Röbi, one of Mark's closest friends, arrived at my door. His voice trembled as he said, "You'd better sit down. I've got bad news. There's no good way to tell you. Mark dropped dead of a heart attack 5 minutes ago. They tried everything. He's gone. I'm sorry." Röbi drove me to the hospital morgue. After viewing the body, I phoned Mark's parents.

I made the arrangements.

Mark would be cremated. His ashes would go into an urn until our daughter, Kaarina, was old enough to choose a location to scatter them. The funeral? No, it would not be held at a church or a funeral home, but rather at The Farmhouse, his favorite restaurant and the place where we'd first met. The mourners would enjoy Magic Hat #9, Stone, and Flemish sour, a few of Mark's favorite brands and varieties of beer. Chef Michael would make my husband's favorite foods, including the butternut squash soup, crusty rolls, and braised lamb. For dessert, there would be hand-stretched strudel. He loved that.

A cinematographer would record the event, filming friends and family as they told stories about Mark. Röbi, for instance, might talk about Mark's love of his bicycle. Taylor would say something interesting about Mark and his bike shop. Maybe Wood would come up with a drinking story. Ken might talk about their many road trips to Formula One races in Montreal. Jeff might mention something about rock climbing or kayaking. Chris could tell a story about Mark and his motorcycle. This film I would store away, somewhere secure, perhaps in the very safe where I kept our life insurance documents and passports. There it would stay until Kaarina was old enough to want to know more about Daddy. Then I would pull it out and let her watch it.

I always got stuck on the eulogy. What could I say? What should I say? It was appropriate to say something positive, of course, but I could only think of the negative. Perhaps I wouldn't say anything. Some widows are too distraught to talk, right? Wouldn't the other mourners notice my dry eyes, though? Wouldn't they think something was odd about my facial expression? Wouldn't the most perceptive among them think, "She's relieved"?

Mark, in reality, was much more likely to die of old age than of a heart attack. Heart disease did not run in his family. His grandmother had lived well into her nineties. Yet staying married until old age felt unbearable, and the alternative, divorce, was terrifying.

The D word—I didn't like to say that out loud. Would I be the first to break my family's tradition of staying married regardless of marital disharmony? My paternal grandparents had been married for more than sixty years. My maternal grandparents, despite how much they'd tormented one another, would probably have reached such a milestone, too, had my grandfather not died in his fifties. My parents had been together more than forty years, and so had Mark's.

Unlike the death fantasy, my divorce scenario was not artificial. It was a plan of escape. Mark and I would amicably share custody of our daughter. He would agree to take his 401(k), and I'd take mine. We'd split the other investments down the middle. He'd keep the waterbed. I'd take the queen we used in the guest room. He'd want the La-Z-Boy. I'd take the rocker. He'd get the leather sofas. I'd take the dining room set and the artwork. He could have the grill.

I'd take the dog, but, if needed, we could work out a custody arrangement. We both loved that dog.

I told myself that I would stay in the marriage until I found myself thinking about divorce every single day. I'd stay until the thought of losing half of our retirement savings to him felt less depressing than the thought of staying married to a man who didn't seem to love me. I'd stay until the idea of our two-and-a-half-year-old growing up in a broken home seemed healthier than the idea of her being raised by two parents who never smiled when they talked to one another, if they talked to one another at all. I'd stay until the notion of telling my parents that we were splitting seemed less uncomfortable than the notion of navigating family gatherings with him by my side.

It was Mother's Day of 2007 that changed everything.

That evening I traveled to New York City to have dinner with Deb, a close friend who was in town for a conference. I'd met Deb, a tall curly-haired brunette, years ago at a book club. We earned our livings as freelance medical writers. We were both workaholics, and over the years, we'd created an informal freelance writing support group. She and I were the only members. We took turns telling work stories that, after a couple glasses of wine, took on dramatic plot twists, lots of animated arm movements, and an incredible amount of laughter. No matter how bedraggled I felt walking into a restaurant for a dinner with Deb, I always felt happier and lighter when I left.

Deb was one of those people who could look at my face and read my thoughts. She would hear me say, "Everything's great. Everything's fine," and then say, "Cut the crap. Tell me the truth." She would listen to me vent for as long as it took for me to run out of steam, and then would ask me a single question that rendered me speechless. Deb had moved from just 20 minutes away from my house in Pennsylvania to Virginia a year earlier. I missed her dearly.

> True friends do not tell you what you want to hear. They are brave enough to tell you what you need to know.

As we waited for our table, we sat at the bar and sipped cabernet. Once at our table, we each ordered a flight of wine and a cheese plate. As we drained our glasses and neared the end of the cheese, we decided to get a bottle. Deb wrote a wine blog and had written a wine book. She was undecided between two wines. She reached into her purse, pulled out her cell, and dialed Keith, her husband, who knew even more about wine than she.

I listened to her talk. I watched her move her hands and smile. I thought about my marriage. I thought about my cell phone, the one that hadn't moved from my purse since my arrival hours before. I hadn't called my husband to tell him I had arrived safely. I had not checked to see how he was doing. I had not thought of him once.

Deb was telling Keith about the conference, about the hotel, and about the restaurant. They spoke as if they hadn't seen one another in weeks. They spoke as if they had so much to tell one another that they could easily talk all night, fall asleep, wake the next morning, and still find more to say.

I would not call Mark. Not now. Not later. Not the following day. I wouldn't because I feared I would hear a voice that was unhappy to hear mine. He would sound harried, as if he had one hundred and fifty more important things to do than to talk to me. I wanted what Deb and Keith had, but I wasn't at all confident that I could ever have it with Mark.

Deb closed her phone. She'd made a decision. She ordered. The wine arrived. Near the end of the bottle, she asked, "How's Mark?" and, in my drunkenness, I related the 7 million reasons why I was unhappily married. She listened.

"Our marriage is dead," I complained. "We have nothing to say to one another."

She nodded.

"Whenever I call him, he sounds unhappy to hear from me, as if I'm bothering him. I think he secretly hates me."

She nodded.

"He never helps with the parenting. He's never home. It's like I'm a single mother. I earn nearly all the money. I do all of the housework and 90 percent of the parenting. I'm exhausted. I can't go on much longer. I want to feel loved, and I don't think he loves me anymore."

"Why are you still together?" she asked.

"I'm only staying with him for Kaarina's sake," I said. "There's nothing left between us. If we didn't have her, we'd have nothing in common."

"You shouldn't stay together for your daughter," Deb said. "If you got divorced, she would be fine. My son was fine after my first husband and I split up. Lots of kids do just fine after divorce. You'll do more damage to her by staying in a loveless marriage than you will by getting out of one."

I asked, "How did you know it was time to give up?"

"I knew it was time when I suggested we try marital counseling and he wouldn't go. I'd run out of options," she said. "Have you tried everything? Have you tried marital counseling?"

There, the question that would leave me speechless. No, we hadn't tried that. Instead of marital counseling, I'd tried crying. I'd tried yelling things like, "Our marriage is in the toilet!" I'd tried saying things like, "I'm miserable in this marriage!" I had once mildly suggested that we try counseling, but I'd said it more as a threat ("We need marital counseling!") than a suggestion.

He'd replied, "If you really think we should try it, I guess I can make time for it." Neither of us had made time for it. I had a business card for a counselor. Had I not made the call because I secretly wanted my marriage to fail?

"You need to try everything," she told me as we paid the bill. "Promise me you will try everything. He probably just needs you to tell him what you want. Men are clueless. Never forget that."

Try everything to save your marriage, even things that you don't think will work. If everything doesn't work or your partner refuses to try anything, consider divorce. No one deserves to be stuck in a miserable marriage—not even you.

I promised.

The next morning, I woke with a wicked headache, a dry mouth, and a heart filled with hope. I was going to fix my marriage. I could do this. I really could. Deb was right.

Later that evening, I sat next to Mark. He was in his usual spot on the La-Z-Boy. The remote was nearby. His muddy green eyes were mesmerized by the motorcycle race unfolding in front of him on the TV. I looked at his thin blond hair, the creases on his sun-baked face, and the slight downturn of his lips.

What had happened to the carefree, grinning guy who'd once found himself hopelessly besotted with me? Where had he gone? Who was this stranger who now shared my bed? What had become of us?

I turned off the TV. I held my hands in my lap. I looked at him, and I said, "We've got problems. We haven't had sex in months. I think about either divorcing or killing you several times a day, sometimes several times an hour. I'm worried that, if we don't focus on fixing things, one of us is going to have an affair, and, I'm worried that the one of us most likely to have the affair is me."

I shed no tears. I made eye contact almost the whole time. I didn't raise my voice.

His features softened. The hardness I'd gotten so used to seeing was no longer there. He looked at me tenderly.

"You're having an affair?" he asked, his voice pinched, an octave higher than usual.

"No, I'm worried that I might. I feel sexy. I notice men looking at me. I want to feel loved, and I don't feel loved by you. I worry that, given the opportunity and a moment of weakness, I might turn to someone else to feel loved."

He asked, "Are you really that disappointed? Are things that bad?"

"Yes, I am. Yes, they are," I replied. "Don't you think so?"

"Things are hard right now. We just moved. Moving to a new home is stressful, but things will get better. Kaarina's getting older. Things will get easier. You'll see."

"No, Mark, they won't, not unless we make them better," I said. "If we don't work on things now, we're going to end up getting a divorce."

"What do you want?" he asked.

What I really wanted, I did not want to say. I wanted to be married to another man. I wanted to be married to someone who came home from work by 6PM, and who came home happy to see his wife and daughter. I wanted to be married to someone who, when he got home, played with his daughter or offered to cook dinner rather than sit in front of Speed TV or get lost in cycling news sites on the Internet. I wanted a man I craved to touch, and who craved to touch me. I wanted someone who noticed that the trash was overflowing and who took it out before the dog got into it and dragged it through the house. I wanted a husband who listened to me when I cried, got angry, or told him I was disappointed with his behavior or our marriage. I didn't want one who, instead, sometimes suggested that I was hormonal and that the mood would pass. I wanted a man who looked at me with love in his eyes and who seemed happy to have me in his life. I didn't want a man who acted as if I was his greatest life complication, the weight tied to his ankles that was dragging him deeper into the ocean.

........................................................................................................

## Dare to dream about the spouse you wish was yours. Dare to ask your spouse to become that person.

........................................................................................................

Could he become the man I wanted? I wasn't sure he even wanted to.

After a long silence, I said, "I want to find things to talk about over dinner. I don't want to eat in silence. I want you to look at me with love in your eyes. I want to have a sex life again. I want to hold hands. I want you to act as if you love me. I want you to make me and Kaarina your top priorities, above your store, above your bike, and above your friends."

"You are my top priorities. I do love you. I love you both," he said, bewildered.

"I need you to show it," I said.

"Maybe I need you to show me how," he said.

"I'll try," I said.

"What should we do next?" he asked.

"Are you willing to do marital counseling?"

"Yes, whatever you think we need," he said.

"You'll make time for it? You won't cancel the appointments? You won't complain about it?"

"I'll make time for it," he said.

Although our marriage felt dead, we didn't suffer from anything that would rule out resurrecting it from the grave. Neither of us was addicted to anything other than caffeine. We weren't co-dependent. He wasn't emotionally or physically abusive, and neither was I. Neither of us was an overspender or gambler. We were both intelligent, reasonable people. Perhaps most important, we both wanted to save our marriage.

That night, I started Project: Happily Ever After. Would it work? Could a marriage as bad as ours actually be saved? Would I ever feel attracted to my husband again? I didn't know for sure. What I did know was this. This project of mine? It required a gigantic leap of faith.

....................................................................................................................

Can your marriage be saved? That depends on the answer to one question: Are you both willing to try to save it? If the answer is, "Yes," then start a marriage project that spans four months. If, at the end of four months, you see any improvement and you are still both committed to making it work, give it some more time and effort. If, on the other hand, there's no improvement, your future together is pretty grim.

# 2

## There Lived a Fair Maiden

### JUNE 1992–APRIL 1995

**"The wise learn from opportunity; the foolish merely repeat it."**

—Anonymous

Our love story starts long before I put on the white dress, slipped my left hand in Dad's right elbow, and took those fated steps down a church aisle. It starts in the early 1990s, a full three years before I laid eyes on Mark. It starts during my early twenties, when I lived in a different state, worked a different job, and was falling out of love with a different young man.

Our setting is Lewes, Delaware, a small Victorian town just north of the popular beach resorts of Rehoboth and Dewey. This is where I lived, in a small apartment that was less than a mile from a beach. If it weren't for the high-pitched fire siren that wailed several times a night, the apartment's unreliable plumbing, and the somewhat strange neighbors (ranging from Mr. I'm Diagnosed With an Intractable Case of OCD to Mr. If You Don't Answer Your Door I'll Peek in Your Windows), it would have been paradise.

It was here that I worked as a general assignment reporter for the *News Journal*, the largest newspaper in the state. I'd wanted to be a newspaper reporter since grade school, and my entire career was already mapped out. After spending a few years at the *News Journal*, I'd get a job at a larger newspaper, and then a larger one until eventually, I ended up at the *New York Times*.

There was a big problem with my career map, though. It was this: I was miserable. As I drove the 20 minutes to the office, my stomach tied into knots, my jaw tightened, my palms became slick with sweat, and my heart lifted into my throat.

I lived in fear of making mistakes, and I made plenty of them. I spelled names wrong, forgot to ask probing questions, failed to retrieve requested information, and repeatedly felt over my head as I reported and wrote about local government, civil and criminal trials, and school board meetings.

I earned about $18,000 a year, which was barely enough to pay the $400 in rent on my apartment along with a car payment and assorted other monthly bills. I frequently bounced checks. I lived on spaghetti and cold cereal. I'd grown up in Northern Delaware, two hours away, and had no friends in the southern part of the state. I worked in a bureau with just three other reporters.

Todd, my college boyfriend, lived in Texas where he was attending graduate school. We talked on the phone many nights a week but, because neither of us earned enough money for airfare, we saw one another only once or twice a year. Many of my friends, of course, suggested I see other people. After all, who goes steady with a guy she sees just a couple times a year?

What can I say? As a fiercely loyal young woman who strongly believed in finishing everything she started, I saw our geographic distance as a challenge. It was a way to prove my unwavering loyalty and love. I could no sooner break up with Todd than I could quit my job at the paper. Both were wired into my identity.

After a few months, Todd dropped out of graduate school and showed up at my apartment with his car, a TV, a stereo, and his clothes. At first, his dark brown eyes, porcelain skin, and perfectly cuddly body were a balm for my dark moods. At night, I nuzzled my nose into his neck, inhaled the scent of Ivory soap, and ran my fingers over the curve of his ear.

That all started to change by the end of the first week, though, when he suggested I attend mass with him rather than my usual form of entertainment, which was reading magazines while my clothes got clean at the local laundromat. He knew I was half-Jewish, half-atheist, but he asked anyway. And he asked again, and again, and again. One Sunday morning while he was at mass, I drove to the bookstore. Half out of spite and half out of curiosity, I bought *Jewish Literacy* by Rabbi Joseph Telushken. I read it each evening while Todd read *The Way* and his Bible.

"You can stop praying for my soul," I told him one night. "I'm becoming more spiritual. See?" I pointed to my book.

"No, I can't," he said.

"Why not?"

"Because you're going to hell," he whispered.

"I am? Why?"

"You haven't been baptized. You don't believe."

Did he really think I deserved to go to hell? Did he think I was a bad person just because I did not share his faith? Was I? I was a good person, right?

Indeed, our relationship suffered from a fatal flaw. He would not marry me unless I converted to Catholicism. I would not marry him unless he stopped trying to convert me to Catholicism.

I could not break up with him, though. I still loved him and I was still blinded by my loyalty. But neither could I live with someone who thought I belonged in hell.

A few weeks more and I was ready to say what needed to be said.

"Todd, you can't stay here forever, you know."

"I know," he said.

The next day he packed and moved to New Jersey where he got a job at a pharmaceutical company. We continued to date long distance.

Now I could do my laundry without complaint, but I was lonely again, and I treated that loneliness with alcohol. One night, I accompanied someone I barely knew to a bar. I started with beer and sadness and progressed to brandy stingers and happiness. The alcohol gave me a blissful temporary amnesia, and I didn't want the amnesia to ebb, so I kept feeding it more alcohol.

I woke the next morning feeling debilitated, desiccated, and exceptionally depressed. I was convinced that I was a failure, a bad person, and weak. My soul was in dire need of a cosmic cleanse, but I scheduled the next best thing—the three free counseling visits that my newspaper health plan covered.

The counselor diagnosed me with low self-esteem, taught me self-hypnosis to help me calm down, and suggested I tell myself affirmations like "I am confident. I am good at what I do." About the low self-esteem: I didn't buy it. I really did suck as a reporter and human being. It wasn't all in my mind. So when she suggested I see a psychiatrist for a prescription for antidepressants, I decided that she was even more deluded than I was.

I couldn't afford to pay for therapy out of pocket so, after my third free visit, I found the one therapist in the county who took my insurance. Over a period of many weeks, I told her about Todd, about how he'd recently applied to Catholic University to become a priest, and later, about how the University had rejected his application.

"How did you feel about that?" she asked.

"I guess I'm a little disappointed. Is that wrong?"

"Why are you disappointed?"

"If he'd gotten in, that'd be it. Priests have to be celibate."

"Why are you still dating?"

"I don't want to hurt him. I don't know what I want. I'm scared."

I waited for her to tell me what to do, but she didn't. Her eyes were closed and her chin was resting against her collarbones. She was asleep.

...........................................................................................................

If your therapist falls asleep on you, it doesn't mean you are the most boring patient in all creation. It means it's time to find a new therapist.

I stopped seeing her. Instead, I went to the bookstore. I bought books about depression, Zen, and Eastern philosophy. I read about meditation and Cognitive Therapy. I read about affirmations. I read about conversation techniques. I read about shyness, self-esteem, and confidence. I even purchased a set of assertiveness tapes from an infomercial and listened to them as I walked around town.

One of the books suggested I could get over my self-consciousness by purposefully eating alone. "What? Everyone will stare at me. They'll think I'm the biggest loser on the planet," I said to the book. Then I read the next few lines, lines that explained that most people don't notice other people as much as we think. I ate alone once, and then I did it again and again and again, finding each time easier than the last.

Another book suggested I get past my shyness by taking the focus off myself and instead putting it on the people around me. I read, "People love to talk about themselves. You'll be the life of any party if you continually ask other people questions about themselves." During a few get-togethers in Northern Delaware, I tried it, and it worked.

Another book suggested I structure my life and sign up for classes or activities so I could meet people. I joined the local YMCA and signed up for Tae Kwon Do and yoga. Yet another book encouraged me to set some goals and take steps to reach them. I wrote one goal list after another, lists like:

Learn Spanish
Plant a tree
Travel the world
Write a book
Get a new job
Break up with Todd
Become more spiritual
Run a marathon
Find the meaning of life
A book about Zen encouraged me to stay in the moment. Another

book taught me how to analyze my dreams. I read Dan Millman's *The Warrior Athlete* and *Way of the Peaceful Warrior* three times. Then there was *When Bad Things Happen to Good People* by Harold S. Kushner. I read, and I read, and I read.

Each book made me a little stronger, a little more together, a little calmer and a little happier.

Now, more than a year after he'd moved to New Jersey, I finally called Todd. I know. Todd was *still* my boyfriend. Did I say I had issues with finishing what I'd started? Did my therapist not diagnose me with low self-esteem? Are you getting why I was still with him at this point in the story?

"Hi, I need to talk to you about something," I said. "I'm not sure how to say it." Silence. He waited for me to go on.

"I'm. . . . This is really hard. I guess, well, I think what I want to say is. This isn't working between us. I don't think we're right for each other. I love you. I do. I really love you, but I'm not right for you. You need to find a good Catholic girl, someone you can feel proud to bring home to your parents. That's not me. I'm not going to convert."

"I know," he said. "I was expecting this call. I knew it was coming."

"I guess this is good-bye?"

"Yeah, bye."

I'd expected to cry as I told him those words over the phone, and I did sob for a few minutes after I hung up. Then, a weight lifted, and I felt incredibly relieved.

........................................................................................

You are not obligated to finish anything. If you are unhappy, own the feeling and do something about it. It's really okay to be a quitter.

........................................................................................

Now, you might think that, with all of my therapy and self-help, I would walk away from this relationship and say to myself, "Self, let's not date for a while. Let's try some self-discovery. Let's get firmly planted on our own two feet before dating again." That would have been the logical thing to do, wouldn't it? Perhaps, but do you know any young woman who actually does that?

Even if you do, I have this to say in my own defense: I was still insecure, and I still craved male attention. Don't we all?

You see, I'd been lusting after Steve, my Tae Kwon Do teacher, for quite a while at this point. All right, I'll admit it. I started lusting after the man on the very first day of class, when I'd first laid eyes on him and heard his voice. I hadn't wanted to admit that little detail earlier in this story because, as you know, I had a boyfriend earlier in this story. Admitting it earlier would have caused you to think not-so-positive thoughts about my character.

But I'm admitting it now.

So when Steve called one night and invited me over to shoot pool, my chest felt warm and my head was light. We drank beer and laughed as I repeatedly hit the wrong balls into the wrong pockets. Later, he walked me to my car, reached his arms around me, and hugged me, holding me long and close. I melted into him and when I looked up, he kissed me. I wanted him in a way that I'd never wanted anyone, but I pulled away.

"I should be going," I whispered.

As I drove home, my thoughts raced. *What are you thinking? He's 18 years older than you! He's been married three times! He has two kids! He's all wrong for you! But he's so hot. I want him so bad. He makes me feel so good.*

I couldn't get him out of my head, but I wasn't sure whether I was strong enough to date a man like him.

About a week later, he asked me to shoot pool.

I shot pool with Steve a lot after that.

For at least a few weeks, I managed to prevent myself from having sex with him and from sleeping in his bed. Doing either would transform me into a young woman who was intoxicated by his presence. I knew that.

But I was already intoxicated. I felt recklessly out of control.

We had sex once, and then again and again. I couldn't get enough of him. There was no bottom to my reservoir of desire.

One night, as we were lying in a tangle on his living room floor, he stopped kissing me, pulled away, and said, "This is just fun, right?"

"What do you mean?" I asked.

"It's fun. It's not serious. You're not getting serious about me, are you?"

Every molecule of my being wanted to meld with every molecule of his. I wanted to be with him every minute of every day. I wanted to birth his babies. I envisioned myself becoming his fourth wife.

It was very serious, but I knew what he wanted to hear. "Of course not. It's just fun. Nothing more."

I continued to buy and read my books, now in search of why an intelligent twenty-four-year-old woman would fall in love with a forty-two-year-old emotionally unavailable man. Did I not get something from my parents that I was now getting from him? Had my father not given me enough attention as a child? Was I sexually pent up from years of dating Mr. No Sex Before Marriage?

Lust isn't rational. It knows no rules. If you are attracted to a man twice your age, it doesn't mean you need to go to couples therapy with your father. If you are attracted to a much younger man, it doesn't mean you are having a mid-life crisis. It just means that you are human. That's it. Stop overthinking it and just feel thankful that you are capable of feeling any lust at all.

As I was trying not to fall in love with Steve, I was quickly falling out of love with my job. While reporting on criminal court cases, I'd listen to the testimony of nine- and ten-year-old girls, bravely detailing how their uncle or father or grandfather or family friend had molested them, only to hear the jury declare this uncle or father or grandfather or family friend not guilty. When reporting on crime stories, I'd knock on doors, asking grieving mothers for photos of their recently murdered children, children who'd been murdered by their own fathers.

One Sunday, Minna, my elderly neighbor saw me on my front porch and said, "Come to church with me!"

"Me?" I asked, my laundry basket balanced on my hip. I was wearing sweatpants. My hair was pulled into a ponytail. Could she really want me inside her church?

"Yes, you," she said. It seemed as if her skin was transparent, with light shining through it.

I thought about the time my childhood best friend Sue had asked, "What is the Holy Eucharist?" and I'd replied, "It's a woman's body part. It's where babies come from."[1] She'd believed me and had written that answer in her CCD homework. I thought about one of the few Sundays that my parents had taken us kids to a Unitarian church. The Sunday school teacher had asked, "Can anyone tell me who Jesus is?" I'd thrust my hand into the air and said, "He's a nice man who lives near my Nana, in the Bronx. He likes to play shuffleboard."[2]

Minna had no idea of the extent of my ignorance. I feared that she would be mortified if she knew I'd never been baptized or that I didn't know the Apostle's Creed from the Serenity Prayer. I, of all people, had no business setting foot into a Christian church, but Minna seemed so caring, so accepting, and so downright excited by the prospect of showing me around.

"Sure, I'll go," I said.

Minna held my hand and led me to a pew. She introduced me to the other churchgoers. She handed me a hymnal and program. I felt calmer than

---

[1] In the event you just read that and don't understand precisely how my childhood mind came up with that answer, here's a little more. I'd never heard the word, "Eucharist" before. The only word I could think of that sounded remotely like the word my friend was asking me about? Uterus. Put the word Holy in front of uterus and what do you get? Mary's womb. It seemed to make perfect sense at the time. Even Sue thought so.

[2] I can't even begin to explain why I thought this, but my mother loves to tell this story at family gatherings.

I'd felt in a long time. I felt complete, at peace, and surrounded by love and acceptance. I did not feel like a failure at work and at love. I felt whole.

I went back the next week and the next, soaking up the pastor's words about forgiveness, kindness, grace, and selfless service. I prayed for the strength to resist my lust for Steve and for the strength to do something about my failed career. "Please help me. Make me strong. Give me strength to do what I know I must do."

My fledgling faith gave me courage. I read the want ads and applied for a job at a company in Pennsylvania that published self-help books and magazines. I was asked to complete a writing test about the importance of dental floss. About a week later, I drove three hours north to Pennsylvania's Lehigh Valley for an interview, and I fell in love. I fell in love with the farm fields and foothills. I fell in love with the location, just an hour's drive from Philadelphia and one and a half hours from New York. I fell in love with the town of Emmaus, which—complete with a functional main street and one-screen movie theatre—seemed permanently stuck in the 1950s. And I fell in love with the company itself. More than a thousand people worked there. Many were in their 20s, and nearly all of them were as dedicated to self-help and self-improvement as I was.

About a week later, I was offered the job. I put in my notice, said a tearful good-bye to Steve, and moved to Pennsylvania.

During lunch at the new job, I chatted with co-workers about doshas, prana, birth order, sunscreen, treadmills, dumbbells, low-fat diets, and fiber. I signed up for the company's volleyball league, took up running again, and met co-workers for hikes, touch football, inline skating and other activities on the weekends. Not a week went by that the company didn't offer some sort of self-improvement course. I signed up for public speaking. I took time management workshops. I went to lectures about the health benefits of honey and quinoa.

And I dedicated myself to Project: Don't Ever Need a Boyfriend Again. I signed up for every hobby and activity available. One night a week I went to a kayaking class. I went to Bible study on yet another night. Another night I volunteered for the Girl Scouts. I took an Aikido class. I was training for a half marathon, too. I filled in every spare space in my life with activity so I would prevent myself from having a moment of spare time to think about calling Steve.

........................................................................................................................

Want to meet the man of your dreams? Stop looking for him. The moment you become a complete person who does not remotely need a man is the moment your future husband will walk into your life.

........................................................................................................................

# 3

## Who Met a Prince

### APRIL 1995–APRIL 1999

**"Never marry a man you wouldn't want to be divorced from."**

—Nora Ephron, *I Feel Bad About My Neck*

By March of 1996, my life was full of friends, hobbies, exercise, yoga, self-improvement, positive thinking, and low-fat, high fiber eating. I'd lost 10 pounds, bought a new wardrobe, and was the happiest I'd been in years.

Despite all of this, I still drove three hours to Southern Delaware to spend occasional weekends with Steve. It was an addiction of the worst kind. For the initial 30 minutes of any visit, I would truly believe that we could have a serious relationship. The rest of the time I would feel miserable about the fact that he was emotionally distant, had commitment issues, and could very well have been my father.

One Friday evening, I was feeling particularly At Risk Of Making a Long Distance Booty Call. If I went home, I knew I would stare at the phone all night, willing myself not to dial Steve's number. That was a battle that I usually lost.

The phone? I needed to put some distance between me and it. That meant that I could not spend the evening in my apartment.

That meant I needed to lean on my fledgling self-improvement skills. I had no plans and no one to call, so I needed to go out—alone.

I went to The Farmhouse, a restaurant and bar many of my co-workers frequented for happy hour. I recognized four women from work. There was also a tall, blond young man I didn't know. He was standing in the corner.

"I think I know you," the man said. "Did we meet at the Core States bike race?"

Nothing about him seemed familiar.

"I don't think so," I said.

He grinned and touched me lightly on the shoulder. "Yes, we met. I shook your hand in the parking lot," he said.

"You must be thinking of someone else," I said.

Still grinning, he asked, "Did you or did you not go to Core States last year?"

"I was there."

"Were you wearing overalls?"

"Yes," I said. *He remembered what I wore?*

"I met you."

He extended his hand. "Mark," he said.

"Alisa," I said, placing my hand in his.

I moved my barstool slightly, so I could face him. He leaned in a little more. We laughed when we figured out he and I shared a nearly identical last name. He was a Bowman. I was a Bauman. I mentioned that my younger brother was named Mark, too. He'd gone to University of Florida. So had my older brother. How very Twilight Zone, right? It was as if we'd been destined to meet.

Later, as I walked up the steps to go home, Mark yelled, "I'm here every Friday."

I liked that he remembered me from a year ago, after meeting me only briefly. I liked how he made me laugh. I liked how he was only four years older than me and college educated with a good job.

And, it must be said, I liked that he really seemed to like me.

I couldn't admit any of this to myself, though, because I'd just completed I Don't Need a Boyfriend Training.

So, when I drove to The Farmhouse a week later, I told myself that I was not going there to see Mark, even though I knew he would be there.

Everything was going really well, too, until I drank my second beer and started endlessly talking about myself. The conversation went something like this:

Me: "I'd be better if I could move on from a past relationship."

Him: "Uh huh."

Me: "I think I'm so wild about him because I'm still sexually frustrated from the guy I dated before him. I knew he was Catholic. Are you Catholic?"

Him: "I'm a recovering Catholic."

Me (laughing hysterically and slapping my palm on the bar): "That's really funny. That's a good one."

Him: "Thanks."

Me: "During summer break, he wrote me a long, multi-page letter explaining why sex before marriage was immoral. When the summer ended and we saw one another in person, he lost his faith once in a while. I didn't tempt him away from it intentionally. We'd start hugging and then we would start kissing and then touching and then, whoops, we did it again. You know? I always told him I was sorry afterwards. I felt guilty, but, looking back on it, I know he was always willing."

Him: "I'm sure he enjoyed every moment."

Me: "By the end of our senior year, sleeping together meant one thing: sleeping in the same bed together. We kissed, but inserting Point A into Slot B was consistently verboten."

Him: "I can see how that might be hard."

Me: "The longer we went without sex, the more Platonic our relationship became."

Him: "Uh huh."

Me: "During one visit he announced, 'I've applied for the priesthood.' I always assumed he'd break up with me, but it never occurred to me that he'd break up with me by becoming a Catholic priest. Who would ever think such a thing?"

Him: "I don't know."

Me: "Anyway, I met this other guy at a Tae Kwon Do Class."

Him: "Uh huh."

Me: "We started dating and, by that, I mean that I started going over his house around 9PM at night and leaving the next morning. Me being in his bed and him making me pancakes the next morning was the sum total of our relationship. I gained 10 pounds that year from all of the pancakes."

Him: "How did you end it?"

Me: "I got the publishing job here. It was geographic therapy."

We talked until the bar was empty.

As I drove home, I felt a mixture of anticipation and fear. Was I on the rebound? Had I even gotten to rebound yet? Or was I still in Addicted to a Man Who Is All Wrong for Me Recovery?

Mark called. We talked for an hour or two, and then he asked me on a date. I was flattered that he could possibly be interested in dating someone like me, considering everything I'd already told him. At the same time, I wasn't sure I was ready to try, yet again, to love someone who might not love everything about me.

"I'm not sure if I have time to go out," I said. "I'm really busy."

"I'm really busy too," he said. A long silence followed.

I would soon be leaving for a week's vacation in California. He would leave after that to attend his brother's wedding in Florida. He said he would call when he returned, and he did. He called and he called and he called. We talked and we talked and we talked. I put off the date and I put off the date and I put off the date.

During these calls, I learned nearly everything there was to know about him. Like me, he rarely opened his mail, so it piled up on his kitchen counter. Like me, he was addicted to the *X-Files*. Like me, he was into fitness.

Like me, he liked kayaking.

He also liked hiking and snowboarding and rock climbing and wind surfing and cycling.

He was really into cycling.

I mean—*really* into it. He told me, for instance, that there was more than one kind of bike. There were road bikes, mountain bikes, track bikes, cross bikes, fixed gear bikes, BMX bikes, cruisers, and more. He also seemed to own all of these kinds of bikes.

"How many bikes do you have?" I asked.

"I'm not sure."

"Well, just give me a guess. How many?"

"Maybe twelve. I'm not sure."

"And you also own a kayak?"

"Yeah."

"And a snowboard?"

"Yeah."

"And a windsurf board?"

"Yeah."

"How much did all of that set you back?"

"I don't know. I didn't buy it all at that same time."

"How much did the most recent bike set you back?"

"You don't want to know."

"Yes, I do. *Tell* me," I purred.

"A few thousand dollars."

Now, I'm usually not a materialistic person. When young women talk about wanting to meet a man with "funds," I usually sigh one of those "if you want funds, then focus on your own career" sighs.

Really, I do. Normally, I'm not the kind of woman who would get all excited by the prospect of dating a guy who has an abundance of disposable income.

Except, at this point in my life, I was still earning less than $35,000 a year, which meant that I still lived in a crappy apartment and still drove a crappy car and still ate cold cereal for dinner.

So, I'll admit, a very materialistic thought did cross my mind and it was this: "He's the kind of person who can afford to spend a few thousand dollars on a bicycle?! Wow. He must be loaded."

And perhaps that thought is what led me to organizing our first date. It's also possible that I was lonely, and he was available. And it's even possible that I was feeling especially At Risk of Making a Booty Call, and to keep myself from calling Steve, I called Mark instead.

Whatever my motivations, I suggested we meet at a bar, and that suggestion set our Bauman-Bowman fate in motion.

I wore my most slimming jeans, my sexiest boots, and my most padded bra.

I felt awkward. I stumbled over my words. I tried to stand a little taller and smile a little more.

Afterward, he walked me to my door. He wanted to see me again. We made a date for the following Friday. He didn't kiss me. I liked that.

I watched him walk away. He seemed sweet and caring and capable. He reminded me of my dad. In a good way. (And, yes, that's really possible.)

We took things slowly. We didn't hold hands. We didn't touch. We didn't kiss. But, once a week, we did something together.

We finally touched a month or so later, when we went to see *The Bird Cage* at the Emmaus Theatre, a one-screen theater next to a set of active railroad tracks. We ate stale popcorn. Freight trains periodically rumbled by, obliterating entire scenes of dialog. He slowly moved his left hand closer to my right. Eventually he slid his fingers around mine. His hand was big. It made mine feel small. His touch was warm and gentle. His hand felt like husband material.

He walked me to the car. He leaned toward me. We kissed. It was tentative and sweet, but also foreign and awkward.

Things sped up a bit after that. A few weeks later, we got hot and heavy on his living room couch. With one hand, he unbuttoned the front of my dress, sending chills down my spine and warmth all over my body. He ran his fingers through my hair. He looked into my eyes and asked, "Would you like to spend the night?"

"I would love to spend the night, but I'm not ready to go all the way, and I probably won't be for a long time. Does that bother you?"

"No, it doesn't bother me. I can wait as long as you need," he said.

"Is it okay if I stay over, even if we don't go all the way?"

"I would love for you to stay," he said.

He took my hand and led me upstairs to his bedroom. In his waterbed, we cuddled and talked. I came to the end of a sentence and waited for him to reply. I turned to look at him. He was asleep.

A few weeks later, at my apartment, we were at it again. He undressed me. He whispered, "You're amazing. I want you so badly."

"I know. I want you, too. But I'm not ready."

"Why not?" he asked, his eyes looking into mine.

"Because I want the first time to be special," I said. After a long silence, I continued, "There's something I should tell you."

He waited.

"Something happened to me when I was younger, something that makes it hard for me to feel comfortable with someone."

I stopped. I wasn't sure I could tell him. I wasn't sure what he would think. He ran his fingers through my hair. He waited.

"When I was fourteen, I dated a boy who was eighteen, and he . . . "

"It's okay," Mark said, his eyes kind, his hand on my head, cradling my face. "It's okay. You can tell me."

"He kept trying to have sex with me. I wanted to be a virgin until I was eighteen. I don't know why I'd picked eighteen. I just had. He kept trying and trying. Each make-out session was a game to him. He'd unzip his pants and pull it out and try to get on top of me. I'd push him away. I told him I didn't want to do it. I told him that so many times. He just kept trying. Then one time, I hesitated. Maybe I was curious. Maybe I wanted to know what it would be like. I don't know why I didn't push him away that time. He got in. It hurt so much. Afterward, I remember thinking, 'This is it?' I didn't understand why anyone would ever want to have sex if that's what sex was all about. I was sore for days. It hurt to sit down. He broke up with me soon after."

I said it all while staring at the ceiling. I couldn't look at him.

"He was an asshole," Mark said.

His words were like a balm. For so many years, I'd told myself the same words over and over, and I'd imagined other people saying them, too, but I'd never believed them. I'd thought that if I'd recounted the story, as I just had with Mark, my listener would come to believe the lie that boyfriend had spread, the lie I had believed about myself for so many years.

"He even told some of my friends that I was a slut," I said.

"You're not a slut. You're not even close. I can't believe you believed that. He was such an asshole," he said.

"I was so disappointed. I'd wanted to be the good little girl in the books I'd read when I was a kid. Whenever I think about him, I get sick to my stomach. I've felt uneasy about sex ever since. If I enjoy it, I feel slutty. If I don't feel slutty, I'm too restrained to enjoy it," I said.

"I understand," he said.

......................................................................................................

If you were sexually abused or molested, it probably did a number on your ability to relax and feel comfortable during sex. Seek counseling. It's worth it.

"I don't usually wait this long to have sex with someone, but things are different with you. I know you care about me. I know you're not just out for one thing, but not every part of me believes that yet. I need every part of me to trust you. I want to feel completely comfortable with you. I want the first time to be something we both remember forever. I don't want it to be something we do out of lust. I want it to be something we do out of love."

"I love you," he said, wiping tears from my cheeks.

"I know," I said. "Thank you."

He was waiting. The tension hung in the air. A few seconds passed, and then the opening was gone. I didn't say it.

As much as I enjoyed spending time with Mark, I held back. I put my job, my hobbies, and my friends first. One Saturday morning after spending the night at his place, he asked me whether I'd like to go hiking later in the day. I told him I would. I drove home and called my running partner.

"When do you want to run?" she asked. I realized I was double booked.

I could have simply told her that I'd forgotten about the run and rescheduled it. I didn't. My friends came first.

I promised to meet her and then I called Mark to find out what time he wanted to go hiking. I got his answering machine. I left a message, and then I left for the run. We ran 10 miles.

I got to his house just before five. He wasn't there. His roommate told me he'd gone hiking. I wrote, "I'm really sorry. Please call me," and left the note by his phone.

He called later that night. He said, "If you didn't want to go hiking, why didn't you just tell me?"

"I did want to go hiking."

"Why didn't you show up?"

"I didn't know what time I was supposed to meet you."

"You had to know that you were too late. It was too late."

And then the tears came. "I'm sorry," I said. "I'm so sorry. I screwed everything up didn't I?"

"What do you mean?"

"You're probably the best thing that's ever happened to me, and I just screwed everything up. I keep pushing you away. I just screwed everything up."

He asked, "I'm the best thing that ever happened to you?"

"Yes," I gasped between sobs.

"It's okay. I forgive you," he said. "Why do you keep pushing me away?"

"Because I'm scared," I said.

"You don't have to be scared," he said. "I'm not going to hurt you."

Don't choose sadness now because you fear sadness later. If everything about that guy screams "Mr. Almost Right," then commit already, for God's sake.

After four full months of dating, I finally allowed myself to trust him. We started planning the first time. We decided to go to New York. We booked a hotel on Central Park East and got tickets to see a show.

Throughout that night, Mark kept one hand on some part of me, holding my hand, touching my arm, or fondling my thigh or my back. We ate. We drank. We walked around. As the elevator took us to our hotel room and I held his hand, I had butterflies. Why had I made such a big deal out of this?

Once we walked into the room and he hugged me, the nervousness eased. I knew he would be okay with whatever happened, even if, after all of this planning, I still wasn't ready.

But I was ready, and it was fantastic. As we lay in bed naked, my head on his chest, I knew what was true.

"I love you," I whispered.

"I love you, too," he said.

........................................................................................................

Plan your first time. Make it special. You'll cherish the memory later.

........................................................................................................

I continued to hold back, just a little, but slowly, over time, he won me over. He supported my dreams and he listened to my fears. He gave me space when I needed it. He held me when I didn't. He honored my independence and accepted my insecurities. He loved every part of me, the ugly and the beautiful, the endearing and the exhausting, the strong and the weak.

He was my companion, the person who watched the TV shows and movies that my girlfriends despised. He'd curl up on the couch with me for entire afternoons as *Goldfinger, Dr. No, The Spy Who Loved Me, For Your Eyes Only,* and *Octopussy* unfolded in front of us. He laughed when I covered my eyes during the scariest scenes of the *X-Files*, and he told me when it was okay to remove my hands and resume watching the show. We sat on his couch on sunny mornings, the light shining through his sliding glass door and onto our skin as we watched birds at his feeder.

He understood my value for giving back and, although he didn't necessarily share it, he readily agreed to help me with various charity projects, such as handing out handiwipes at the Port-o-lets during a music festival to raise money for a senior center.

He accompanied me to huge dinner parties, often one of the only guys in a room full of chattering chicks. He'd leave these gatherings feeling drained. "Just when I thought I had a comment on one topic, you had already jumped forward two topics. How do you keep up?"

"I feel so charged up when I'm around them. I find the conversations interesting and stimulating. You don't?"

"No," he said. "It's stressful. You are all talking fast and interrupting each other, and you change topics within seconds. I can't follow the logic of it at all."

"But you don't mind coming with me, do you?"

He held my hand. "I don't mind going anywhere with you."

It wasn't until I ran the half marathon in late September—two full months after our trip to New York—that my fear of commitment completely evaporated. It was then that I allowed myself to fall for him in such a way that I would hurt badly and for a very long time if things didn't work out. The race fell on the last day of Mark's vacation, a vacation he was taking in the Outer Banks to wind surf.

At mile eight in the race, I was struggling. I had gone out too fast. I looked to my right and there was Mark. He was riding his bike along the side of the road.

"Hey," I said.

"Hey," he said.

"Thought you were on vacation?"

"I left early so I could see you race," he said.

"Thanks, I can't talk anymore," I said, huffing.

About 20 yards ahead of me was a woman I knew. She was wearing Nike shorts, and "Just Do It" was printed across her butt.

"Alisa, you can catch her," he yelled. I never did, but the encouragement helped. I picked up my knees, pressed through my feet, pumped my arms and hung on.

I began staying at Mark's place more and more often. One night, after I complained of the traffic and the twenty minutes it took to drive from my place in Bethlehem to his place in Emmaus, he said, "Why don't you move in?"

I asked, "Are you sure you are ready?"

"I'm sure," he said.

"I've never lived with a boyfriend before. If I move in, then it's a first step toward a bigger step."

"I know," he said.

We decided that I would move in at the end of April, roughly a year after we'd first met. During the month leading up to the official move, I sold my furniture and some of my appliances. I packed small boxes, carried them to my car, and made a number of trips back and forth from Bethlehem to my new home. I sorted through photo albums and shoeboxes, too, throwing away photos of Todd, Steve, and other old boyfriends. I tossed old love letters.

I couldn't, however, part with my journal. In it I'd written my life goals and quotes and sayings I wanted to remember. In that journal, I'd captured the minute details about my love affair and eventual breakup with Steve, along with the initial details of my love affair with Mark. I would have been mortified if he'd read any of it, but I also couldn't throw it away. When I brought the journal to Mark's house, I put it in his shelf between the two books I knew he'd never feel tempted to read: my Bible and my Disciple workbook.

On the official first day of our co-habitation, I moved my clothes in. I arrived at his place and, with shirts and pants draped over my arms, walked upstairs to his bedroom. He wasn't home. I'd wanted him to be there to share the experience with me, but it hadn't occurred to me to ask him to be there.

I opened the closet door to the left. It was full of clothes. I opened the closet to the right. It was full of clothes, too. I sat on the floor, the pants and shirts in my lap, and I cried, disappointment filling every part of my being.

He arrived home a couple hours later. He found me in the bedroom, my clothes in a pile. As soon as I looked at him, I started crying again and, without a hello, I yelled, "You knew I was moving in today. I told you the date!"

"What are you talking about?"

"You didn't even clean out a closet for me," I sobbed. "Not even a closet."

"I'm sorry. I've been busy," he said.

"Busy? But you knew I was coming. For the past month I've been packing, selling my things, and carrying stuff over here. You haven't helped. You've done nothing."

"But the timing wasn't the best."

"Do you want to live together? It doesn't seem like you do."

"I do want you here. I do want to live with you."

"How can I believe you? You didn't even clean out a closet."

"I'm sorry," he said. "I really am."

He hugged me and promised to try harder. He offered to borrow a pickup and get a few friends to help move the one piece of furniture I was not willing to sell, a queen bed that I'd purchased a few years before. It had been my first furniture purchase, and I'd saved every nickel and dime of my newspaper reporter's salary to buy it. I couldn't part with it, not even for love.

He removed his clothes from one closet and carried them to the spare bedroom upstairs. He helped me hang my clothes. Then we sat next to one another and stared at the closet, my closet.

"I'm the one who's taking all of the risk," I said. "I got rid of almost all of my things. The only change you had to make was cleaning out a closet."

"But you didn't want me to move into your apartment, right?"

"No, it's just that it feels as if it's your place, not our place. I am surrounded by masculine black and white. Your bed is black. Your couch is black. Your walls are white. You have a waterbed. It's like I'm living in a fraternity."

"This is our place," he said. "It's not my place. It's our place."

"It doesn't feel that way to me," I said.

"How about we buy something together? I've wanted to buy a loveseat for a while. Do you want to buy one together?"

It took a lot of shopping to find a loveseat that didn't say "frat boy" but also didn't say "I let my girlfriend handle all of the decorating." We eventually found a green and red loveseat. The fabric was itchy, and we bought it from someone who was selling furniture on the side of the road. It wasn't perfect, but it was neither overly masculine nor overly feminine and, perhaps, most important, it cost only $200.

Little by little, I left other lasting impressions. We added blinds to the windows, painted the molding contrasting primary colors, and replaced his gray sheets with cream. We hung lots of colorful photography and artwork, and I painted a Matisse-like mural on the bathroom wall.

........................................................................................................

If you want him to help you move in, tell him. If you want to celebrate you moving in with a candlelight dinner, tell him. If you want him to be home when you walk into your new home for the very first time, tell him.

........................................................................................................

During those initial months of co-habitation, I occasionally found new hiding places for my journal. Finally, one day, I said, "Look, I have this journal. I wrote some really personal stuff in there, stuff that I don't want you to read. You'd never try to read it, right? I don't have to hide it from you, right?"

"Right," he said, "Just like I have a date book. You'd never open it and read it, right?"

"Right."

A few months later, he went away for a weekend-long cycling trip. One night, I couldn't stop thinking about his date books. What was so personal that he didn't want me to know? What secrets was he keeping from me?

I started in his closet. There I found bike parts, car parts, medals, and trophies. There were photos, directions to various locations, financial documents, tax records, and bank statements. As I moved his stuff around, I carefully made sure to memorize its original location, and put it all back in its proper place.

It took a while, but I eventually found the date books. It would be okay if I just took a little peek, wouldn't it? After all, we were living together. We shouldn't have secrets, right? I knew nothing about his past girlfriends. He'd been so mum about his previous romantic life that one of my friends was convinced I was his first girlfriend ever.

I hesitated. I tried to stop myself. "These are his private things," I told myself. "I shouldn't be doing this." I stared at the books. I stared and stared, and then I gave into temptation. I picked up the book for 1996, the year we'd met. The first twenty or so entries described different workouts. On January 13, for instance, I learned he'd gone on a two hour mountain bike ride with Jay in the snow. On February 4, he'd ridden four hours to Spring Mountain and back.

Then I read the entry for February 28. "Had dinner with Eileen at JP O'Mally's. She called. I went. Very interesting dinner. Amazing, wonderful, beautiful woman!!"

*WHAAAT?!*

I read one more entry about Eileen before coming to March 8. "Met Alisa at Farmhouse. Interesting."

*Eileen was amazing, wonderful, and beautiful and I only get an interesting?*

March 15: "Met Alisa at Farmhouse. Talked until 11PM Very interesting and intelligent. Quite the conversation."

*No beautiful? No amazing?*

I consoled myself. *Perhaps he'd run out of room in the little square to write the word "amazing."*

April 3: "First date with Alisa. She asked me out! Went to Harry's. Played pool. Shot the shit. No kiss."

*No amazing?!*

April 25: "Met Alisa and her friend at The Farmhouse."

*Still no amazing?*

May 3: "Went with Alisa to Robata's. She came to my house (1st time) and drove. Food ok. Conversation very good. No kiss. . . wimp!!"

*Come on, humor me. You still didn't think I was amazing? That was our third date!*

May 10: "Saw Birdcage. Held hands. 1st kiss. Magical. Soft. Lovely."

*Now we're talking!*

May 16: "Went to Bach Choir. Back to my house. Wrestled on sofa for 2 hours. Alisa spent the night. Wow! This may lead somewhere."

*Getting better.*

June 29: "NY W ALISA. AMAZING! 1st time!!"

*Finally!*

I read through his account of the rest of our first year. On one page, in a random space, he'd written, "Mark + Alisa." Then next to it, he'd written, "Alisa + Mark." On one of the back pages, next to a hand-drawn map to his house and directions to Philadelphia, he'd written: "Alisa Bauman 5'3", 6P, 36B/C, 25-inch waist, 8/8/70."

I flipped through the book again and again, waffling between feeling jealous about Eileen, guilty for reading the date book, and touched that he'd chronicled every date we'd ever had, not to mention my measurements and clothing size.

Now he had no secrets. But I did. And while my husband was quite comfortable with keeping secrets, I wasn't.

∞

Near the end of the week, I told Mark that we needed to talk.

"When you were away, I did something I shouldn't have done," I said.

"What did you do?"

"I read your date book. I read all of them. I read everything I could find. I looked at everything in your closet. I opened and searched every drawer in the house."

"You did? Why?"

"Because I wanted to know more about you. You're so secretive about your past. You won't talk about your past girlfriends. I'm so curious about your life before me," I said.

"There's nothing to know about my past. My life started the day I met you," he said.

I wavered between feeling touched, feeling as if Mark had something to hide, and feeling guilty.

"Are you mad?"

"I'm not mad. Is there anything that you read that you want to talk about?"

"I didn't know you liked Eileen," I said.

"I didn't like her that much," he said.

"You said she was amazing. You never wrote that I was amazing," I said.

"You are amazing. You're way more amazing than Eileen. You're the most amazing woman in the world. I love you more than anything. I don't love Eileen. I love you. She meant nothing to me. You mean everything to me."

"What did you like about me when you met me? You said Eileen was beautiful and amazing, but you only said I was intelligent."

"You are intelligent. You're really intelligent. I think you're probably smarter than I am. I like that about you. I find that attractive. You're also funny. You're nice. You're hot, and you have a great ass."

"I do?"

"You have a really great butt. Your butt was one of the first things I noticed about you."

"But my boobs are too small, aren't they?"

"Your boobs are perfect, and your butt is even better."

We hugged, and he squeezed my great ass.

..............

You can tell whether or not he's marriage material by how easily he forgives. A wedding band doesn't prevent you from doing and saying stupid things. If he holds grudges over minor stuff during the dating stage, he probably doesn't have what it takes to stay happily married to the likes of you.

..............

As our first year of cohabitation neared an end, I couldn't think of a single reason not to marry him, and I was crumbling under the pressure from friends, church members, and my parents, many of whom kept mentioning that line about the cow and the milk.[3]

One day I read an article in *National Geographic* about the diamond industry. I asked him never to surprise me with any type of diamond jewelry. "I don't want to patronize an industry that destroys third-world countries," I said. "Plus, it says here that diamonds aren't even rare. They are only expensive because the industry controls how many enter the marketplace at any given time." He agreed, adding that a diamond ring was a pretentious show of wealth. Was he my soulmate or what?

---

[3] My mother would like you to know that she never once uttered the phrase, "Why buy the cow when he can get the milk for free?" She says she'd never before heard that phrase until she read a draft of this book. I believe her.

"We've been living together for a year," I said.

"I know," he said.

"It's time we started talking about the next step. What do you think?" I worried that he might tell me he wasn't ready, worried that he might tell me that he would never be ready.

"I think I want to marry you," he said.

"I think I want to marry you, too," I said.

We set the date for April 10, 1999, roughly a year away.

That summer, it rained for a week, water seeping into the carpet in the living room. The carpet remained damp for days and eventually started to smell like an adolescent boy who hasn't showered for two weeks. We pulled it up and threw it away, revealing the cement slab underneath. We decided to install tile rather than new carpeting, in case the house flooded again. We picked out the tile and had it delivered. To save money, Mark wanted to install it himself.

I spent the rest of the year tasting wedding cakes, interviewing caterers, touring reception halls, and pleading with him to install the ceramic tiles. I would love to have been the type of person who could laugh off a cement floor when entertaining my grandparents, aunts, uncles, and cousins in my living room. I wasn't that person. I was the kind of person who looks at a bare cement floor and wonders, "Am I about to make a huge mistake?"

The summer turned to fall. Fall became winter. Winter became spring. Still no tiles.

My church required us to meet with a premarital counselor. The week before our final appointment, she suggested we continue with counseling and put off our marriage date. She wanted us to resolve two issues. Issue number one: I was on the fence about children; Mark was not. He did not want them. Issue number two: I'd mentioned that, at times, I wished Mark and I spent more time together; he'd mentioned that he had many interests and hobbies, especially the hobby that involved riding his bike, and that I'd known about these interests and hobbies when we'd met.

"Can you believe she had the nerve to do that?" I said as we drove home afterwards.

"What do you want to do?" he asked.

"I'm not doing the extra sessions," I said. "I'm not postponing the wedding."

At our final appointment, I confronted her. "Mark and I have been very forthcoming with you. We decided to use premarital counseling to solve a few issues. We could have easily lied, as most couples probably do, and told you that everything was just peachy. We didn't, but we can solve our problems. They are minor, and we're both frustrated that you've decided to manipulate us into getting more counseling at a time that should be filled with joy."

"If you can be that assertive with me, there isn't a doubt in my mind that you will be able to communicate with each other. You have my blessing," she said.

And two days before the wedding, my fiancé pulled an all-nighter and installed the ceramic tiles.

...........................................................................................................................

If your premarital counselor suggests you need more counseling, you should probably get more counseling.

...........................................................................................................................

During our wedding reception, our pastor separated our guests into small groups and asked them to offer advice for the married couple. Our guests reminded us to "never go to bed angry," to "always remember why we fell in love," and, in Mark's case, to "always answer 'yes, dear.'" One of the last guests to offer advice was my eighty-four-year-old grandmother, who had recently celebrated her sixtieth wedding anniversary. "Patience," she whispered to me. "Patience."

The day after our wedding, the temperature dropped below 30 degrees, and it sleeted.

Most women spend the first third of their lives praying that some guy somewhere will just pop the question already. Then they spend the second two-thirds of their lives wishing that they had not said, "yes" to that question.

# 4

## She Married Him, and He Turned into a Frog

APRIL 1999–MAY 2007

**"In a relationship in which two people become one, the end result is two half people."**

—Wayne W. Dyer, *Your Erroneous Zones*

Just before Mark and I were married, I had landed a job as an editor at *Runner's World* magazine. Within a year, I was promoted to senior editor. Since meeting Mark, my salary had nearly doubled. Mark's career, however, had stagnated. He'd been a product manager at a biotech company when we'd met, and now he was still a product manager for the same company. He'd never been promoted and he'd never gotten a decent raise. I now out-earned him by more than twenty thousand dollars.

As I traveled the world on press junkets, attended extravagant parties in New York and elsewhere, and brought home lots of swag in the form of running shoes, clothing, and backpacks, Mark was having an email war with his company's vice president over the merits of casual Fridays and overtime pay. Whenever I saw his tense face and cold eyes, I thought he was mad at me. It was only after persistent questioning that he revealed his problems at work.

"My company is getting rid of some overstock. They had a silent auction for the employees. I had the highest bid for a drafting table, but my boss told me I couldn't have it."

"Why?"

"You might as well just read it," he said. He handed me a printout of an email exchange.

Mark to VP: "When can I claim my drafting table?"

VP: "You can't have the drafting table. Sorry, there's been a misunderstanding."

Mark: "Why not? I had the highest bid."

VP: "You may have had the highest bid, but the table is worth more than your bid of thirty dollars. You didn't bid high enough."

Mark: "When you organized the auction, you never mentioned there were minimum bids. I followed the rules of the auction. I had the highest bid. The table's mine."

VP, replying and courtesy copying Mark's immediate supervisor, Len: "I don't care whether or not you had the highest bid. The table is worth more than your bid. You're not getting the table."

Mark: "You can't do that."

VP: "Yes, I can. I'm the boss. You're not getting the table."

Mark: "You're breaking your own policies."

Len to Mark only, emailing from his vacation in Aruba: "Stop emailing the VP. You're playing with fire."

VP: "The matter is closed. I don't want to hear from you again about this matter."

I lowered the printout to my thighs. "Do you want to quit?"

"No, I can't lose my job," he said.

"You're going to lose it if you keep this up. I'm making enough to support us until you get another job. Life's too short to stay in a job you hate."

"I can't quit," he said. "I can't let you support me."

Two days later he asked, "Were you serious when you said I could quit?" He looked even more miserable than usual.

"Yes, I was," I said.

We hugged. "We're in this together," I said.

He put in his notice the next day.

During his unemployment, I periodically asked him what he thought he'd do next. He generally answered that question with an "I don't know."

"Are you reading the want ads?" I'd ask.

"Yes," he'd say.

"Have you applied for anything?"

"No."

"Why not?"

"Because there's nothing that fits my skill set."

"Maybe you could try something different."

"Like what?"

"You love to ride your bike. Maybe you could open a bike shop. Or maybe you could start a bike touring business."

"I don't want to mix work with pleasure. If I get paid to do my hobby, my hobby will become work and it will stop being fun."

"You really think so? I don't."

We had the conversation that you just read about 679 times, not that I counted or anything.

I tried to become comfortable with the idea of Mark being a house-husband. I was a feminist, right? Gloria Steinem would have been so proud of me, you know? We were the true modern couple.

Weren't we?

Okay, I'll admit it. I kind of wanted him to get a job, like right away. I wanted him to get a good job, too, one that provided a salary that was *a lot more than mine.*

Sure, I'm shallow, but at least I'm honest. I could have just lied to you here and told you that I was brave and accepting and all of those other things that we all like to imagine that we will be in such a situation. Or I could just tell the truth, which is that him not working made me see him as weak.

But that was okay, because he was only going to be weak for a short while. He would get a job really soon. I mean, what real man loses his job and sits on the couch and watches TV while his wife does everything else? Sure, that happens *to other people's husbands*. My husband? He was a provider.

More important, while we waited for the perfect high-salary job that fit his skill set to appear in the want ads, he had plenty of time to paint various rooms in the house and finish any number of long languishing special projects that neither of us, until then, had the time to tackle. That's what I would have done if I had been in his situation.

But, as I soon learned, Mark was not me.

He did make my lunch and dinner. He did put away the sneakers, wash the clothes, and remove the socks from the bedroom floor. He did everything I asked him to do.

But he did no more than that, and he continually put off big projects, such as painting my home office or building some bookshelves, because, as he put it, he was "busy." This "busy" excuse? I didn't buy it. Before he'd quit his job, I had managed to clean the bathrooms, straighten the house, make my own lunch, and make dinner most of the time, even with a full-time job and freelance projects on the side. He had to have free hours that he could put toward painting my office.

"What exactly do you do all day long?" I asked.

"I do housework," he said.

"How long does it take you? It can't take you all day to pick up the shoes and socks."

"It takes a lot longer than you'd think."

"It takes thirty minutes, tops."

"It takes a lot longer than that."

"I think you watch TV all day, and when you're not watching TV, you're riding your bike."

"I do a lot around here."

"It feels like I'm working all of the time so you can have the easy life."

"That's not true."

That was a difference of opinion that we never did resolve. According to my husband, it still takes all day to straighten up the house, and it takes at least a year to build and install bookshelves.

And after that year—a year filled with near-daily complaints from me about his work ethic, he F-I-N-A-L-L-Y installed those bookshelves, painted my office, and started reading the want ads.

He applied for and was hired to work for the marketing department at *Bicycling*, a magazine owned by the same company where I worked. The new job required him to travel to cycling races and events around the country.

It was then, with him working at this new job, that I felt this pang of disappointment. Despite how much we'd bickered about the housework, despite how weak I saw him, despite how taken advantage of I felt, and despite how scared I was of not making enough money to pay the bills, I'd still liked having him around. I'd gotten used to him being home when I came home from work. I'd gotten used to eating dinner together. I'd gotten used to snuggling on the couch as we watched television each evening.

Now I was making my own lunch, eating frozen dinners by myself, and missing the househusband I'd driven back into the workplace.

In the new millennium and nearly three years into my job at *Runner's World*, a book editor offered me a ghost writing assignment that would earn me more than half of my salary in just a few months. Other editors called, asking if I was willing to take on other projects, projects that paid just as handsomely.

It wasn't hard to see that I could make a lot more money working for myself than I ever could by working for a company.

I put in my notice.

The following year was a blissful one for us, with me loving my work and him loving his, and both of us loving each other. We had more money than we needed, and we indulged ourselves with weekly massages, expensive dinners, regular trips to New York to see shows and eat out, and vacations to Hawaii and Yosemite.

We didn't argue very often, but, when we did, the arguments were always about the same topic: housework. Because I was working where I lived, I couldn't stand the mess. He kept telling me to ignore the clothes on the floor and the dishes in the sink, but I just couldn't. Around 7AM, I found myself methodically lining up shoes in closets, cleaning out cabinets, tossing socks in the hamper, and washing the ever-present pile of dishes in the sink. If I managed to get through the day without feeling the need to straighten up the house, then I'd fall apart at night. He'd want to get busy with me. I'd go through the motions of foreplay, all the while thinking about the mail piled up on the dining room table.

I was absolutely sure that I spent double or triple the amount of time as he did on household chores. He didn't believe me. I didn't like that he didn't believe me. Didn't he know that I was always right?

Most of the time anyway.

Definitely this time.

To prove my rightness to him, I created a poster that listed all of the tasks that needed to be done around the house on a weekly or monthly basis. It included cutting the grass, yard work, vacuuming, dusting, cooking, grocery shopping, cleaning the bathroom, cleaning the kitchen, doing laundry, paying the bills, dealing with the accountant, and more. Whenever one of us completed a task on the list, we checked it off and wrote down the amount of time we'd spent on it. When we tallied the numbers, Mark couldn't deny that I really did do more than twice as much as he did. I believe his exact words were, "Wow, you kicked my ass."

We split up the tasks more evenly. Cutting the grass would always be his job, considering I had hay fever. We shared the responsibility of weeding the garden. He agreed to deal with the leaves in the fall and the snow in the winter. He also agreed to vacuum, do the laundry, and wash the dishes. I did everything else.

..........................................................................................................................

Make a list of all of the indoor and outdoor chores that you both think need to be done on a daily, weekly and monthly basis. Talk about which ones you will do, which ones he will do, which you might do together, and which you can outsource (to a cleaning lady, gardener or lawn care service).

..........................................................................................................................

After my first year of freelancing, I told Mark that I was lonely working by myself, and that I wanted a dog to keep me company. He resisted, telling me that a dog was a big commitment.

Eventually he gave in, though, and one day we drove to the SPCA. There we saw a brown Doberman with floppy ears. His tail was tucked and his head hung low. He was filthy. He looked up at me with pitiful yellow eyes that spoke of a lifetime of pain and suffering. I took one look at him and had one thought. It was this: "I have to take that dog home with me. He's my soulmate."

We paid our fifty dollars and slowly walked the dog that would later be known as Rhodes (i.e., Rhodes Scholar) to the car.

Three days later, our passive, docile dog lost his shelter trauma and wanted to play and run 24 hours a day. He pushed my hands away from the keyboard with his snout and jumped his feet on my lap. He ate every tissue box in the house, emptied the contents of the downstairs trash can multiple times a day, and chewed up the remote access key to my car, setting off the alarm. He dug a hole in the loveseat that Mark and I had purchased together. When I walked him, he was constantly interested in squirrels, bunnies, and other attractions and proceeded to yank me off the road. During one walk, he pulled forward so quickly that my feet came out of my shoes. I landed in a belly flop on the pavement.

I signed us up for obedience boot camp. On the first night, Rhodes yanked me around the room, pulling me from one dog's butt to another. The other dog owners seemed to have such passive, docile dogs. And then there was my dog, the one whose owner kept yelling, "No!" and "Bad dog!" Was there hope for him? For us?

There was.

He learned quickly. He became my personal project. I bought and read every dog-training book that had ever been printed. I practiced commands with him every single day.

By the end of obedience training, he was a well-behaved and loving 60-pound lap dog who cuddled with me whenever I sat down. He lounged in my office all day while I worked. When I was sick, he was by my side. When I went to the bathroom, he was right there with me. When I left him home alone, he howled in protest.

And get this. He was voted "Most Improved Dog" at obedience class graduation! My dog! An award winner!

I fell in love with him, and for a few years, he filled the void inside of me. Until he didn't.

Mark had told me when we'd met that he did not want to become a parent, but now, after three years of marriage, I wanted a baby. The need for a baby became an ever-present yearning. It was stronger than any craving I'd ever had before. Without a baby, I felt as if my life would never be complete.

He'd changed his mind about the dog, right? Would he change his mind about a baby, too?

"I want to be a Mom," I told Mark one night. "I'm supposed to be a mom."

"A baby's a really big commitment. It's a lot of work," he said with a sigh.

"I know," I said, "But I still want one. When I'm on my deathbed, I don't want to look back on my life and realize that all I did was work and earn a lot of money. I want to know I did something important. I want to know what it feels like to be pregnant. I want to know what it feels like to give birth. I want to know what it feels like to nurse. I want to know what it feels like to have a child who loves me more than anything else in the world."

"I'll think about it," he said.

Was he putting it off intentionally, hoping that, by biding his time, my eggs might eventually shrivel up and die? Was he thinking that I would change my mind, that I would stop wanting this baby? Could I wear him down? Did I really want to try? Was he really father material?

That last question? It scared me.

...........................................................................................

Little known fact: a man who tells you that he doesn't want to have children really doesn't want to have children. If you want to be a mother and he doesn't want to be a father? Reconsider your relationship.

...........................................................................................

Still, the desire for a baby was strong. I couldn't ignore it. I couldn't let it go. I persisted in asking for one, eventually promising that we would take a second honeymoon in New Zealand before having a child. I took on freelance job after freelance job during the next few months, turning absolutely nothing down, even if it meant that I'd have to work seven days a week for two months straight, and even if it meant that I had to work until 3AM a couple nights a week. In roughly six months, I saved $8,000, enough to cover the airfare and an eco-hiking tour with a guide. We planned to go for two and a half weeks in January.

The week after Thanksgiving, I arrived home from running errands. Mark was in the living room. It was the middle of the day.

"How come you're not at work?" I asked.

"I need to talk to you about something," he said. "You should sit down."

"What is it?" I asked. "Did someone die?"

"No," he said. "No, no one died, but I need to tell you something, and I don't think you are going to like it."

"Just tell me," I said. "How bad could it be?"

"I lost my job. They outsourced my position."

I was silent for a long moment.

"Mark. We'll. Get. Through. This. We'll. Be. Fine."

The words were forced. I wanted them to be true. In reality, though, I was thinking, "Christ, not this again! What have I done to deserve this? How could I marry someone who ends up unemployed not once but twice?"

I tried my best to hide such thoughts, though. I tried my best to seem strong. I tried my best to seem supportive. I tried my best to seem so very positive.

We hugged.

The following day he met with someone from human resources to go over his severance package and extended health benefits.

We postponed the New Zealand trip, just in case. We postponed the baby, too.

You can tell what kind of parent your partner will be by how your partner interacts with your pets. If you do all of the pet care—feeding, grooming, training, petting, and cleaning—you can wager a good guess that your partner will stand back and let you do all of the baby care, too.

∞

I worried that the layoff would bruise Mark's ego, destroy his self-confidence, or send him spiraling into a depression.

And, it must be said, I worried that I might very well spend the rest of my life supporting my unemployed husband. Yes, that thought did plague me, more than I care to admit.

So I continually prodded him.

"What do you want to do next?" I'd ask.

"Dunno," he'd say.

"How about opening a bike shop?"

"I don't know."

"What don't you know?"

"I don't think it would work."

"Why not?"

"It just wouldn't."

I got nowhere with that discussion, so I changed course.

"You could work for me," I suggested. "I have more projects than I can handle. I could use an assistant."

Between the lines, though, I said, "That is, until you find another job." I was pretty sure he heard them, too, so I only channeled them to him 162 times.

He agreed to give it a try.

I tried to seem confident about the working arrangement but, inside, I was filled with fear. Years before, when he'd been unemployed, I'd had a full time job with weekly paychecks and health insurance. Now, I earned more money, but I earned it sporadically. I got paid in large lump sums, sometimes going months without a paycheck. When I learned that health insurance would cost us $750 a month, the fear magnified. I consoled myself by imagining worst-case scenarios. *What if I can't pay the mortgage? We'll dip into the New Zealand money. What if we run out of New Zealand money? Then we'll sell a stock or borrow against the 401(k). What if we sell all of the stocks and still need money? Then I'll ask my parents for help.*

Mark agreed to take on nearly all of the household chores. He dropped off deposits at the bank, ran packages to Fed Ex, and delivered various packages and discs to some of my local clients. He wrote and edited material for a few of my projects, too. I supervised and read his work, but he turned out to be a better writer and editor than I'd anticipated.

He always did whatever I requested, but he waited until the absolute last minute to start or finish any task, which meant that I often discovered him in front of the TV. I would demand that he turn off the TV and do the work I'd given him, and he would respond, "I'll get it done by the deadline, okay?"

This infuriated me.

Of course I'd given him a deadline. Of course, I didn't really need him to finish it earlier than the deadline. But finishing it earlier than the deadline would have been nice. If he'd seemed busy, as if he'd been working hard to help us earn our money? It would have been nice. And if he'd finished things earlier than expected? Then I could have given him more work. You are with me on this point, yes?

And sure, I was jealous, too. There was definitely a little of that going on. I wanted to sit in front of the TV, too. Only I didn't want to watch cycling races and car races. I wanted to watch *Oprah*.

For once, I wanted to know what it felt like to watch *Oprah* without feeling like I needed to get back to work. I wanted to be a kept woman. I didn't want this for very long. A year? That would have done the trick. Yes, I would have settled for a year of keptness.

But in no way was I going to say that because saying such a thing would have made me seem whiny, greedy, and in-need-of-a-Puritan work ethic, don't you think?

As the months passed, I began to resent him more and more. I didn't like telling him what to do. I didn't like seeing him in the La-Z-Boy. I didn't like the jokes that his friends and mine made about him being my househusband, my kept man.

I was embarrassed. I felt taken advantage of.

I wanted to be proud of him. I wanted my parents to be proud of him.

I wanted his parents to be proud of him.

I wanted him to do things that made other people proud.

So I kept bringing up the bike shop.

"There's rental space available on Main Street," I said.

"It's not a good space," he said.

"Why not?"

"There's no parking."

Another rental space would open up. I'd suggest it. He'd tell me it was too big. Or too small. Or too in-the-wrong location.

Was he going to camp out on the La-Z-Boy forever?

It's always better to talk about your wants, needs and feelings—even if they make you seem like a despicable human being—than to keep them to yourself. Marriage is about growing closer. It's about understanding each other—even the ugly parts. Have the courage to be ugly.

I added family budgeting and financing to his to-do list. I loaded Quicken onto a laptop, taught him how to use it, and explained the basic budget I'd formulated, the one that allowed us to put away a large portion of my salary into the Roth IRAs, annuities, stock purchases, and SEP IRAs.

As days became weeks and weeks became months, I periodically asked how we were doing financially, and he always answered, "We're good." One day he asked me if he could go on a skiing trip with his old boss, and I answered with a question, "How are our finances?"

"We're good," he said.

"Then, go," I said.

Some time later I withdrew money from the ATM and looked at the account balance. We had less than $200 in our account. With the balance slip crumpled in my fist, I drove home. He was in his usual spot in front of the TV.

"How are our finances?" I asked, unable to hide the anger in my voice.

"What do you mean?"

"You've been telling me that they are fine. They are *NOT* fine."

"How are they not fine?"

"We have less than $200 in our account."

"So?"

"We started with $8,000 only a few months ago, and I've been cutting myself regular paychecks and making regular deposits into the checking account.

*WHERE DID ALL OF THE MONEY GO?*"

"I guess we spent it," he said.

"On what? How do we blow $8,000 in only a few months and have nothing to show for it. Nothing! Where did it go?"

"My ski trip was kind of pricey?" he said reluctantly.

"How pricey?"

"The hotel was expensive."

"How expensive?"

"My share was $2,000 for the week."

"What else?"

"We went Snowcat skiing."

"What the heck does that mean?"

"We rented a Snowcat to take us up and down the mountain. We didn't have to wait for a lift. We had a private run to ourselves."

"How much did that cost?"

"My share was $500 for the day."

"You paid $500 for one day of skiing?"

"Uh huh."

"What else?"

"We ate at some really expensive restaurants every night, and there was the airfare."

"You didn't think to ask me if that would be okay?"

"You told me I could go on the trip."

"That money was supposed to finance a trip that we could take together. Do you know how hard I worked to earn that money? Do you know how many things I didn't buy so we could save that money? Didn't you think about that? Didn't it ever occur to you?"

"I'm sorry," he said.

"I am, too," I said.

A rift had opened between us, with me taking on the role of parent and disciplinarian and him becoming a despondent child whose mean old Mommy wouldn't let him go out to play. I hated my role of responsible adult. I wanted him to act responsibly without me forcing him to do it. I took back the job of managing our finances and put him on a budget, and I hated every minute of it.

Talk about the value of money. Agree on how much of your income to save and how much to spend. Create a discretionary spending budget for each of you to use in whatever way you want. Place no limits on what you can each buy with your personal allotment. He can blow all of his on a beer hat if he wants to, as long as the beer hat doesn't cost more than his monthly allotment.

I still wanted a baby, though. I just wasn't sure if I still wanted my husband. I didn't feel as attracted to him as I had in the past, and I rarely wanted to have sex. If he suddenly had become impotent or disinterested, I wasn't sure whether I would have noticed. I wanted us to grow closer and become the couple that we once were. But how? Where and when had things gone so wrong?

For some reason, a second honeymoon seemed like the only possible solution to our problems. Marital counseling? That never occurred to me, probably because only really screwed up couples needed that. We weren't really screwed up. We were just not as happily married as we'd once been. That's all. A second honeymoon? It would cure every single problem we had. It was going to transform my husband into a doting, responsible person with an income. Poof. Just. Like. That.

New Zealand was, of course, out. Not only was it too expensive, but going there would have proven me wrong about my husband ruining our chances of going there.

No, I would not reward him by working my rear end off to go to New Zealand.

But Iceland? That was enticing, not to mention a lot more affordable.

The small, volcanic island, despite its name and location just south of the Arctic Circle, had temperatures in the fifties and sixties most of the summer. We'd be able to see geysers, whales, waterfalls, and hundreds of different types of birds. We could hike on glaciers and relax in hot springs. It was only four and a half hours away by plane. We were close to putting down a deposit when Mark traveled to Mount Snow, Vermont, to compete in an annual mountain biking event.

I was sitting at my computer when he called.

"First, I'm okay," he said, slowly. He sounded groggy, as if he'd just woken up. "I'm okay," was the line he used whenever he crashed his bike and was calling me from an emergency room. A nurse, I assumed, was probably scrubbing dirt and gravel out of a very open and very gross wound as we spoke.

"What happened?"

"I broke my ankle," he said. "I was coming downhill on a practice run and I wrecked." He explained that he was going into surgery and would call again when he got out. He reiterated that he really was okay, and he told me he loved me.

"Wait," I said. "How badly is it broken? Should I cancel the Iceland trip? How long will you be in a cast? Can you hike on glaciers?"

"Yeah, you should probably cancel it. I'm sorry."

"I'm glad you're okay. Do you want me to drive up there?"

"No, you don't need to. I'm fine. I'll be fine."

"Are you sure?"

"Yes, I'm fine, shortcake."

I stared at my computer. I didn't have time to drive to Vermont, but this was my husband, and he was in a hospital, and his leg was broken. It was his right leg. He drove a stick shift. There was no way he'd be able to drive home.

But I had a lot of work to do, too. And I was the only one of us who had work. Plus, he knew mountain biking was dangerous. A not-as-understanding wife might even say he got what was coming to him.

And even though I was certainly not such a not-as-understanding wife, I did want to pay the mortgage. And I didn't want to miss my deadline. I didn't miss deadlines. Missing deadlines? That was what other wives did when their husbands broke their legs. So I typed awhile more.

And then this strange sensation took over my being.

It was guilt.

Mixed with fear.

Along with some worry.

And a dose of empathy, too.

The guilt-fear-worry-empathy sensation got me emailing and calling a few of Mark's friends, asking for advice. They all told me that I'd better get my sorry-excuse-for-someone's-wife's ass to Vermont.

Except they said it more like, "He's really going to need your help. You'd better go."

Röbi offered to drive to Vermont with me.

We'd been driving for about thirty minutes when Mark called.

"I've got two plates and twenty-three pins in my leg," he boasted.

"Wow, you didn't break it. You shattered it. I'll be there in a few hours," I said.

"No, you don't need to come," he said. "I'm fine."

"Mark, how are you going to get home? You can't drive. Röbi's with me. I'll drive you home, and he'll drive your car home. We're coming. We've already been driving for a half hour."

"No, I don't need you to come. I can catch a ride home with a friend. I'm fine," he said. "Let me talk to Röbi."

I handed Röbi the phone. They talked for a while and then Röbi hung up.

"What do you want to do?" Röbi asked.

"I guess we should turn around," I said.

Due to a misunderstanding, Mark's friend didn't show when Mark was released from the hospital. Wearing only a hospital gown, Mark hailed a cab, asking the driver to take him to a pharmacy (to fill his prescription) and then a hotel. The next day, his friend finally retrieved my repeated voice mail messages and drove to the hotel to retrieve Mark and drive him home.[4]

I felt incredibly guilty, but I got my project done on time.

.................................................................................................

If your husband is hospitalized, stop whatever you are doing and go to the hospital. Do it even if he tells you he doesn't need you. He needs you. He just doesn't want to sound like a one of those evolved men who cry when they watch *Beaches*. He wants to seem strong. A Navy Seal wouldn't tell his wife he needed her, even if he was in a full body cast, right? Neither will your husband, except he's not a Navy Seal.

.................................................................................................

Mark would need to keep his leg elevated for a month. After that, he'd be able to hop around on crutches, but he was not supposed to put any body weight on the right leg for three to four months. If he did, he risked shifting the pinned bones out of alignment.

Can you say invalid? Good, because that was the situation. Let's just get one thing straight. I did make a vow about sickness and health when we married, but I'd assumed the sickness thing wasn't going to happen until after retirement. I wasn't prepared to nurse a man in his thirties, especially while I still working more than forty hours a week.

---

[4] When I originally wrote this section, I described Mark taking the taxi to Wal-Mart to buy clothes, a fast food restaurant for food, and a pharmacy. I'm almost positive my original version is the same version of the story he told me so many years ago. When he read and fact-checked this book, however, he told me that he only went to a drug store. I can't decide if he told me a tall tale so many years ago to elicit my admiration or if I just remembered it incorrectly. At any rate, I've used his version of the events in the book rather than my own, even though I like my version better.

But I was going to do it. And I was going to smile through every moment of it. And I was going to tell my friends and family that I was doing "Great!"

Because that's the kind of woman I am.

I worked my usual long hours and also cooked and cleaned and did the yard work. I drove him to his orthopedic and physical therapy appointments, and I tried my best to be supportive and understanding.

But he didn't make things easy for me. I'd just be getting into a paragraph when Mark would yell, "Can you bring me a coffee?" I'd walk downstairs, make him a coffee, go upstairs, get into writing, only to hear him again.

"I finished it. Can you put my mug in the sink?"

One day, about a month and a half into his convalescence, I arrived home with the groceries and noticed a coffee mug by the La-Z-Boy.

"How'd you get the coffee?" I asked.

"I took the stool and pushed it with my hands as I hopped on one foot to the kitchen. I made the coffee and put it on top of the stool and hopped back."

He seemed so proud of himself. He looked as if he were waiting for a hug or, at the very least, a fist bump.

What he got was my resignation.

"Good, then you can get your own coffee, beer, food, and whatever else from now on. You don't need to call me while I'm working."

I also called a cleaning lady, something I'd been threatening to do for a long time and, for a long time, he'd been asking me not to do. He'd claimed that we didn't need a cleaning lady, that he didn't want a stranger in our house. I knew better. He didn't want his friends teasing him any more than they already did.

Well, tough. My sanity was more important than his reputation. And, for the record, he really was an unemployed slacker whose wife supported him.

By the end of the summer, his leg healed and the cast came off. It had now been more than a year since we'd talked about becoming parents. I'd written a freelance article about how a woman's fertility started to drop during her late twenties. Already, at age thirty-three, my chance of getting pregnant if I managed to have sex on my most fertile day of the month was only 40 percent. This would drop to 30 percent by my thirty-fifth birthday.

We abandoned Project: Second Honeymoon and started Project: Conception. I purchased a basal temperature thermometer, bought and read *Stay Fertile Longer,* and got naked with my husband every other day. I gave up coffee. I gave up alcohol. I ate less tofu. I peed on a lot of sticks.

One month went by. Two months went by. Three months went by.

Should we consider adoption?

In early December I traveled to Phoenix on business. I was due to get my period during the trip, so I packed pads, tampons, and a pregnancy test.

My second morning in Phoenix marked day 27 of my cycle. It was too early for a pregnancy test, but I couldn't wait. I just had to know. Out came the stick and down went my pants. Within a fraction of a second, a dark and undeniable plus sign appeared.

I dialed Mark's cell.

"Honey, I'm pregnant," I told him.

"You are? How do you know?" he asked.

"I peed on a stick and got a plus sign," I said.

"But can't you get a false positive?"

"I don't think so. I'll get a blood test when I get back, but I'm not the least bit doubtful. I'm pregnant. There's a baby in my belly. I can feel it."

"Oh, all right," he said.

"I should get back to the conference. I just wanted you to know," I said.

"Yeah, okay," he said.

Did that conversation seem wrong in every single way to you? It certainly did to me. I'd imagined him getting just as excited about my pregnancy as he would get excited about, say, finding out that we had enough money in our bank account for him to take a snowboarding trip to Crested Butte.

But instead, he sounded about as happy as he generally sounds when a big piece of household equipment breaks—say a boiler or a refrigerator—and must be replaced with money that could have been spent on a snowboarding trip.

He seemed resigned. Defeated. Beaten down.

Or was I just imagining this? Maybe the pregnancy hormones were making me super sensitive.

I packed the stick in my suitcase.

When I got home, I showed him the stick.

"You kept it?" he asked, his eyebrows raised.

*He wants this baby. He wants this baby. He wants this baby.*

This was just one of those peculiar differences between men and women, I told myself. Women saved urine-covered pregnancy sticks, inserting these sorts of things into scrapbooks along with ultrasound photos, hospital bracelets, and dried-up umbilical cord stumps.

Men? They threw such things away. Just because he didn't want to inspect every inch of the stick didn't mean he didn't want the baby.

Right?

A week later I went to my family doctor for a blood test. Maybe I asked Mark to come with me. Maybe I didn't. Maybe I said something like, "I'm going in for the blood test tomorrow," and he said, "Do you want me to come?" Maybe I said, "You don't have to be there," even though I really meant, "I'd like you to come." Maybe he didn't know that "You don't have to be there" meant, "But I'd really like you to be there," and that's why he wasn't there.

I just don't remember. I do remember that the idea that he really should have been there, right next to me, holding my hand, did not occur to me until the nurse said, "Congratulations. You're pregnant!"

It was then that I yearned for someone to wipe the tears of joy from my cheeks, to hug me, and to say, "Wow, this is so cool."

Mark had been unemployed for well over a year. Don't you think it was about time he found paying work?

I certainly did, so I asked him to look for a job. I didn't care where he found work. He could be the fry cook at a fast food restaurant for all I cared. I just wanted him to have a paycheck when the baby came. I wanted a husband who worked. Like other people's husbands did.

I periodically found him browsing the want ads. By the end of the first trimester, however, he still hadn't applied for paying work.

One night, he said, "There's a storefront available downtown. It's the perfect place for a bike shop."

I'd been suggesting he open a bike shop for I didn't know how long. He would be perfect at owning and managing a bike shop. Him owning a bike shop? It was what he was meant to do.

I'd known that for a long, long time.

But now? While I was pregnant? Now, when I was hoping to work less and take time off?

Why hadn't he done this earlier? A year earlier? Two years earlier? Why had he waited until such an inconvenient moment to decide that, yes, indeed, he wanted to open a bike shop?

"Why didn't you do this earlier?"

"A space wasn't available earlier."

"Yes, there was. There were lots of spaces available."

"They weren't the right spaces. This is the right space. It's on Main Street, and the rent is cheap. It's the perfect location, and it just became available."

"You won't have an income when the baby is born," I said.

"I know," he said, his hands folded in his lap.

"How much is it going to cost to get it up and running?"

"We can remodel the retail space for nearly nothing, but we'll need about $40,000 to buy inventory."

I was a saver. I'd saved more than 20 percent of my salary since I'd gone freelance. I'd invested it well, too. We had the money. Money was not technically an issue. I just wasn't sure if we had enough money for him to open a bike shop and for me to take at least six weeks off for maternity leave. Was there enough for both?

"I don't want to stand between you and your dream. I do feel the need to say that the timing sucks. We're both going to be making a lot of sacrifices for this. Is it really that important to you?"

"Yes," he said.

And so, as I was researching birthing classes and reading *What to Expect When You're Expecting*, he was meeting with a financial counselor, accountant, and lawyer. Our financial advisor and accountant recommended taking a second mortgage on the house rather than selling off our stocks or borrowing against our 401(k)s. As I signed the papers to open the line of credit against the house, I felt a mixture of anticipation and fear. I hoped we were doing the right thing, but I couldn't help but think that we were making a huge mistake.

My La-Z-Boy-loving husband quickly morphed into an early riser who was at his soon-to-be bike shop before sunrise. There he and a couple friends stayed for hours—knocking down walls, installing sinks, building a marble coffee bar, spackling, and who knows what else.

He often arrived home long after I'd gone to bed. Then he'd be back at it the very next day.

As he focused on birthing his bike shop baby, I focused on birthing a baby of the human variety. I practiced prenatal yoga, meticulously counted my protein grams, and read everything I could about pregnancy and childbirth.

As I painted our hallway, he painted the walls of his bike shop. As I rearranged and got rid of furniture, trying to empty out one of the bedrooms so it could become a nursery, he bought and installed an espresso machine and set up a bike mechanic work area. As I obsessed over baby names, he obsessed over what to call his new store.

We were two people living in two parallel universes.

We were losing touch in other ways, too. Pregnancy had made me exceptionally horny, but Mark continually brushed off my advances.

Had he fallen out of love with me? Had I fallen out of love with him? Did he care about anything other than bikes, his bike shop, and his friends?

I'd heard about The Bradley Method, a 12-week program that teaches husbands how to coach their wives through a natural childbirth. I hoped the class would somehow help us to grow closer. I hoped it would encourage him to take an interest in the baby that was growing in my belly.

"Twelve classes? Does it really take that long to learn how to have a baby?" he asked.

"One of my friends raved about it. I think it will be really helpful."

"I'm busy getting the store ready. Twelve classes every Saturday morning is a lot."

"I'd really like to do the Bradley classes," I said.

"O-*kay*," he said with a sigh.

He accompanied me to the first class. The following week, he told me he was too busy to come. He accompanied me to some classes and missed others.[5] During the second to last class, we simulated the birthing experience. Mark rubbed my back as I held an ice cube in my hand, but I

---

[5] My memory and my husband's memory differ regarding how many birthing classes he attended. I remember him missing nearly half of the classes. He tells me he only skipped one or two. Given that I'm the one who is more likely to remember walking in alone (why would he remember not attending a class?), I've kept this section closer to my memory of what happened than his.

could tell that he didn't want to be there. I imagined early labor, calling him to announce that my water had broken. Would he ask one of his friends to drive me to the hospital? Would he be able to find the time to attend his own baby's birth?

My brother emailed. He asked if I knew anyone who might want his purebred Weimaraner, complaining that the dog barked too much.

"If that's all that's wrong with her, I'll take her," I wrote back, thinking that Rhodes could use a playmate while I was busy with the baby.[6]

"You will?" he asked.

"I need to talk to Mark about it. I'll get back to you."

That night, I told Mark that my brother was getting rid of his dog because she barked too much. "She probably just needs obedience training. Remember how unruly Rhodes was in the beginning? I tamed him. I can tame her. What do you think?"

"If that's what you want," he said.

I soon realized that adopting Jasmine during my third trimester would obliterate any notion of having a relaxing pregnancy. She barked incessantly. She bullied Rhodes, too. She nipped him in the ass for no other reason than the fact that his butt was there and she could reach it with her teeth. She stole food from his bowl. She took over his crate. She chased him off chairs, off beds, and out of sunny spots. She took his bones. He skulked around the house with his ears back, tail tucked, and head hanging low. The poor thing.

She terrorized household visitors, too. She'd lie on the floor in a calm and content-looking ball. Then, someone would make the mistake of walk-

---

[6] Yes, reader, I know. This was an insane notion. What can I say? I was pregnant! I wasn't thinking clearly.

ing too close or too loudly or too something, and she'd strike, nipping that person in the rear. Not a day went by that I didn't have to chase her down, tackle her, and wrestle her to the ground to stop her from sinking her teeth into someone's back-side. Whenever I yelled, "No! Jasmine! No!" I felt the baby move inside of me, and I worried about the nervous little being I would eventually birth.

................................................................................................................

Only take on one marital stressor at a time. If you are pregnant, don't get a puppy. If you are starting a new business, don't get pregnant. No matter what, never, ever in a million years consider starting a business, having a baby, and adopting a bad-behaving dog all at once.

................................................................................................................

By May, Mark had opened for business. He worked 7AM. to 7PM Monday through Friday, 8AM to 4PM on Saturdays, and 9AM to 2PM on Sundays.

He had to be at work before seven, though, in order to get the coffee machine warmed up. He was often there long after closing, too, as he vacuumed, took out the trash, and did accounting.

As far as getting ready for the human baby went, it was all me.

I acquired hand-me-downs—a crib, clothing, a baby swing—from friends. I registered at Babies R Us. I bought diapers, crib sheets, and butt balm. With the help of my parents, I painted and decorated the nursery.

And I obsessed about baby names. I read baby name books. I made lists of baby names. I asked other people what they thought of various baby names. I asked Mark what he thought of baby names, but I never got much input other than a cursory, "We don't need to pick a name yet. It's still early."

Were other fathers just as uninterested in the name-picking process as mine was? Did he care more about his store than he did about me? Did he care about this baby at all?

Did he want this baby?

Was my marriage falling apart?

Those questions? I thought them, but I tried very hard not to think them. I pushed them into a dark corner of my brain, the same dark corner that holds other questions like, "Does anything really happen after death?" I tried to pretend that everything was perfect, that my husband loved me and that, like me, he was overjoyed by the idea of becoming a parent.

By August 5th, though, two things were clear. I was going to have a C-section and the baby would be born without a name. Our baby was breech, its head facing up and bottom facing down. I'd tried every "baby turning" remedy out there. I'd spent hours with my legs and hips elevated on the couch and my head on the floor. I'd gone to a hypnotherapist. I'd tried a chiropractic technique thought to help turn breech babies. I'd visited an energy healer and I'd undergone an uncomfortable procedure that involved two doctors pressing their hands deep into my abdomen in an attempt to force the baby to flip over. None of it had worked. I was scheduled for surgery the following day.

My parents were staying over so they could attend the birth. After dinner, Mark asked me if he could meet some friends at a bar.

"You don't want to have this baby, do you?"

"How did, 'can I meet Wood and Beevis at The Farmhouse?' turn into, 'I don't want to have this baby?'"

"The crib still hasn't been assembled. The bassinet is still in pieces. We don't know what we are going to name this baby. I'm terrified of surgery. The birth is tomorrow, and instead of staying home and helping me get ready, you want to go out with your friends," I said between sobs.

"You're going to be in the hospital for a few days. I can get all of that done before you come home. Plus, we won't need the crib for a while," he said.

I exhaled slowly, trying to pull myself together, trying to find words that would sound logical to him. "I'll feel more relaxed if everything is ready before I leave for the hospital. Can't you just do this one thing for me, for us? Is it that important that you go out with your friends tonight?"

"This may be my last night out in a while," he said.

The tears until then had been sliding slowly down my cheeks, but now I was gushing. Some parents painted and assembled entire nurseries by the end of the first trimester. Some did it before conception. Our baby would be born in fewer than 24 hours. Did normal, well-adjusted people generally wait until their wives were recovering from major abdominal surgery and their babies were just hours from coming home before they assembled the crib and bassinet? Was it just the hormones of pregnancy that made me feel there was a huge rift between us? Did my husband really love me or did he resent me?

"Whatever," I said, feeling a hot rage building in my stomach and rising up into my throat.

"If it's that important to you, I'll stay," he said, talking slowly, as if the wrong word would send me into a maniacal fit. "I think there's pa-*len*-ty of time, but if you want it all done right now, I'll do it, okay?"

He assembled the bassinet easily and quickly, but the crib proved more time consuming, given we'd gotten it secondhand and it no longer had an owner's manual. As Mark and Dad put parts of the crib together, thought better of it, and took them back apart, he continually muttered, "We don't need to be doing this tonight. We have plenty of time."

They finished the job around ten, and then he left to meet his friends.

The following morning, Mark drove me to the hospital at 5AM. The three hours between our arrival and my trip to the operating room were busy ones, with various nurses coming to hook me up to an IV and to heart rate and blood pressure monitors, shave my pubic hair, get me dressed in a hospital gown, and perform other pre-op tasks.

Just before 8AM two nurses walked me to the OR.

At 8:11AM, my obstetrician pulled the baby from my belly. He dangled her over the sheet that separated my chest from my lower body. She was still attached, by umbilical cord, to my womb.

"This is your daughter," he said.

"It's a girl?" I knew Mark would consent to only one child. A girl? I was overjoyed.

"I love her," I said, and just in case anyone got the wrong idea about my crying, I added, "I'm crying because I'm happy."

"What's her name?" a nurse asked.

"I don't know," I said.

Later that morning we settled on Kaarina Izabel. We arrived at that decision just moments before Mark called his parents to tell them that we'd just had a baby.

During my first night in the hospital, my IV and Foley catheter were still attached, along with a blood pressure cuff and pressure hose on my legs to prevent blood clots. I couldn't get out of bed without a nurse's assistance. That night, Mark left around 9PM to go to an outdoor festival. Mom slept on the cot next to me, offering to get up in the night and bring the baby to me to nurse.

She asked me why Mark had not offered to stay. "He's the one who should be here with you. What's wrong with him?" I was still buoyed by new mom bliss. I told her she didn't know what she was talking about.

I stayed in the hospital for two and a half days. I was ecstatically happy there. I had a beautiful, healthy baby girl, a room to myself, and as much support as a new mom could ever need. When my abdomen started to hurt,

I pressed a button and a nurse would come and inject a wickedly effective prescription painkiller that numbed the pain faster than it took me to count to ten. When I wanted to take a shower, I wheeled the basinet to the nursery, dropped off the baby, and had as much time to myself as I wanted.

Whenever I had the slightest problem—a gas pain here, a sore nipple there, a sore back, a question—a nurse was by my side in seconds with an Gas X, lanolin, Tylenol, or an answer. My obstetrician agreed to release me from the hospital a day early so I could celebrate my birthday at home. Early on the eighth, I called Mark and asked him to pick me up.

"I'm busy. There are a lot of customers here. How about 3:00?"

"You can't come sooner?"

"No, that's the best I can do."

I spent most of my birthday alone, rocking Kaarina over and over again. Finally, a little after 3:00, Mark and my parents retrieved us.

When we got home, Mark, his friend Ken, and Dad went to a "Customer Appreciation Party" for Mark's business. I encouraged him to go, saying as they all walked out the door, "Be back in an hour for the cake." Ken's wife Gail stayed behind with Mom and me.

At some point during the next hour, my milk came in. In case you've never nursed, here's a quick education on milk making. When a baby is born, the mom has no milk. She has colostrum, a high protein goo. Mom's boobs only provide a teaspoon or two of this yellow drink per nursing session. This encourages the newborn to suck and suck and suck and suck. Eventually, after twenty-four to seventy-eight hours, the constant and fierce sucking triggers the mammary glands to make milk, and mothers, for whatever reason, refer to the first shipment of milk as "coming in," probably because it comes in so goddamn quickly.

My barely B-cup breasts swelled to beyond double Ds. Really, they looked much larger than Pamela Anderson's artificially augmented size. I exaggerate not. They were huge and they were heavy and they were hard and they hurt. It felt as if someone had filled them up with lead. My breasts were so full of milk that my nipples stuck out like cones. They were deformed, and they were ultra sensitive. They were also starting to chafe from multiple days of her hard little gums grinding themselves on my areolas.

Kaarina happened to be hungry. I put her to my breast and stuck the nipple in her mouth. Pain shot through my boob and up and down my body. I felt as if I was being electrocuted through my nipple. No, of course I've never actually been electrocuted through my nipples, so of course I wouldn't truly know if breastfeeding feels like being electrocuted through one's nipples.

But it makes sense. Ask any mother who has ever breastfed a child.

I tried, through the pain, to relax, as I had been told that one needs to relax for the milk to let down. Again, if you've never nursed, here's a quick primer on the whole letting down thing. It might seem logical that milk would just sit stored up in Mom's boobs, ready for the taking, but if that were the case, Mom's boobs would leak milk all day long. Instead, it is stored in the milk glands. Sucking stimulates the letting down, which is when the milk drops from the glands and into the ducts.

My milk would not let down. Kaarina kept spitting out my nipple and then crying. I would stick it back in her mouth, she'd clamp down and suck, I'd shudder with pain, and she'd spit it out again. At some point, Ken and Dad arrived home. "Where's Mark?" I managed to ask, between bouts of nipple torture. "He's still at the party," one of them told me.

"What?"

"He's still at the party."

I called Mark's cell.

"Why didn't you come home with Dad and Ken?"

"I need to greet a few more customers. I'm working the party. I'll be home soon," he said.

"But I said to just go for an hour."

"I need to work the party."

"I'm having problems here."

"I'll be home soon."

Ken and Gail wanted to stay until Mark got home so we could all eat birthday cake together. My mother warmed washcloths and placed them on my breasts. Kaarina whimpered and then cried.

"I think she's still hungry," Gail said.

I thought some not so nice words about that little comment. I won't print those words here because Gail will probably read this book. Gail? I was in a really pissy mood and my nipples were killing me and I felt like my cone-shaped nipples were on display for all the world to see. That's why I thought those words, okay?

I hoisted myself out of the chair. I walked outside and dialed Mark's cell. I growled into the phone, making a sound that even surprised me, "Get your ass home."

He did.

I ate my cake. Ken and Gail left. I slowly ambled upstairs. There I found small pieces of plastic and little bits of yarn all over the bedroom carpet. I knew the mess was the work of Jasmine. Rhodes did not destroy things anymore. It took me quite a while to put together precisely what they had been before she'd chewed them into pieces. Once the revelation hit me, I ached with loss. The debris was from a baby care video that I hadn't yet watched along with a pair of hand knit booties Mom had purchased in Italy.

The nursing problems continued. I sat in the rocking chair in our bedroom with my husband on one side trying to suck the milk out of one breast with a hand-held breast pump and my mother on the other side, trying to massage the milk out with a warm wash cloth.

My thoughts pinged back and forth from "Please, please, please let the milk come out" to "Is this normal? Do other mothers have this much trouble?" to "I'm not sure I can last much longer" to "I can't believe I'm letting my mother massage my breasts" to "See? He really does love me. He wouldn't be holding a breast pump to my boob if he didn't love me" to "I wish I could watch that baby care video. Now I will never know how to be a good mother."

Finally, the baby latched on, sucking one boob and then the other to considerably smaller sizes. When she finished, she started crying. She was still hungry.

Now, I'd run marathons. I'd done a lot of really hard things in my life. Normally I'm not a quitter.

But I could *NOT* take it any longer.

"What do you want me to do?" Mark asked. "Tell me what to do. How can I help? What can I do?"

"Get formula," I cried. "Just get formula. I can't take it anymore. Get formula."

Mark found a pharmacy open at 2AM, bought formula, bottles, and nipples, drove home, boiled it all, and then made a bottle. The baby drank it and fell asleep with the bottle in her mouth.

See? Good father. A bad father would have gone to sleep rather than going to the pharmacy. A bad father would not have boiled the bottles and nipples. A bad father would not have given the baby the bottle.

He loved me. He loved her.

I was exhausted. I knew that we should probably talk about him not being home when I'd needed him. But it was 3AM and I was too tired. "We'll talk about it tomorrow," I told myself, drifting off to sleep.

The following morning, Mark left for work at 6:45. I resumed breastfeeding, Mom repeatedly bringing me warm compresses to soften and soothe my sore nipples. Mark did not return until after 8PM. Mom baked a chicken, and we all ate in silence.

..................................................................................................

If you plan to nurse your baby, sign up for a breastfeeding lesson before birth and get the contact information for a lactation consultant before birth, too. Breastfeeding might not be rocket science, but it's certainly not like taking a shower either. Most breastfeeding mothers absolutely need professional help.

As my estrogen levels plummeted from one thousand times above normal during pregnancy to less than the usual amount during breastfeeding, I was waking repeatedly in the night to nurse for thirty to forty-five minutes, change a diaper, and then rock a baby back to sleep, only to do it all over again in less than two hours. The first couple of nights were the hardest. I'd hear her cry, try to move, groan from the pain, roll over onto all fours and slowly ease myself out of bed. Each time I woke, I took Gas-X and Motrin, hoping one or the other would ease my next journey from the bed to the bassinet. I lost track of how many pills I'd taken or when.

Mom had planned to stay for two weeks. With each passing day, however, tension grew between Mom and Mark. He'd leave for work at 6:45AM and return after 8PM. When he wasn't working, he was on his bike or hanging out after hours at the shop with friends. Mom did the grocery shopping, cooked all of the meals, and periodically muttered something or other about how it would be nice if the baby's father actually held his baby every once in a while.

A week after the birth, as we drove up the hill to the house, I heard Mom say, "Oh shit."

"What's wrong?" I asked.

She said, "Something strange just happened."

"What do you mean?"

"Where were we just now?"

"What do you mean?"

"What did we just do?"

"We went to the pediatrician and then we got coffee and then we drove home," I said. "You don't remember?"

"No," she said.

I called Dad to get the name and number of her doctor, who explained that it was probably nothing but that we should take her to the ER.

"You're not going anywhere," Mark said. "Hospitals are filled with germs. It's not safe to take a newborn there."

"But how are we going to get her there?" I asked.

"I'll take her," he said.

With a lump in my throat, I hugged Mom and then stood and watched them walk to the car.

I called Dad. I sat on the couch and stared into space. Two friends stopped by to meet the baby. For a while, I felt better. They even had me laughing. Mark called a few times from the hospital, asking me where my dad was.

"I caught him in the middle of making lasagna," I said. "He'll be there as soon as he can. He had to pack a few things. It's an hour and a half drive, and I'm not sure he knows where the hospital is. What's the deal? Do you need to go back to work?"

"Yes," he said. The yes was drawn out and cold. It was a "Yeh-*essssss*." Between the lines, it said, "Are you a moron? Of course I have to get back to work."

"Then I'll come to the hospital. I don't want her there alone."

"No, you can't do that."

"Don't leave her alone," I pleaded.

"He better get here soon," he said.

Dad eventually arrived and Mark went back to his shop. My friends left, one of them accidentally hitting Mom's two-week-old Subaru as she backed out of our driveway. She scraped off some paint and pulled off the side view mirror. I told her to not worry about the damage, and then I cried until my eyes swelled.

Mark arrived home. He tried to cheer me up by telling me stories about the hospital.

"This doctor came in and gave your mom a glass of water. Then he left the room and came back five minutes later and asked her if she knew who gave her the water. She didn't," he said.

"Oh," I said.

"She kept asking the same questions over and over. Did Alisa have her baby? Was it a boy or a girl? It was so annoying that I wrote down the answers to the questions and numbered them. When she would ask one of those questions, I'd say, 'Number 2' and she'd read the answer," he said.

"Um-hum," I said.

"One time, when she asked me if it was a boy or a girl, I lied and said it was a boy. She did not like that."

After a number of tests, the doctors diagnosed her with Transient Global Amnesia, which is just a fancy name for "you have no short term memory and we have no bloody clue why." She was not having a stroke. She was not having a hemorrhage. She was not having a seizure. They predicted that her memory would start to come back within twenty hours of the onset of the memory loss. She would eventually be able to remember nearly everything. Her condition was not dangerous. It was just a pesky little nuisance that would go away all by itself.

Around 9PM or so, whatever had been interfering with her memory cells stopped interfering with them. She called. I cried when she asked, "Have I been of any help this week?" I cried as I told her she'd been an amazing help, that I never would have gotten through the week without her.

Then I hung up and cried even more.

The doctors released her the following day.

Later that day, Mom went home with Dad. A part of me was relieved. Mom couldn't keep her opinions about Mark to herself, and I wasn't getting enough sleep to be able to talk to her about my marital issues without getting snippy. A part of me, however, was also sad.

Within a few weeks, Kaarina developed colic.[7] The crying would start around dinnertime. If Mark was home, we'd take turns walking and rocking her until ten or eleven, when he went to bed. Then I was on my own until midnight, one, or two, or whenever it was that I finally got her to sleep. If he wasn't home, I held her nonstop.

During the worst week, the crying started around noon. I rarely could figure out if she was crying from colic or crying from hunger, so I continually offered her the nipple. And, so, there I was, one day, switching her from boob to boob for hours. Once, just as I'd almost gotten her to sleep, the dogs barked, startling her awake. I screamed at them and shut the door to the nursery.

Mark arrived home around 8PM. I heard him climbing the steps. I heard the dogs get up, wag their tails, and pant. The door opened a crack and then all the way. He was standing in the doorway, his arm leaning against the frame.

"Did you make anything for dinner?" he asked. "And why are the dogs in the hallway?"

"I've been sitting in this chair with her on one boob or another for the past eight hours," I said through gritted teeth. "I haven't even gotten up to go to the bathroom."

In his happiest most cheerful tone of voice, the one he might use if he were talking someone off a roof or a bridge, he said, "I'll order some takeout and pick it up!"

Then, just like that, I turned from a milk factory into a tear and snot factory.

His eyes soft and his mouth still pulled in a smile, he asked, "Can I get you anything? What can I do for you? How can I help?"

---

[7] Despite popular belief, colic is not a stomach ailment. No one knows what causes it, although various people have their theories, ranging from stress during pregnancy to trauma during the delivery (such as a C section), either of which cause the infant to feel overstimulated by light and sound and cry nonstop.

"I can't do this anymore," I sobbed. "I don't have what it takes. I'm a terrible mother. I can't do this."

He walked toward me, knelt by the rocker, and put his hand on my shoulder.

"That's not true. You're a fantastic mother. You just had a bad day."

He held me in a half hug until I calmed down. Then he got takeout.

Hand off the baby to your spouse, even if that means your baby gets formula. Do it even if it means your spouse doesn't hold the baby right or the baby always cries when you are not around. Do it even if your spouse puts the diapers on backward. No mother is unbreakable. Give yourself a break before you hit your breaking point.

The phone rang repeatedly during the day. I eventually unplugged all of the phones from the jacks and stopped checking messages. When friends offered to come over, I begged off, telling them I was too tired for visitors. It was all I could do to nurse, change diapers, and clean spit up. I didn't have the mental wherewithal to manage talking and listening, too.

When the rage erupted, it was strong, violent, and almost uncontrollable. One afternoon, I woke with a start. Jasmine was barking, yet again. I flew out of bed, saw a rawhide bone on the floor, picked it up, and hurled it at her. It hit her in the head, knocking her sideways.

Then there was the night that I woke to Kaarina's crying. It seemed as if I'd just gotten to sleep. I felt as if I'd just nursed her five minutes ago.

"What do you want now?" I said through clenched teeth as I reached my hands under her tiny little body. I felt an overwhelming urge to shake her, throw her, or smother her. Shaking her would feel so good. Shaking her would show my husband that he should have given me more support. Shaking her would teach him to appreciate me more. I grasped her tiny body firmly with my fingers. I was squeezing her. Then the tears came. I sat in the rocker. I put her to my breast. The tears slid down my cheeks. They slid onto her little head. I snorted. I heaved. She nursed. I was scared of myself. I was scared of my anger. I was scared of the person I was becoming. I no longer knew myself, and the person I saw now, I didn't like.

The next day, the night felt like a dream. I remembered the details of what had happened, but it felt as if it had all happened to someone else. I was a calm person. I was a happy person. I was a nice person. I was a generous person. I was intelligent.

I was not a baby shaker.

But I knew I needed to tell Mark. With my voice shaking, I explained that I'd come close to hurting the baby. I said that I'd wanted to shake her. I said that maybe I had shaken her, just a little, before coming to my senses.

I said that I didn't know who I was or what I was becoming.

He told me to wake him whenever I needed him.

Afterward, I did try to wake him a couple times. One night, for example, Kaarina spit up nearly all of the breast milk she'd just consumed onto me, the afghan, and the rocking chair. I could not get her back to sleep, and I didn't think I could hold her and clean up the mess at the same time. I was cold and wet, and I stank of sour breast milk. I told him I needed his help.

"I'll be up in a minute," he mumbled, and then he went back to sleep. I got changed, threw everything in the washer, and swabbed down the rocker. I did it all while holding the baby.

There were plenty of other similar nights. Poop or pee or both would be all over the crib, and I'd need to change the baby, wipe her down, nurse her, and put her on the floor while I changed and cleaned the crib.

In retrospect, I could have tried harder. I could have asked for help more often, more loudly, and more insistently. I could have, but I didn't. Did I not do it because I was too tired to talk? Perhaps. Did I not do it because I was ashamed to ask for help? Maybe. Did I not ask because I wanted to think of myself as the perfect mother, the one who could do it all? Probably. Did I not ask because I was already training myself for divorce and single motherhood? It's all very possible.

Saying, "I need help" does not mean you are weak. Rather, having the courage to say those words means you are very, very strong.

$$\infty\!\infty$$

One morning, I put Kaarina on the floor on a blanket. Jasmine was sleeping nearby. I did not trust that dog, so I placed my body between the dog and the baby.

I felt something hard whack the side of my face.

"Ow," I said, my hand to my cheek. Jasmine was now standing. My cheek throbbed.

"You didn't just? You didn't?" I stared at the dog. "Did you just bite me in the face?"

I picked up Kaarina and walked to the bathroom. In the mirror, I could see teeth marks along my cheekbone. She hadn't broken the skin, but she'd bruised me.

I put Jasmine in her crate and called Mark.

"Jasmine just bit me," I said dejected. "It's just a matter of time before she bites the baby. I don't know what to do."

"I'll call Jim," he said.

Jim was a survivalist. He had tanks of water buried in his backyard, a massive gun collection, and three adopted and somewhat vicious dogs.

Later that day, he came with his pickup, a crate loaded into the back. He took Jasmine. I didn't miss her one bit.

.........................................................................................................

## Everyone should know a Jim.

.........................................................................................................

By five weeks postpartum, we were running out of money. I had no choice but to start working again. I'd put our names on a waiting list for one of the best daycare centers in the area when I'd learned I was pregnant, but they were still booked for at least a few more months. With my parents in Delaware, no family in the area, and a husband who was working twelve hour days, seven days a week, I tried to work around the baby. I worked while she slept, which was not often. She took two twenty- to thirty-minute naps each day. I worked whenever she was content in her bouncy seat or in her little play gym. I worked while I nursed, and I worked while I held her.

I worked, and I felt guilty, guilty because I wanted to focus my attention on her and not on the keyboard, guilty because I thought she deserved a mother who actually paid attention to her rather than shushed her constantly, and guilty because, even when I was not working, I had not one ounce of mental energy. I'd read that baby girls were expert at reading facial expressions, that they craved smiles and eye contact. I knew I was a shell of my former self. My face was expressionless, mirroring the absence of thoughts in my head. I worried that she would see this blank expression and somehow grow to believe that she was not lovable.

By the time she was eighteen weeks old, we were still on the daycare's waiting list and I was informed that it might be six months or longer before a space opened up. I called all of the centers listed in the Yellow Pages. Most had long waiting lists. I finally found a daycare center with an opening for two days a week. I dropped her off early one December morning.

Then I walked to the car. I'd expected to feel guilty, but I didn't. I felt relieved.

Kaarina got her first cold three days later, and her nose didn't stop running for the rest of the year. The constant colds, fevers, and GI illnesses disrupted her sleep. By January, she'd regressed to two wakings per night, and then three. By seven months, she was back to waking every two hours. Early one late winter morning I found myself at the end of the driveway, in the dark, with her in her car seat. We'd woken early and I had decided to take her to daycare, even though it was only 6:30AM. I sat in the car motionless for a very long time. I couldn't leave the driveway because I couldn't figure out how to turn on my headlights.

Something was wrong with my brain. Every month I invariably opened a late notice for a bill that I swore I had already paid, but eventually found hidden under another piece of paper. I would make lunch dates with friends, and then forget about them. I lost Kaarina's pink eye medication within moments of coming home from the pharmacy; I found it a year later in the medicine cabinet. I lost track of what I was saying within just a few words of starting a sentence.

I also occasionally fantasized about driving my car into trees and telephone poles. I'd see a pole ahead and think, "God, it would feel so good to just accelerate and drive right into it." I'd consider it, but then I would not be able to get up the nerve to unlatch my seatbelt.

By the time she was eight months old, I had tried all of the advice in the *No-Cry Sleep Solution*. None of it had helped. Various friends and even my pediatrician had suggested I let her "cry it out," but I'd resisted. Now, I was desperate. I would have given away my house, my furniture, my retirement savings, my jewelry, and, yes, definitely my husband for one decent night's sleep.

On the first night I sat on the floor just outside her door as her whimpers grew into a screech and then into a constant wail. She stood in the crib and shook the sides as she wailed, yelling "Mama!" between screams. She cried so violently that she choked on her saliva and snot, periodically sounding as if she was going to throw up.

*I am doing the right thing. I am doing the right thing. I am doing the right thing.*

Mark closed her door and then his. I opened her door. He opened his and asked why I'd opened hers.

"I need to hear her," I said. "I can't ignore her."

"I can't sleep," he said. "The crying is too loud."

"Mark, I haven't slept in eight months. This is going to take three nights. This is three nights out of your life. I hate when you close the door."

"Why?" he asked. "I just want to sleep. Sleep is normal. Everyone sleeps at night."

"Okay then," I said, exhausted and unable to put my feelings into words. "Go to bed. Close the door."

I sat in the hallway, alone, for two and a half hours that night, until she finally stopped crying.

Her sleep improved. Rather than waking every two hours, she woke just once. Her health, however, deteriorated. She picked up a new germ every time I dropped her off at daycare, and every other week she was home with a fever or diarrhea. I was convinced that the daycare center staff was not properly sanitizing the teething rings or washing their hands. I couldn't prove it, mind you. But I felt that truth in my bones.

So I began searching for a better daycare center, and soon I was touring a center recommended to me by my pediatrician. The infant room was more than twice the size of the cramped little room at Kaarina's current daycare center. It was also quiet. Not a single infant was crying. They were listening to Mozart.

"Oh my God," I said. "I need to change centers now."

The center director told me she had an opening in August, around Kaarina's first birthday, three months away.

Soon afterward, Kaarina developed a 102 degree fever that lasted seven days. Once the fever eased, she developed diarrhea. I kept her home for two weeks, trying to work around her as best as I could.

Mom suggested that I take her out of daycare permanently so she could recover in a germ-free environment.

"But I have to work," I said, despondent.

"Then move in with us. We'll watch her so you can work. We need to get this baby healthy."

"You'd really do that?" I asked.

"Yes," she said. "We'd enjoy it."

Relief washed over me.

The following week, I began driving the one-and-a-half hours to Delaware on Mondays, staying the week with my parents, and driving back home Fridays or Saturdays, so Mark could have some time with his daughter. In Delaware, I felt relaxed. I was no longer lonely. I felt happy and cared for. I did not miss Mark.

I considered moving to Delaware permanently.

I moved back to Emmaus just two months later, though. My parents were getting anxious to return to their real lives. Dad mentioned that he missed riding his bike. Mom wanted to get back to her painting. The new daycare had a full time opening earlier than expected.

I could list example after example that paints a picture of a detached, neglectful husband and father, but I'm fairly certain at this point that you get it. If I clubbed him over the head and told him that what I wanted him to do was nonnegotiable, he did it. If I was any less firm about it, he didn't.

Because of this, I'm sure it will seem quite counterintuitive when I tell you, as I am doing now, that my husband had made a project of getting Kaarina to walk almost since the day she was born.

Yes, I'm quite sure it seems like odd behavior from a man who would rather ride his bike, have a beer with his buddies, or hang out at his store than go to one of his child's well-baby appointments. It's not to me. It's because I know that my husband is possibly the most competitive man on the planet.

And when the most competitive person on the planet has a nephew who walked at seven months, that competitive father becomes bent on having his child break the family record.

To encourage her to walk by six months, he put her through walking exercise training. He'd hold her back or hips with his hands and stand her up, trying to strengthen her legs by placing her wobbly body weight on them.

Month six had come and gone without walking. So had month seven. She'd crawled at month eight. By her first birthday, she was still on her belly, and Mark had long given up hope of having her break the world's record for the earliest walking baby. She was making progress, though. She could pull herself up and stand unassisted for a few seconds. Her first steps would be soon, and I couldn't wait to see them.

One evening in late September, her caregiver proudly told me, "Kaarina took a few steps today." "She did?" I asked, feeling a mixture of joy and sadness. Now that she was in daycare fulltime, it made logical sense that she would start walking there. I knew that, but I'd assumed that they would not tell me about those steps, allowing me to cling to the illusion that the first steps I saw were the very first ones, even if they were the one hundred and first steps.

I carried her to the car and strapped her into her car seat, kissing her on the head and whispering, "I'm proud of you." I wanted to be happy, but I was disappointed. I wanted to see those steps. I'd seen the rolling over. I'd fed her the first solid meal. I'd been there for the crawling. I'd heard the first words. I wanted the steps.

I drove to Mark's store.

I walked into the store, said a collective hello to the various customers, knelt on the floor and stood her on her feet, as Mark had done so many times the previous year. I held her until she felt steady, and then I let go and walked a few steps away, reaching my arms out to her and hoping that she'd walk toward them. She took a step and then fell over, crawling the rest of the way. Did that count? Did it? I so wanted it to count. I said, "Did you see it? Did you see it?"

Mark, engrossed in putting away inventory, said nothing. I'd thought he'd been looking at us when I'd put her on the floor, but maybe he'd turned his head and I hadn't noticed. As he walked past, I softly said, "She took a few steps today."

One customer yelled congratulations. Another customer said, "That's great!" Mark said nothing. I tried one more time, "She took a few steps today."

"I heard you the first time," he said and walked away.

Various people looked away or toward the floor. I waited a few more minutes, trying not to look too conspicuous, and then I turned and walked out without saying good-bye.[8]

As I drove up the hill to our house, I made plans to move to Delaware, to buy a house somewhere near my parents or near my older brother. Some part of me must have felt wounded, but I covered up that wound with anger. I told myself that I did not need him. I told myself that I could leave him. I told myself that I would be better off as a single mother than I would be married to a man who didn't love me. I was already a single mother anyway, practically. I was earning all of the money that flowed into

---

[8] About two years later, not long after our marriage project, I mentioned this fight to one of the customers who'd been at the shop that day. He said, "You know, I remember that day. Just before you walked in, a customer ripped your husband a new one for not having his bike fixed on time." Why my husband never mentioned this to me, I'll never know. Perhaps it was a point of pride. I can tell you this: had I known that? I would have been a smidgen more understanding. Just a smidgen, though.

our bank account and doing roughly 90 percent of the parenting. What was 10 percent more? I'd gotten this far. I could do this without him.

I pulled into the driveway, a profound sense of calm coming over me. I unstrapped Kaarina from her seat. I carried her inside, and I made only enough dinner for myself.

Around 8PM, I heard his car in the driveway. Then, the sound of the TV. Then the thunk of the footrest extending from the recliner. He yelled something. I said nothing. I had nothing left to say to him. If I started talking, I'd start crying. I wanted to take a pair of scissors and cut him out of my life. I didn't want to go through the trouble of discussing it all with him. I just wanted to be done.

He yelled something else. Then there was the creaking noise made by his feet on the stairs. The door opened. His eyes were stony and cold. His lips were pressed together in a flat line. His cheeks were expressionless.

"Why didn't you answer me?"

"Because I'm mad at you and I don't feel like talking to you right now."

"What about?"

"How you treated me at the shop. How you bit my head off."

"How did I bite your head off?"

"You really don't know?"

"No, I don't know what you are talking about."

"I told you about her steps."

"Yeah, you kept saying it and I heard you."

"But you didn't respond."

"*BECAUSE* I was *BUSY*," he said.

"You were too busy to talk to me? You were too busy to say hello or acknowledge me in any way?"

"I was really busy," he said.

I didn't know where to go with this. I felt sick to my stomach.

"Our marriage is in the toilet," I said. "It's trashed. There's nothing left between us."

"What are you talking about?"

"I'm talking about our marriage and about how it's over. There's no love between us anymore."

"I love you."

"You do not."

"Yes, I do."

"You don't show it," I said, sobbing in huge gasps.

He sat next to me and put his arms around me. "I've been busy. This has been a hard year. We're both tired and stressed out, but our marriage isn't over. We still love each other. I promise to help out more. It won't always be this hard. What can I do to help?"

"Be home more," I said between sobs. "Prioritize me and Kaarina. Make us the most important things in your life."

"You are the most important people in my life."

"No, we are not. Your store is your top priority. Your bike is your next priority. Your friends and social life come next. Then us."

"That's not true," he said. "You are at the top of my list. You are."

For a few months, he put us closer to the top. When Kaarina was home sick, he offered to come home for a couple hours and watch her so I could work. When I was exhausted at night, he suggested I go to bed early, and that he could get her to bed without my help.

For a while, I thought things were actually going to work out between us. I told a couple of my closest friends that I'd come very close to leaving him, but that we were working on our problems and that we were doing much better.

........................................................................................................

When you want your husband to do something, be specific. "Prioritize me," is not specific. Come home from work every day at 6PM and stay up every other night with the baby? That's specific.

That good spell? It lasted for about six months. Then, slowly and steadily, Mark regressed. He began staying later and later at the shop, hanging out with his friends more and more, and asking, "Can I go ride my bike?" at the most obviously inopportune moments. For instance, Kaarina and I would both be throwing up from the stomach flu and he'd walk up to me, dressed in his cycling gear, and say, "I'm going for a ride, okay?"

Oh, the bike. I grew to hate the bike. To me, the bike was the other woman. The store was the illegitimate child. His greatest loves were my greatest enemies. I hated that he put me in the role of being his conscience. I wanted him to understand that I needed his help without me having to ask for it.

I began to feel as if there was nothing left between us, and as this feeling grew, I began fantasizing about a life without him. The fantasies came on spontaneously. I'd be walking the dog and I'd be thinking about splitting up our savings accounts and who would get what pieces of furniture. I'd be driving to the grocery store and I'd be thinking about moving closer to my parents or to my older brother. I'd be running and I'd find myself fantasizing about myocardial infarction.

Mark came home from work one afternoon a few months after Kaarina's second birthday. I was sitting outside. Kaarina was napping. He asked, "How's things?" I'm sure he was expecting, "Fine." He got, "I'm miserable."

"What's wrong?" he asked.

"Mark, I'm miserable. I'm miserable in this marriage."

"Are you going to have your period?"

"No, Mark, this isn't a hormonal thing. I'm miserable, and I'm miserable every single day. It doesn't matter what day of the month it is. I'm still miserable."

"You're just tired," he said.

"Yes, I'm tired, but I'm also miserable," I said. "We keep having the same argument over and over again. Things change for a while and then they slide back to a state of misery."

I started crying.

He said slowly and coldly, "You need to get a life." [9]

"What?"

"You need to get a life. You're too focused on me for your happiness."

"How am I supposed to have a life when I have to work to earn the money to pay the bills and then I'm the only one here in the morning or evening to be Kaarina's parent? How am I supposed to go out? Do you want me to just leave her here alone?"

"I can watch her," he said.

"But you never do," I said.

"Because you don't ask me to," he said.

"You're always busy or just not here to ask," I said.

"Maybe you need to pick one night a week that's your night. Then you can always have that night. You don't have to ask."

"I guess we'll do that," I said.

Unlike our previous "our marriage is in trouble" discussions, this one did not end with a hug. It did not end in a "Yes, you're right, I still love you" place.

No, this one ended as coldly as it had begun.

I gave up on fixing my marriage and instead began plotting its eventual end.

But I promised myself that I would try to pull myself together and get healthy before I left him. Oh, and, yes, of course I took the night that he'd suggested I take. Why not? I signed up for a meditation class, went to book group once a month, and ran with a friend one morning a week.

---

[9] A few weeks into Project: Happily Ever After, I mentioned this particular argument to my husband, and how I had thought it was the turning point that signaled the end of our marriage. "When you told me to get a life, I thought you didn't love me anymore," I told him. He responded, "I never told you to get a life. I told you that you needed to get out of the house more often." To this day, I'm not sure if I was so sleep deprived that I heard him say different words than he actually said, or if he *thinks* he said something other than what he actually said.

As you might have suspected, Mommy's Night Out did not solve our problems. In an odd, tortured way, it made them worse. Once I established a life outside of motherhood, I became stronger, more independent, more confident, and less needy. All good, right? Not necessarily. Now, I was much less afraid of divorce. If anything, I craved it. Instead of one night a week to myself, I'd get two, as I assumed Mark would settle for the typical custody arrangement of two nights a week and every other weekend.

Mommy's Night Out also gave us one more thing to fight about, as Mark repeatedly tried to steal my night away from me. I'd be getting ready to go to meditation class and he would say, "I forgot to tell you, I'm going for a night ride with the guys. I can't cancel it. I'm sorry, you're going to have to skip your class." You want to know how I responded to that? I said a few words that my editor has asked me not to print here, and then I got in my car and I drove to meditation class, leaving him to figure out what to do about the ride he'd scheduled on my night.

Indeed, we argued over me-time as if it were a precious commodity.

And eventually we were arguing about pretty much everything.

One late winter evening, for instance, when Kaarina was about two and a half, the three of us went grocery shopping. We were in the cereal aisle when Kaarina made a run for it. I chased her, slowed my pace to grab her, only to watch her run off again. She stopped in front of the shelves of pasta sauces. "Mommy, look at this!" She was holding a jar of red sauce.

"Honey, why don't you give that to Mommy?"

"No! I want it!"

"Sweetie, Mommy would really like to look at that. Can I see?"

She hugged it to her chest. "No!"

"I'm going to count to five. If I get to five and you have not given me the sauce, I'm going to pick you up and I won't let you get down again.

One, two, three. . . ."

"Here, Mommy." She handed over the sauce. By the time I got it back on the shelf, she was at the end of the aisle and the chase had resumed.

I finally tackled her, tucked her under my arm in a football carry, and found Mark, hovering near the refrigerated chicken. His face was tight.

"What?" I asked.

Slowly, with that cold voice of his, a massive eye roll, and quite a bit of loud throat clearing, he said, "While *YOU* two have been having a good time, *I'VE* been here trying to decide what groceries we need."

"Don't talk to me like that," I said.

We maneuvered the rest of the store in silence. He tossed some stuff into the cart. I tossed some stuff into the cart. All the while, words and phrases were racing through my mind. *I was having a good time? He thought I was having a good time? Where exactly did he think I was having a good time, at the martini bar in aisle 4? Am I supposed to do everything? Chase down the kid and put all the groceries in the cart while he does nothing? Is that what he wants, because if that's what he wants I have no use for him.*

We drove home in silence. I got Kaarina ready for bed. I sat at on the edge of her mattress. I held her hand, and thought, "Now I know why some people murder their spouses."

And then, just like that, salvation hit. "This would make a great novel," I thought. "I could write a novel about how an otherwise good person (me) could do a terrible thing (kill him)."

After she fell asleep, I went to my office, turned on the computer, and started writing. The words flowed. The only sounds in the room came from the tap tap tap of the keyboard and from the words in my head.

*I wish I hadn't kept this from my children all these years. I should have told them. At least I think I should have. All my life I thought the difference between right and wrong was the difference between black and white. I thought I always knew which was which.*

*It wasn't until I met Lionel that the right began to blend with wrong, and that black and white mixed together into a shade of gray. I would like to think that I made the right decision that day. I wonder if my children would agree. I wonder what you will think. Before you make any judgments, I'd like to tell you the whole story. I'd like you to hear it all before you call me a sinner. Just listen with an open mind. That's all I ask.*

*Most people probably think they do the right thing most of the time. Most people think that the evil people, the sinners, do wrong all day long and think wrong every minute of the day. These are the serial killers and the thieves, the drive-by shooters and the rapists. Looking back over my life and thinking about what happened, I wonder if we aren't all a little of both. I wonder if we don't all have some sin and some saint in us.*

For the first time in a very long time, I felt happy. Each day, I wrote a little more. The novel soothed me. It was a refuge. Whenever I worked on it, I became so engrossed in the plot that I forgot about my personal misery.

But when I wasn't working on the novel, I was still exceptionally miserable about my home life. I felt trapped—in my marriage, in parenthood, and even inside my own house. Indeed, the house felt like a prison, probably because I spent so much time stuck inside with a clingy, whiney toddler who seemed to have an ever-present runny nose. I had more time than any mother truly needs to obsesses over the smallness of the rooms, the inconvenient layout, the lack of a backyard, and the bugs. Oh, the bugs. It seemed as if some sort of bug invaded the house during every month of the year. Sometimes I'd find a wall covered with ladybugs or a floor covered with ants. If it wasn't flies, then it was mice. If it wasn't mice, then it was stinkbugs.

A house with a backyard and a swing set that had recently been visited by an exterminator? I was convinced it would solve nearly all of my problems.

About that, let me explain, because at this point, you're probably questioning my sanity. Why on Earth would I buy a house when my marriage was so obviously in trouble? Wouldn't buying a house make it even harder to end this bad marriage? It depends on your perspective. I did not consider buying a more expensive home a sign of a deeper commitment with my husband. In fact, it was quite the opposite. It was an escape.

In my divorce fantasy, I put an offer on a house. We kept our old house until we moved in. Mark and I got into a fight. I told him to leave. He did, and he went right back into the old house. He'd buy half of our old bug-infested house from me. We'd split our investments. We'd share custody. My family, particularly my mother, would start visiting me again.

It all seemed to make perfect sense.

So one February day a realtor walked us through one house after another. It seemed as if each one had a fatal "No way can I live here!" flaw. One didn't have a backyard. Another didn't have a garage. Yet another had a view of a paintball factory. Would there be a house in our (my) price range that was just right? Or would I have to settle for a Less Than Perfect House, just as I seemed to have settled for a Less Than Perfect Marriage?

Settle I did not.

Near the end of the day we walked into the last house on our touring list. I saw the 500-square-foot sunroom, hardwood floors, and walnut paneled den. It was my match made in heaven.

We closed a month later. We talked about putting our old house on the market in a few weeks. This, I reasoned, would give me a full month to decide whether or not I wanted to stay married.

Two days after closing on the new house, however, one of Mark's customers asked to see our old one. He made an offer that day. We accepted it. My divorce fantasy vanished.

Once in the new house, we began bickering about every little thing. He wanted the bathroom counter completely clear of clutter; I didn't. He didn't think I washed the clothes correctly; I didn't like the way he folded them. I accused him of shrinking my favorite sweater; he blamed it on the cleaning lady.

And when we weren't bickering, we had nothing else to say. We'd go out to dinner and stare at our food, the silence between us as thick as our butternut squash soup. I began to hate when he was home. His eyes were so cold and his jaw so set. I assumed he resented me. I believed that, in talking him into becoming a father, I'd ruined his life.

At the same time, I was finally rested after the early years of motherhood. I was excelling in my career. I was exercising and getting fit. I was feeling sexy. I noticed men looking at me. I fantasized about my soulmate, the perfect match who just had to be out there somewhere. Mark had been a mistake. I'd married him because he'd come along at the right time. We had nothing in common, I told myself.

By the time I met Deb in New York, I was 15,000 words into the story of how I would eventually kill my husband. After Deb made me promise to work on my marriage, I said, "You know, I was at the grocery store one night, and I got so mad at him, I decided to write a novel about how I would eventually kill him."

"Oh my God, that's great. You're writing a novel? That's great! Tell me more."

"It's about this naïve girl who gets knocked up by a player, marries him, and then eventually finds herself stuck in a terrible marriage. She doesn't want to divorce him. I'm not sure why. I still have to figure out why divorce isn't an option. Anyway, she decides to kill him."

"How does she kill him?"

"I don't know. I'm stuck on that because I want her to get away with it. Maybe she poisons him?"

"No, that's too cliché. Let's see. How about he has diabetes and she puts an overdose of insulin in his coffee."

"You can die from an insulin overdose?"

"Yes, and it would be impossible to trace."

As we walked back to the hotel, my mind was cluttered with thoughts about how Grace would do in Lionel and about how I would undo everything that was wrong with my marriage.

# 5

## So She Started a Project

### MAY 2007–JUNE 2007

**"All marriages are mistakes that we then spend time repairing."**

—Salvador Minuchin

I'd promised Deb that I would try everything, but other than giving my husband the ultimatum, I tried nothing. This went on for about two weeks.

Then, early one evening, Mark and I got in a fight about whether he had retrieved our daughter from daycare at the right time. I thought he'd picked her up too late. He thought he'd gotten there in plenty of time.

This sort of argument might seem mild to you. Perhaps you are thinking that it seems like the type of fight that is over as quickly as it starts and is completely forgotten after a good night's sleep. For me? It was anything but mild and forgettable. It was a sign that our marriage was beyond repair.

Indeed, feeling empty, misunderstood, and completely alone, I sat outside in the dark. "Why did I have to go and tell Deb about my marriage?" I thought. "Now she's expecting an email from me explaining how marital counseling is going."

Deb, though, would not be getting that email. Mark and I were not seeing a counselor. More important, I had no plans to ever see a counselor. I
had no plans to see one because I didn't see the point. We were obviously
destined for divorce. Why prolong the inevitable?

How could I stay married to a man like him? How?

Minutes passed. A half hour passed. An hour passed. The crickets
chirped, and as I listened to them, I heard Deb's words: *Have you tried everything? Have you tried everything? Have you tried everything?*

Did I owe it Deb to try? Did I owe it to my daughter to try? Did I owe
it to myself to try?

Dang it all.

I got up. I walked inside. I went on the Internet and typed "marital
improvement" into Amazon.

I ordered two books by John Gottman, who directed the so-called
"Love Lab" at the University of Washington. I ordered a book from John
and Linda Friel, a husband and wife marital counseling team. Years before
I'd attended a lecture by David Schnarch, PhD, so I put one of his books in
the cart. I also got a book by the aptly named Patricia Love, EdD.

Then I thought about marital counseling.

Should we go there?

Did we really have to? Couldn't we just read some books and be done
with it?

I wasn't a fan of marital counseling for many reasons. One was that, as
a teen, I'd watched my parents go through the paces of marital counseling.
They'd gone to weekend-long retreats, individual therapy sessions, and couples therapy. I'd grown up with parents who talked about "I statements"
and "speaker listener techniques" and journaling. They'd talked about the
relative merits of talk therapy, feminist therapy, and cognitive therapy.

And they'd fought. I would sit at the end of the driveway in the summer, especially on the days when the windows were open, listening to
Mom screaming at Dad. How far would their soundwaves travel? Would

they reach the neighbors next door? Would my best friend, who lived across the street and two doors down, be able to hear?

My parents eventually worked things out. One day Mom hugged Dad and decided to move back into her marriage bed. I'd been both relieved and thankful when Mom decided to become a member of our family again, but I hadn't been thankful for the therapy. Had the therapy really done anything positive? Had it helped them at all? Hadn't it just given my mother a bunch of fake reasons to despise my very doting father? It wasn't until Mom stopped trying to change Dad into an outgoing, talkative, and charismatic man, and had accepted him for the quiet, nearly wordless Mr. Fix It Family Man that he was that their marriage had strengthened. Their reconciliation gave me hope for my marriage, but it didn't give me hope that marital counseling was the solution.

My reluctance also stemmed from my memories of the sessions Mark and I had with our premarital counselor. Back then Mark had clung to his yeses, no's, and one-word jokes. When she asked about our biggest differ-ence, for example, Mark, without a hint of a smile or change in tone of voice, said, "Height." (He's nine inches taller than I am).

If my dad was quiet, Mark was an emotional vault.

Every time I thought about scheduling an appointment, I envisioned our initial exchange with the marital counselor.

"What's wrong with your marriage?" the marital counselor would ask.

"Nothing," Mark would reply.

"Why are you here?"

"My wife made me come."

"Does that bother you?"

"No, she's not happy. I want her to be happy."

"Why do you think you're having marital problems?"

"I don't know. Ask my wife. She's the one with the problem."

Mark did not reveal feelings. Feelings? Him? I'd only seen him scared once, on the night before he'd had a questionable mole removed and biopsied. I'd never seen him sad, depressed, excited, or angry.

He seemed to only have one feeling. It was even. Day in and day out, he was even Steven.

How could I take *HIM* to talk therapy? He. Didn't. Talk. I could drop him off on a deserted island and pick him up a month later. I could try to make a conversation by asking, "How was it?" After a month without a single person to talk to, he would still give me a one-word answer. It would be, "Good."

A brilliant counselor just might have been able to coax Mark to talk candidly about our problems and his feelings. I worried, however, that we would have to visit four or five mediocre counselors before we found the brilliant one, and that we would give up on counseling and on our marriage long before we found our Marriage Whisperer.

I thought back to my early twenties, when I had low self-esteem and dysthymia. I'd bought into self-help so strongly that I'd eventually made a career of writing self-help books. I'd repeatedly used self-help books to solve every problem I'd ever had. I'd used them to train Rhodes. I'd used them to get pregnant. I'd used them to solve nursing problems. I'd used them to get Kaarina to sleep through the night. I'd used them over and over again.

I wondered, "Could self-help save my marriage?" Reading my way to a better marriage seemed a lot less intimidating than asking a total stranger for help.

Maybe the books would be enough. Maybe, after reading the books, I would know so much about marriage that I could become our Marriage Whisperer.

Yes, that was likely. I believed in my ability to become our Marital Whisperer about as strongly as I believed that I should change my daily behavior based on my horoscope. (Just in case you aren't sure about that analogy, it means that I didn't believe it all that strongly.)

From that less than optimistic start, I went about creating a marital improvement plan. A top priority: resurrecting our sex life. We were in the midst of a six-month-long dry spell. Another priority: forgiveness. I was wounded from the past, and I'd covered those wounds with adhesives that were so thick and so strong that I could barely feel any emotion, good or bad. Yet another: romance. When I fantasized about other men, I didn't think about sex. I thought about romance—about being told I was cherished, about being caressed, about being proposed to. Heck, I fantasized about handholding. Could my husband ever sweep me off my feet again? Was that possible?

Another issue: communication. We couldn't seem to communicate the mundane facts of life, such as the fact that we were out of toothpaste or milk. Our level of emotional intimacy was so low that I often avoided eye contact.

I decided to tackle forgiveness, sex, romance, communication, and intimacy. Once we made progress in one area, we'd move onto the next.

And then, freelance writer that I am, I decided to set a couple deadlines. I worried that without deadlines, we'd never get started. We'd say we were working on our marriage, but the books would sit in a pile, unopened and unread. Our marriage would become the bare cement floor of so many years ago. Without a deadline, we'd never set the tiles and spread the grout.

I set two. One, July 25, was just two months away. That was the night that my husband had been planning on traveling to New York City to attend a cycling event. I decided to go with him, asking my parents to babysit. Mark and I had not spent a night alone—with just each other—in two and a half years. We probably needed a week, but I was willing to settle for a night. A night away would allow us to focus on nothing but each other. It would also serve as the symbolic rebirth of our married sex life. Most important, it would give us a date to write on the calendar, something that would motivate us to read the books and put their advice into practice.

The second deadline would be Labor Day. That would mark four months of trying. It was after Labor Day that we would take a good hard look at our progress. If we were making some progress—any progress—I would keep trying to save our marriage. If we had made no progress or Mark did not seem to be trying, I'd take another look at divorce.

..........................................................................................................

> For a set period of time, give your marriage project every ounce of your attention. Try everything. If you see any improvement during that time, keep trying. If not, consider divorce.

..........................................................................................................

# 6

## To Forgive Him

### JUNE 2007

**"In the Bible it says they asked Jesus how many times
you should forgive, and he said 70 times 7. Well, I want
you all to know that I'm keeping a chart."**

—Hillary Rodham Clinton

I sat down with *The 7 Best Things (Happy) Couples Do* by John and Linda
Friel, not because it was about forgiveness, but because it was the first
book Amazon.com delivered. I flipped through it, not looking for anything
in particular, other than, perhaps, a chapter titled, "Alisa, this is the answer
to all of your marital problems." I didn't find that chapter, but I did find
one titled, "We always pair up with emotional equals."

"Yeah, right," I muttered, convinced I'd be able to refute everything the
authors had to say. "John and Linda, this here is a woman who definitely
did not pair up with her emotional equal. She married an emotional
moron."

John and Linda countered, "Many people get themselves stuck in the
quagmire of actually believing that their long-term relationship partner is

significantly . . . more dysfunctional than themselves."

"In this case, he is," I thought.

John and Linda suggested that I ask myself, "What did I do to contribute to the failure of my marriage?"

Me? *ME?* ME?

I thought, "Look, John and Linda, you've got things all wrong here. This marriage failed because of *HIM,* not because of *ME.* It's not *MY* fault. It's *HIS.* He's the one who didn't clean out the closet when I moved in. He's the one who left me alone with a newborn. He's the one who abandoned me. I'm guiltless. I'm blameless. I'm just a hardworking woman who was somehow conned into marrying the world's biggest slacker!"

"Emotionally mismatched couples don't survive dating," said John and Linda.

I wondered, "Could they actually know what they're talking about? Did I do something, maybe a tiny little something, to contribute to the failure of this marriage?"

John and Linda wrote about overly independent people and overly dependent people. Both types were equally problematic.

I thought, "What's wrong with independence?

I thought, "I'm independent."

I thought, "Mark is independent."

And then my imaginary John and Linda smiled, their eyes twinkling with understanding as I thought, "Mark and I have no connection. We're both too independent."

I thought about why I valued independence. That brought me to my mother. She'd been so unhappy with her marriage and her life that she'd slept in the basement for a year. She hadn't earned enough money to pay rent on the smallest of apartments. She hadn't been able to spend a weekend alone without suffering a panic attack. She dreamed of a life without Dad, but she stayed because she was too needy to leave.

I'd been angry with Mom for wanting to leave Dad, but I also pitied her for not having the courage to do it. To prevent myself from ever becoming as needy, I asked Dad to teach me how to change my oil, oil filter, and spark plugs. He taught me how to change a flat, how to find a stud in a wall, and how to hammer a nail. He taught me how to drive a stick shift. He taught me how to balance a checkbook and how to understand money markets, certificates of deposit, savings accounts, and other investment options. He taught me how to do my taxes. He taught me how to read a road atlas.

When I met Mark, I valued his independence. He hadn't wanted to envelop me. We spent time together, and we spent time apart. He'd always been a shade more independent than I was. He spent more time on his bike than I spent running, reading, volunteering, or working, but our independence had worked for us until the rules changed. It worked until he lost his job, and became financially dependent on me. It worked until we had a baby, and I became emotionally and physically dependent on him.

I wanted to be independent, but I couldn't, not after parenthood.

I needed his help.

I hated that I needed his help. I didn't want to need it.

"If I have to need him," I thought, "I want him to know it without me saying it. Saying the words makes me feel weak. I want him to read my mind. I want him to help me without me asking for help."

I could almost see John and Linda shaking their heads, waiting for me to come to my senses. "All right, I know," I told them, "He can't read my mind. I know that, but I still want him to! John and Linda, you're right! Stop rubbing it in! I need to learn how to feel comfortable with my dependence. I need to learn how to be more vulnerable. I need to learn how to ask for what I need without feeling guilty.

"When I'm physically exhausted and he asks whether he can go for a bike ride or out with his buddies, I need to learn how to say, 'No' and to not back down. When I can't make it through an entire Saturday of solo parenting, I need to learn how to call him at work and ask him to come home, and when he tells me he is busy with work, I need to learn how to say, 'Tough shit. Come home now.' Okay, John and Linda, I get it. I'm not just part of the problem, I own the problem. I'm not happy, and the only person who can make me happy is me."

In fact, John and Linda had said very little. It was one of their easiest therapy sessions ever.

I wanted to forgive, and I'd tried many times to do so. After the big fight around Kaarina's first birthday, I tried. After the big fight around her second birthday, I tried. After our discussion around Mother's Day, I tried.

I got nowhere. Whenever Mark did something that pushed one of my buttons—perhaps he rolled his eyes, left dishes in the sink, or didn't come home at a pre-designated time—I remembered every single slight during the 11 years I'd known him, and forgot about his every good quality. I dropped into a state of total recall coupled with partial amnesia. I turned him into Deceased Husband #1 a.k.a. Man Formerly Known as Alisa's Husband a.k.a. Mr. Ex.

I turned to Google.com. I typed in "forgiveness." Most of the pages dealt with major acts of forgiveness, such as forgiving your father for repeatedly beating you. None dealt with forgiving a husband for being an insensitive numbnut.[10]

I eventually found one page that listed the process of forgiveness. I printed and read it. I learned that forgiveness required more than just wanting to forgive. I would first have to deal with my pain, anger, and disappointment. Then, I would have to relate this pain, anger, and disappointment to Mark, and he would have to acknowledge that his actions had

---

[10] When I wrote this sentence, I asked my husband, "How do you spell numbnut?" He asked, "Are you writing about me again?"

resulted in these feelings. I needed to hear two very important words come out of his mouth, "I'm" and "sorry."

I made a list of all of the memories that brought up negative feelings. I wrote "the closet incident." I wrote, "your bike." I wrote, "the store." I felt the anger all over again. I felt the hurt all over again. I felt the pain all over again. By the time I was done, my list covered an entire piece of paper.

Mark was watching the Tour de France on the television and keeping tabs on the race on a live coverage Internet site. I asked him a couple of questions. He didn't respond. I gave up and walked to the bathroom to brush my teeth and wash my face.

Already defeated, I gave up on The Project. I turned him into Mr. Ex.

But John and Linda were there, too. They were gently whispering to me, prodding me, telling me that I had fallen into my old bad habit. They were telling me to try harder. I was about to tell them to just shut up already when Mark walked into the bathroom to take a leak. I had his full attention.

"I need to talk with you about something. Can we talk about it in the sunroom? Will you be able to pay attention?"

"Yeah, sure."

He met me in the sunroom.

"When I get really mad at you, I don't just get mad about the one thing you did that day. I also get mad about one hundred or more other things you've done that date back to the day I met you. I also block out every good thing you've done in the past ten years."

He laughed.

"I need to let go of the past, so I did some research today," I said, waving my printouts in front of him. "To let go of my anger, I need to do something. I'm not sure this will help, but I want to try it. It might seem silly, but I'd like you to go along with it. I'd like to list all of the things I'm still mad about, and I want you to tell me that you are sorry."

"Oh . . . *kay*," he said. I decided to ignore the sarcasm.

"Are you sorry that on the day I got home from the hospital with the baby, you went to the customer appreciation party?"

"Yes, I'm sorry. I should have stayed home with you."

"Are you sorry about spending our New Zealand money on that skiing trip?"

"I didn't spend all of it. We could have still gone to New Zealand."

"Yes, you did and no, we could not."

"Okay, I'm sorry. I should not have done that."

"Are you sorry you didn't even have a closet cleaned out for me that day I moved in with you?"

"I didn't have a closet cleaned out?'

"No, you didn't."

"I'm sorry. I should have been ready for you. I don't know why I wasn't."

I'd expected him to argue with me. I'd expected him to rationalize his behavior. I'd expected him to accuse me of being overly sensitive.

"Are you sorry you didn't want to have sex with me when I was pregnant because you thought I was a big fat cow?'

"I never thought you were a big fat cow!"

"You didn't want to have sex with me."

He was silent.

"So?" I asked.

Silence.

"If it wasn't because you thought I was a big fat cow, what was it? You definitely didn't want to have sex with me."

"It was weird."

"Define 'weird' for me."

"You know, just weird."

I wish I were a patient woman. I'm not. No, if I see someone struggling to find the right words, I don't wait for that person to find them. I hand them over.

"Was it weird because there was a baby in my belly?"

"Yes, that's it," he said with a relieved smile.

Was that really it? Now I had no idea. Why couldn't I have just waited for him to say something?

"But it was safe. Sex wouldn't have hurt the baby," I said.

"How do you know?"

"Because I do. You could have asked the obstetrician."

"I'm sorry I didn't want to have sex when you were pregnant."

I ended with a question that John and Linda would probably have declared, "unfair." I put him in a "never" situation, even though it was truly a sometimes.

"Are you sorry that you were never there for me when I needed you?"

"I didn't know you needed me."

This answer surprised and frightened me. I'd almost killed our baby one night. I'd snapped at the people who loved me the most. My hair had clogged up the bathroom drain with each shower, and that was when I'd remembered to shower.

I'd disintegrated into an angry, unhappy, mentally compromised and physically sick person, and I turned into this person while he watched.

He'd heard me scream at him, at the dog, at the baby, and at the world. He'd seen the circles under my eyes. He'd seen the fatigue. He knew, when the phone rang, that I sometimes didn't answer it because I didn't feel like standing up. He'd seen me startle at the slightest sound.

Hadn't he?

How could he not have seen it?

"Do you remember when I could not figure out how to turn on my headlights?"

"Yes, but I just figured you were sleep-deprived. What should I have done?"

"I needed your help. I needed you to be here. I needed Kaarina's father to be her father. I needed a husband."

As I said the words, I felt the anger leaving me. I felt the hurt leaving me. I felt the frustration leaving me.

"I'm sorry. I'll try my best to be there for you in the future," he said, looking at me with tender eyes.

"Is there anything else?" he asked.

"I don't know. I'll tell you the next time I get mad at you."

"Sounds like a plan."

I kissed him on the forehead.

........................................................................................

Make a grudge list and share it with your partner. Talk about those old wounds and then let them heal.

........................................................................................

We'd made progress, but I wasn't sure it would be enough. It was one thing for him to tell me that he was sorry. It was another for him to become a better husband, a better father, and a better man. Him earning back my trust would take time.

I turned to a meditation I learned through yoga. I sat with my back against the wall, closed my eyes, and relaxed my body. I focused inward on my breathing and on the sensations I felt in my chest. My heart felt tight, as if someone's fist was wrapped around it. I wondered if it would ever feel normal again.

I brought one person at a time into my mind. First, I focused on myself. Then, I brought the image of Kaarina to mind. Then, the image of a friend. With each image, I told these beings, "I offer you my loving kindness. I wish the best for you. I give you my unconditional love." I visualized myself sending a comforting white energy to each person. I watched that energy envelop each person.

I saved my husband for last. I couldn't see his face. It came through in patches. I sent him my unconditional love. I wrapped him in my loving kindness. I released him to his greater good.

I focused on my heart again. It wasn't as tight.

When we settled into bed that night, I held my husband's hand. It was big and warm. In his hand, I could feel our marriage healing. I could feel a connection between us growing stronger. I thought, "Maybe, just maybe, I will be able to love this man again."

A week and a half later, we traveled to Cape May, New Jersey for three days. On the Sunday morning that we were supposed to leave, Mark worked a half-day. While walking out the door that morning, he'd asked me to look for the battery charger for our digital camera.

I looked in the first place that came to mind, the junk drawer in the kitchen. Here I stored batteries, empty PEZ dispensers, birthday candles, our ever-growing collection of lip balm, old cell phones, and unused Post-It pads. If I'd put the battery charger anywhere, I would have put it there.

It wasn't there.

I looked in the hallway closet. I looked in our bedroom.

The last place to look was the one place I didn't want to look—the walk-in closet in the basement. This was Mark's territory. It was his closet. It was a man space to beat all man spaces.

Looking for the battery charger in the walk-in closet would be like trying to find a lost child in Wal-Mart on Black Friday. I opened the door. Unworn suit jackets, dress pants, ties, suspenders, and an assortment of skiing, motorcycle riding, and cycling apparel hung from the closet rods. Every assortment of shoe—ski boots, motorcycle boots, cycling cleats, sneakers, hiking boots, and flippers—were piled on the floor. There were boxes, stacks of papers, plaques, helmets, climbing ropes and harnesses, shin guards, body armor, trophies, briefcases, and stacks of framed photos.

Toward my right, I saw a transparent plastic bag. Inside was a box that said, "Olympus."

The charger!

But what was that on the floor in the corner? I picked up a stack of greeting cards. They dated back to the year we'd met.

*HE'S SAVED EVERY LETTER I'VE EVER WRITTEN HIM?*

One card read, "Oh it's lovely weather for a sleigh ride together..." On the inside of the card it said, "Now correct me if I'm wrong, but I don't think we've ever done it in a sleigh." I picked out this card? Me? I felt this way? About him? I sighed. I wanted this to become the sort of card I would pick out for him now. I wanted to feel that kind of tenderness and sexual energy again. Was it possible?

The next card had a photo of two zebras with their heads pressed together. On the inside, I had written, "Thanks for sharing your past six months with me. You have been patient with me, and you have made me very happy."

I found a piece of paper with a face drawn in ink. One eye had a penny taped to it. Another had a dime taped to it. A nickel was taped where the nose should have been. A mouth was drawn with a tongue sticking out. I had written, "Because I could not be there in person, here's a picture of me. I'm so glad you are in my life. The penny is for thoughts, the nickel for hugs, and the dime for a kiss. So you've almost got everything, but, well, you'll get that when you see me in person."

I had no memory of ever making this card. Had I ever been so goofy and so in love?

The last one was a sappy card with lots of words on it about what it meant "To love a man like you." I had written, "It means having someone I can look at and ask, 'Wanna go hear classical music with me?' and he'll say 'Yes,' even though he doesn't like classical music, just because he loves me. It means when I'm sick, smelly, and look like shit, he'll cuddle up next to me and keep me warm, even if it means making himself sweat. It means

I am very happy thankful and blessed to have met you and have you in my life." I carried the cards upstairs and put them on my desk. I'd sent these cards to Mark, but now I wanted them for myself. They reminded me of a woman I'd once known. Perhaps if I read those cards over and over and over again, I could become that woman again.

On the way to the beach, I found myself thinking about the cards and the long-lost woman who'd sent them. Why had I fallen in love with him? Was he just as perplexed about how he'd ended up with me?

I asked, "Do you know why you feel in love with me?"

I expected, "Dunno."

I got, "That's easy."

"Really?"

"Yes," he said, counting the reasons on his fingers. "First, you're hot."

I blushed, and I stopped him from moving onto reason number two. Hot was not how I felt about myself. I'd never felt comfortable with my looks or my body. I'd always thought of my face as too square, my body too squat, my breasts too small, my thighs too thick, and my arm hair and eyebrows too bushy.

Since the baby, I'd also thought of my abdomen as a bit too puffy. I obsessed over the fine lines that seemed to multiply overnight around my lips and eyes. I hated wearing bathing suits because of cellulite. Hot? No, I was a 36-year-old station-wagon driving mother who wore cotton underwear. Mothers were not hot, and this particular mother had endured years of never hearing her husband hint that he'd like to get busy. Could he actually still be attracted to me, fine lines, cellulite, C-section scar and all?

I craved to hear him say, "You're hot" again. I needed him to see me as a sexual being just as much as I needed to become a sexual being again.

"Are you just saying that to make me feel good?" I asked.

"You are definitely hot."

I shifted a little in my seat and sat a little taller. I turned toward him and rested a hand on his thigh.

"What else?"

"You're smart."

"What else?"

"You're nice."

"What else?"

"You're athletic."

"Honey, do you think you could write it down?" I asked. "Can you write me a love letter? I'll write one for you and you write one for me. Just write why you love me."

"When's my deadline?"

"By the time we go to New York."

"Okay, I'll do it."

I watched the road for a while. I listened to music for a while. I stared at Mark for a while, and then I finally said, "Sweetie, there's something I need to tell you."

"What is it?"

"Do you remember the time we were shopping in the grocery store and Kaarina ran away? After I chased her down and found you by the chicken, you said something snotty."

"I'm not sure. Maybe," he said.

"Well, I was so mad at you that I wanted to kill you. Instead of killing you, I started writing a novel, one about a desperate wife who is plotting to murder her husband."

"Do you still want to kill me?"

"No, I'm not going to kill you. I just wanted you to know about the novel. I've kept it a secret from you. Sometimes when you come home and ask me what I'm doing, I tell you I'm working, but I'm really writing the novel. I've been secretive about it, and I've lied to you about it. I've always wanted to write a novel. I've wanted to be a novelist since childhood. This is so big for me. And I hid it from you. I hid the most important thing I was doing for myself from you. I'm sorry."

"I'm really happy for you," he said. "I really am."

...................................................................................

Why did you marry your partner? Think about it for a long time. You had a reason, in fact you had many reasons. Write them down and share them with your partner.

...................................................................................

During our time in Cape May, Mark suggested I take a couple hours for myself each morning to run, shop, work on the novel, or read. He rode his bike in the afternoon, while Kaarina and I napped. At the beach, I relaxed in a chair and read a book while he built one sandcastle after another for Kaarina to knock over. When we were out at restaurants, he kept her busy with coloring. He held Kaarina's ice cream cones, letting the ice cream melt down his hand and wrists as her tiny tongue licked imperceptible amounts at a time. He even accompanied her to the potty, a job that was usually 99.9 percent mine.

One evening, we were walking along Cape May's main drag when I saw a lingerie store. "Hey," I told Mark and Kaarina, "Mommy wants to go in this store." Mark saw the mannequins in the window. "I'll take Kaari into the next store. You take your time," he told me.

I immediately felt overwhelmed. I didn't know which panties would become food for my butt crack and which ones would stay put. I didn't know which outfits would make me feel self-conscious and which ones would allow me to feel sexually self-confident. I was about to give up when Mark and Kaarina walked in.

"I don't know what to get," I told him.

"This," he said, picking a tight black teddy that came together at the waist with a silky ribbon.

"Why?" I asked.

"You have a great waist, Momma," he said. "This will show it off."

"I have a great waist?"

"Yes, you do."

Kaarina ran out of the store's open door.

"Gotta go," he said. "Take your time."

I picked out a few more outfits. In the dressing room, I fumbled with all of the hooks and closures, and I fretted over the best way to stuff myself into various waist cinchers. Should I clasp it together around myself, as if I was putting on a jacket? Should I step into it, like a dress? If so, how would I get the damn thing past my rib cage without ripping it?

I got dressed, found more lingerie to try on in a larger size, and went back to the dressing room. I eventually settled on a form-fitting teddy that stopped at my waist and a pair of panties that made my butt look like two firm apples and showed off the part of my body that had caused my husband to become so hopelessly besotted with me so many years before.

As you work on your marriage, focus on the small positive changes—the smile, the compliment, the empty dishwasher, the hug. Champion what is changing for the better rather than obsessing over what is still left to change.

We returned from Cape May with a stronger, warmer, and happier connection, but I knew the post-vacation glow would fade if we didn't continue to move forward with The Project. I'd been able to shed some of my anger, but I still had more forgiveness to work through. I knew this because of John Gottman. Gottman was known for his ability to talk with any random couple for roughly five minutes and then predict with 91 percent accuracy whether or not the couple would divorce. I was curious how he made such predictions and what he might have to say about my marriage, so I read his book, *The Seven Principles for Making Marriage Work*. In it he listed a number of telltale signs that a marriage would end in divorce, and it was the sixth of these signs that gave me pause. He wrote, "Couples who are deeply entrenched in a negative view of their spouse and their marriage often rewrite the past. . . . History gets rewritten for the worse. . . . Another bad sign is when you find the past difficult to remember—it has become so unimportant or painful that you've let it fade away."

In other words, they forget what they ever saw in one another.

I thought of the advice from our wedding. *Never go to bed angry. Always say, "Yes, dear." Never forget why you fell in love.*

I'd forgotten.

Did I really fall in love with him? Did it really happen?

It must have. We hadn't married young. We hadn't married out of desperation. We hadn't married for money or status. We'd married for many rational reasons.

Right?

What were they? I must have fallen in love with something. I must have.

I turned to Google.com. No, I didn't think I'd find a web page titled, "Why you fell in love with your husband." I was searching for information about the science of attraction. I hoped that in learning what attracted one human to another, I just might be able to remember what had attracted me to Mark. From the Internet, I learned that humans are all attracted to the same qualities. We all like dependable, kind, healthy, smart, educated mates.

Men are attracted to youth and beauty, too. Women, at least on some level, like men who earn a lot of money and are influential.

I remembered that when I met Mark, he seemed dependable and kind. I remembered that I thought he was smart. He was educated, had a job, and owned his own home. That's not why I fell in love with him, though. I knew a number of men with the same characteristics, and I didn't marry them. I married Mark.

I thought about the cliché, "Likes attract." I liked that he was a liberal, was physically fit, and enjoyed watching James Bond films. I liked his independence. I liked that we both loved food and we both loved to travel.

I thought about the cliché, "Opposites attract." I liked that he was calm. I liked that he was confident. I liked that he was not a work-a-holic.

None of this explained why I married him. Why him and not any number of other guys I dated?

The question sent me right back to, "I don't know." Did I choose him because I was ready and he was there? Did I marry him because I couldn't find any reason not to marry him?

I eventually dug down to a deep tender knowing place, and when I reached that place, I got goose bumps. The knowing place told me that I was drawn to him because he he'd loved me without conditions. He loved everything about me, including, in his words, the way I smelled. He loved me in every hairstyle, in makeup and without, with heels and in flats, sweaty and freshly showered. He loved me through many illnesses. He loved me happy and angry. He loved all of me.

With the exception of when he asked me to change out of a stained T-shirt before visiting with his parents, he'd never asked me to change.

Perhaps it's not what would have attracted you to a man and certainly not what would have convinced you to marry him. I'm sure you have your own set of "must haves." One of my friends, for instance, says she'll only date men who are between the ages of thirty-eight and fifty, taller than five foot eight, fit, have a thick head of hair, and are avid novel readers—and those are just the list of dating specifications.

As it turned out, my requirements in a mate were quite simple. I just wanted to be adored. I just wanted to be loved for who I was, and not for who I could become. I wanted someone who believed in me.

When I lost my virginity at age fourteen, I'd been so ashamed that I told no one. A year after I lost my virginity, I wrote a note to a friend telling her that I wasn't a virgin. I lost my courage and threw the note in the trash, and that's where Mom found it. My parents had the discussion in the kitchen. It had started with, "We're so disappointed in you" and had ended with me being grounded. In retrospect, I suspected that if they'd known more details about how I'd lost my virginity, the discussion might have gone differently. I hadn't told them. I couldn't look them in the eyes.

It was my shame that had met Mark that day at The Farmhouse. He courted my shame, and he accepted it, and he loved it. He loved all of me. He accepted everything about me. He listened to me. He never judged me. He never asked me to become something I wasn't. He never pushed me away from my dreams. He loved me unconditionally, and that's why I married him.

Mark and I were opposites in many respects and, when I was mad at him, it was the opposites that I fixated on. I'd get steamed up about the fact that I noticed the socks on the floor and felt the need to pick them up, when he didn't even see the socks or me picking them up. I'd get angry if he left his empty beer bottles, yogurt containers and banana peels on the floor or on the countertop instead of just putting them in the trash or recycling where they belonged. I'd feel miffed that he only seemed to remember his mother's birthday the day before, and always seemed to need me to rectify this problem, begging me to not only buy her something, but to overnight mail it to her. I'd get even more miffed that, because I didn't want her to feel heartbroken about her son forgetting her birthday, I always did it. I'd get irritated that I could hear Kaarina's middle-of-the-night cries within nanoseconds, and he rarely heard them at all.

Yet I also realized that the same opposites that drove me crazy were the ones that had attracted me to him so many years ago. When we met, I loved that he was calm. It had offset my nervousness. I thought back to many incidents during Kaarina's first year of life when, if I was being honest, I had to admit his calm nature had kept me sane.

In the beginning, I loved that he knew how to relax. It kept me from burning myself out. I loved that he was assertive. It meant that I didn't always have to be. I loved that he knew how to have fun. It kept me from being so serious, and allowed me to laugh and have fun, too.

I hadn't married myself. I'd married Mark because he wasn't me. I'd married him for a reason. I'd married him for many reasons. I was ready to write my letter.

### Why I Love You

*I love your eyes, how they are sometimes gray and sometimes greenish brown, as if they can't make up their minds.*

*I love that you like to drive, and don't mind if I sleep the entire way.*

*I love how your face looks when you have stubble.*

*I love that you remain calm in crisis—always. I love that you understand that I will probably never be calm in crisis, and that you never think to mention it.*

*I love that you haggle so well with car salesmen.*

*I love how, if we are getting bad service in a restaurant, you assertively but not aggressively ask for the manager and somehow always get us a discount, free meal, or coupon for a free meal.*

*I love that you pack light.*

*I love that you can pack an entire garage worth of stuff into the smallest of spaces in a car.*

*I love that you love burritos, sushi, Indian food, hummus, octopus, and butternut squash soup.*

*I love that you love to travel as much as I do.*

*I love that you don't believe in spanking (our daughter, that is).*

*I love that you kill mice and rats, and don't tell me the intimate details of how you do it.*

*I love that you know how to rotate my tires, change my brake pads, and change my oil.*

*I love that you can talk "car mechanic."*

*I love your nose.*

*I love your hands.*

*I love that you are the type of man who would save my love letters.*

*I love that you know how to tie all sorts of knots, and that you never get frustrated with me for not being able to figure out how to tie anything other than my shoelaces.*

*I love that you never raise your voice.*

*I love that you know how things work, especially cameras and cell phones.*

*I love that when I ask a rhetorical question like, "I wonder how an air conditioner actually makes air cold," you know the answer and tell me.*

*I love that you will build an endless number of sandcastles for Kaarina to knock over.*

*I love that you know how to install shelving, build planters, hit nails with hammers, and put the right-sized bit in the electric screwdriver.*

*I love that you seem to always know whether something needs a screw or a nail.*

*I love that you never lose your patience.*

*I love that you've finally found a way to teach me how to use the quick release on the garden hose.*

*I love that you know that I shop at J Jill.*

*I love that you rub my shoulders or get me a drink when I tell you I've had a busy day or that I'm working with a difficult client.*

*I love that you love to watch* The Grinch Who Stole Christmas.

*I love that when something breaks, Kaarina always says, "Daddy will fix it," and she's usually right.*

*I love that when something big needs someone to blow it up, and Kaarina wants it blown up fast, you will sit and blow and blow and blow until it's done and she's smiling.*

*I love that you bought matching orange Florida Gators crocs to wear with our daughter.*

*I love that you taught Kaarina to say "Go Gators!"*

*I love that you never tell me I look tired, even when I do.*

*I love that you can reach everything on the top shelf of the kitchen cabinets, without having to stand on a chair.*

*I love sharing dessert with you.*

*I love that you have no fear, except of snakes.*

*I love that you wouldn't think of asking me to put chemicals in the hot tub or to cut the grass.*

*I love your scars.*

*I love that you can open any jar.*

*I love that you know how to wrap a sprained ankle, dress a scrape, and other basic first aid.*

*I love that you don't cry or whine when you fall off your bike and get hurt.*

*I love that you always have an answer for everything, even if you really don't know what you are talking about.*

*I love your baked ziti.*

*I love that you love me.*

# 7

## To Desire Him

### JULY 2007

**"For women, foreplay is everything that happens in the twenty-four hours preceding insertion. For men, it's everything that happens three minutes before."**
—Louann Brizendine, M.D., *The Female Brain*

Mark was never my Casanova. Even during our earliest days of dating, I was not drawn to him in an intense, chemical, lose-all-sense-of-reality kind of way. When I'd dated Steve, for instance, I couldn't keep my hands off him. I craved him. I was intoxicated with lust. Mark? I was drawn to him *just enough.*

Just enough was okay though, because I assumed I was getting something in return. Mark may not have revved up my sexual engine in a big way, but he was not going to hurt me, either. He was caring, doting, responsible, sensitive, smart, and kind. Mark was husband and father material. Steve and Todd? Definitely not marriage material.

It never occurred to me that Mark, one day, might stop fulfilling his end of the bargain.

It also never occurred to me that my small attraction to my husband could eventually evolve into no attraction whatsoever.

But that's what happened.

I went from wanting sex a few times a week to once a week to twice a month to once a month to once every few months to never. His sex drive, however, stayed the same and, as a result, he continued to initiate. I felt guilty and inadequate whenever he spooned me from behind, rubbing his boner against my rear end. Over time, however, I grew tense and irritated. Couldn't he tell I was tired? If I wanted to get it on, would I be wearing a ratty old T-shirt and granny panties? Did he have to spring it on me by rubbing himself against me? Couldn't he just ask like a normal human being?

When the baby came, my sex drive disappeared completely. I was getting no sleep and I was going through a temporary menopause, complete with hot flashes. My prolactin levels were high and my estrogen and testosterone were low, drying up lubrication. By then, I'd rebuffed his sexual advances so consistently that he'd stopped initiating.

I was fine with that. I felt guilty about being fine with it, though.

I assumed my sex drive would return when I stopped breastfeeding. Kaarina weaned at sixteen months, but my sex drive was still nonexistent. I assumed it would return once I got more sleep. It didn't.

I would see parents with two children—a toddler Kaarina's age and an infant—and think to myself, "They are still having sex. What's wrong with us? What's wrong with me?"

When my sex drive returned between my thirty-sixth and thirty-seventh birthdays, I was quite unprepared. I commiserated with that stereotypical adolescent boy who walks up to the chalkboard to complete a math problem, all the while hoping no one notices the woody in his pants. For the first time in years, I found myself spontaneously fantasizing about sex and getting horny in very inappropriate places. I thought about sex as often as 10 or 15 times a day, but my fantasies never involved Mark. They involved waiters, male friends, or men I made up in my mind.

Possibly more important, I felt sexy. I was one of those enviable women who ended up skinnier after childbirth than before. I'd also grown out my hair. And, because I'd shrunk a clothing size, I had bought a new wardrobe. I was attracted to myself in an odd, should-I-really-admit-this-in-my-book sort of way.

But my husband? Could I ever feel that kind of attraction for him? Would I, for the rest of my life, only desire men I could not have? Could Mark ever become the man of my sexual dreams?

Apparently, all of this was appallingly normal. From the Kinsey Institute I learned that roughly 3 percent of married couples were just like us—smack dab in the middle of a great big long dry spell. Another 13 percent of couples had sex only a few times a year and nearly half of married couples said they did it less than once a week.

About a third of them did it two to three times a week, and just 7 percent humped nearly every day. I had no interest in trying to get into the top 7 percent. I figured that segment of the married population was composed of those youngsters who meet in Vegas, marry after knowing one another for just a few hours, and then proceed to have sex multiple times a day for the next 8 months before begging the church to grant them an annulment.

I didn't even aspire to get into the top third. After a six-month-long dry spell, the idea of doing it two to three times a week seemed absolutely terrifying.

A few times a month? That, I thought, I could handle. Could we achieve that statistic? Did we have it in us? Did I? I lusted for that stat. At the time, I probably lusted for the stat more than I lusted for my husband, but at least I felt lust for something. And maybe, just maybe, I would develop a hearty lust for my husband, too.

According to Louann Brizendine's *The Female Brain*, men had between 10 and 100 times more testosterone than women and consequently, their genitals actually became quite uncomfortable if they didn't get a regular release. Women, on the other hand, tended to have high levels only during the second week of our menstrual cycles, just before ovulation. Had the writers of Genesis missed an important detail when they listed God's punishments for eating the apple? In addition to painful childbirth, he also inflicted us with mismatched sex drives. Our men wanted it every day or, at the very least, weekly. Women, however, only felt this way roughly once a month, and that was if we were actually attracted to our husbands in the first place.

New York—where we pledged to rev up our sexual engines again—was now just a few weeks away. What had I been thinking? We'd been cursed since the beginning of time, and I somehow thought that we could take a little trip to a big city and, magically, the Curse of Genesis would lift and we'd want to play hide the salami for hours on end? It was much more likely that Mark and I would find ourselves in our New York hotel room, stare at one another, and say, "I wonder what's on TV?" I worried that, if New York didn't go well, we'd become demoralized and never find the motivation to try ever again. I'd become one of those old ladies who, when her girlfriends are talking about sex, says, "You're still bothering yourself with *THAT*?"

I didn't want to put off having sex forever, but after a six-month-long dry spell, what's a few more weeks? I reminded myself that I'd wanted this deadline. The date on the calendar was supposed to motivate us to do our homework, and it had. I was officially obsessed. I had Patricia Love's *Hot*

*Monogamy* in my purse. I read it whenever I had a free moment. I read it while Kaarina napped. I read it late into the night. I read it while waiting for hair appointments. I dog-eared and highlighted page after page.

Dr. Love explained that sex involved three distinct stages: desire, arousal, and orgasm. Desire was the sexual fantasy. It was the lightbulb moment that got me thinking about sex. Arousal for men was the hard-on. For women, it was the lubrication and engorgement of the genital region. Orgasm was the short-lived but intense muscular contractions that felt so out-of-this-world wonderful. According to Dr. Love, most women had no problem with orgasm. Rather, we had problems with the first stage, desire. A third of all women rarely initiated, she said, because they rarely felt desire.

I high-fived Dr. Love and told her she was right-on. I asked her where she'd been all of my married life. I told her that I'd rarely had a problem enjoying orgasm. Orgasm was a total body, totally pleasurable sensation. Yet, the pleasure of one orgasm wasn't enough to entice me to want another one. I likened my feelings about the lure of the orgasm to my feelings about chocolate. Researchers had shown that the pleasure center in women's brains becomes twice as aroused when women eat chocolate than when they kiss their spouses. This made sense to me. Chocolate came in a nice little package. It took almost no work to unwrap it, put it on the tongue, and reach a state of salivary bliss. Kissing and foreplay were completely different and, even with the best of techniques, they didn't always lead to physical ecstasy. If I had to grow the cocoa and sugar-cane, harvest it, smash it up, and mix it with cream that I hand-milked from a cow, I'd stop eating chocolate, too.

We needed to find a way to turn Mark into a Dove Bar.

I put aside Dr. Love and again picked up *The Female Brain* by Louann Brizendine, M.D. This good doctor told me that our weekend away in New York was exactly what she prescribed. In women, she told me, sexual desire only fired up if the worry center in the brain, called the amygdala, was switched off. It was only once the amygdala was off that the brain's pleasure center flipped on. Flipping off the amygdala was difficult in chronic multi-taskers like me. The thought, "There are dirty dishes in the sink" fired up my amygdala. So did the thought, "Kaarina might wake any moment." Same with the thought, "I forgot to do x, y, and z today," a notion that plagued my brain almost constantly.

New York would remove most of these amygdala thoughts. In New York, I would have no dishes to wash, no dog or child to interrupt us, and no email to check. A weekend getaway, she told me, was one of the most potent aphrodisiacs.

So it wasn't such a crazy idea after all. New York just might be the magical remedy we needed to lift the Curse of Genesis, but only if we were ready for it, which brought me back to Dr. Love. She told me that Mark and I had to discuss what we enjoyed in bed and what we didn't. To ease us into this discussion, she provided a few conversation starters. One was, "What I'd like more of in our love-making is . . ."

Did I know what I wanted? It didn't take long for a fantasy to surface. I could see Mark's hands on me. He was doing all sorts of things, things he rarely ever did, even during the best of times.

Did he have similar needs and wants from me?

I tapped Mark on the arm.

"Sweetie, could you think back months to when we used to actually have sex? What would you have liked more of?" I asked.

"I don't know," he said.

"Well, I would like you to blindfold me, tie me up, and then pleasure me, making sure to stimulate all of my senses."

He turned to face me. "You want *THAT*?"

"Yes, I do. Now, your turn."

"I don't know."

Had we never had a conversation about sex before? Surely we'd talked about what we liked and what we didn't like. Surely, in all of these years, it hadn't just been a silent game of trial and error.

"Think about it," I told him.

"How long do I have to give you an answer?"

"Have one ready by the time we get to New York."

A man who did not have erectile dysfunction, I learned, could generally get it up just about anywhere and anytime. It didn't matter if his woman had just irritated him. It didn't matter if she'd just called him a string of very creative curse words. It didn't even matter if she torched his favorite ball cap.

If she wanted him to rise to the occasion, all she had to do was this: take off her clothes.

Women? We were a bit more complex. It took a lot more than a naked man to turn us on. In fact, for many of us, the thought of our naked husbands did just one thing: make us want to hide.

Women, Dr. Brizendine wrote, can't feel desire unless we believe our men adore us. Fear, anger, and shame all kept the amygdala flipped on. These emotions killed desire. Happiness, joy, and comfort, on the other hand, flamed it.

No wonder Mark and I had stopped having sex! I'd been mad at him at least once a day during the past six months, if not longer. We hadn't had a twenty-four-hour time span for foreplay. We'd had constant anti-play. As a result, he was not my Dove Bar. He was my Brussels Sprout.[11]

I didn't necessarily need to buy lingerie or erotica (although both were definitely on my to-do list). Rather, I needed to solve the problems that brought up the anger, frustration, fear, and shame. In the beginning, I knew

---

[11] I feel the need to state that I'm one of the few people on the planet who actually likes Brussels Sprouts. The only food that I absolutely despise is grapefruit, but somehow the word "grapefruit" just didn't sound quite right in that sentence.

I was the most important person in his world. Over time, something had shifted. His bike became more important. His store became more important. His friends became more important. I needed to feel more important than the bike, the store, and his friends, and I needed to feel as if Kaarina was more important than all three as well.

I needed to hear him say, "I love you." I needed to hear him say, "You are so beautiful." I needed him to tell me that he appreciated me. I needed him to ease my life by straightening the house, handling more parenting, rubbing my shoulders, and making us breakfast. I needed him to spend time with his daughter, and I needed to see him enjoying every minute of that time. Most important, I needed him to tell me that he was the luckiest man alive because I was in his life. I needed to hear it in his words, and I needed to see it in his actions, and the only way I was going to get either was to ask. I could hear Deb's sage words echo in my head, "Husbands can't read our minds. They're clueless."

Clueing him in didn't come easily for me. I would have preferred he have a divine revelation one day or figure it out on his own. I would have preferred to find a self-help book titled *How to Worship Your Wife* and have him read it.

But I was willing to give it a try.

That night, as I was putting Kaarina to bed, I thought to myself, "Why is it that I always do the bedtime routine from beginning to end while he sits in the La-Z-Boy and watches TV?" I almost kept this thought to myself, adding it to the pile of problems that generally made me feel taken advantage of and underappreciated. After I finished settling her into bed, though, I sat next to him, muted the TV, and said, "I don't think it's fair that I get her teeth brushed, her jammies on, read the books, and get her settled while you're watching TV. Do you want to read the first book and I read the last book, or the opposite?"

"The last book," he said.

Once we traded book reading, Kaarina made a game of racing me to find Daddy after I'd read the first book, and then she raced Daddy back to the bedroom. Because he read the final book, he took on the job of corralling her whenever she snuck out of her room, complaining, "I'm not tired." I got more time to myself at night and felt more relaxed and talkative, too.

I again had to clue him in as we planned the trip to New York. You might think that picking a night to go away together would have come easily. Wrong. We were still in the very early stages of this marriage project, after all, which meant we could come to a stalemate over just about anything.

The stalemate took place because cycling, yet again, found a way to wedge itself between us. You see, I'd asked my parents to babysit July 25, which was the day Mark had told me he'd wanted to go to New York in the first place. Then Mark checked his calendar and realized that the cycling event was not the twenty-fifth. It was the twenty-sixth.

I asked my parents whether they could watch Kaarina on July 26. They agreed, but on the condition that we drove Kaarina to them; they were not willing to drive to us.

"Why won't they just drive here?" Mark whined.

"Because they're leaving that weekend to drive to Atlanta to visit my brother, and they don't want to drive one and a half hours Friday night only to drive all day on Saturday."

"Then we'll drive to them," he said.

I stared at him. Was the cycling event that important? Couldn't he just skip it and go into New York on a different day? Wasn't our marriage more important than his love of cycling?

"Mark, do you realize how much time we're going to be spending in the car?"

"What do you mean?"

"We're going to be driving an hour and a half in the wrong direction to drop off Kaarina, and then we have to drive two plus hours to New York from my parents' house, which is farther from New York than our house. By the time we drive to New York, check in, unpack, and attend the cycling event . . ."

I trailed off, too disappointed to go on. Maybe he didn't care about sex, love and marriage. Maybe he really only cared about cycling.

"Are your parents willing to drive to us if we go Wednesday instead of Thursday?"

"I think so," I said.

"Why don't we skip the cycling thing and just have a romantic night?" he asked.

Was that foreplay? I thought it was.

The Friday before the trip, I went to the salon. I had an appointment with Carmen, an esthetician who, one friend had told me, could expertly wax one's bikini area into the sexiest of shapes. This particular friend had suggested I talk to Carmen about a "Martini Glass." The pubic hair that lines the lips of the vagina is waxed down to thin lines that resemble the stem of a glass. The hair along the top is waxed into the shape of an upside down triangle, the bowl of the glass.

I was a few minutes too early, so I feigned interest in the skin care products. I heard someone say my name. Then I saw Carmen. Everything about her—from her long eyelashes and full lips to her slender hips and high-heeled boots—dripped of sensuality. She walked me to a room with a table covered in a white bed sheet.

"You want the Martini?"

"Yes," I told her.

She stared at me, apparently waiting for me to do something.

"You're going to have to tell me what to do. I've never gotten a bikini wax before."

"Just take off your pants and get on the table."

As I unbuttoned my pants, I was thinking that I could use a little privacy. Even at the gynecologist's office, the nurse handed me a little gown and sheet and then stepped out of the room. The gynecologist was going to get up front and personal with me, but the little gown and sheet gave me the illusion of not having someone staring closely at my nether regions.

As this ran through my mind, Carmen was waiting. She was standing with her arms crossed. She was staring at me. I took a deep breath, dropped my pants, stepped out of my panties and climbed onto the table.

"Spread your legs," she said. I did. She walked around the table and looked at me from all angles. As she walked, she periodically tussled my pubic hair. She checked out my front side the way my mother, a visual artist, looks at a still life.

"Do you want a very thin stem or a wide one?" she asked.

"I don't know. I've never done this before. I'm a little worried about the pain, so maybe I should go with a wider stem?"

"Yes," she said, looking at me. "This is going to hurt. You are *VERY* hairy."

This news did not exactly surprise me. My father had descended from hairless English and Germans. My hair follicles apparently inherited none of his genes. I'd inherited the genes from my Russian maternal grandfather, who had hair on his chest as thick as a poodle's. If I didn't wax my eyebrows, they'd grow together.

She pulled out a tongue depressor, dipped it in the hot wax, and spread it over the left side of what would soon be the stem of my glass. She placed a cloth on top and pulled fast and hard. "That's not bad at all," I said. Then she did the right side, and I almost jumped off the table. "That side was a lot more sensitive."

"One side always is," she said.

Then she ripped off the hair along my C-section scar. I flinched. She ran her index finger over my scar and said, "You're a mom, yes?"

"Yes."

"How old?"

"She's three."

"No, how old are you?"

"I'll be thirty-seven in a few weeks."

"Thirty-seven and a mom? You look great!" she said, pointing to my abdomen.

I decided to forgive her for calling me hairy.

She continued to wax and rip, wax and rip, all the while instructing me to move my legs into different positions. At one point, she wanted them "froggy" with my feet together and knees out to the side. Then she wanted my legs straight, but pressed together. Later, spread eagle. "Ah, beautiful," she said. She'd transformed the ugly duckling into a swan. I stepped off the table and got dressed.

Later, after I arrived home, I dropped my pants and looked in the mirror. For the first time in my post-pubescent life, I actually liked what I saw. I felt a bit guilty in my newfound awe of my nearly hairless front side. If Gloria Steinem knew about it, what would she say? Would she declare me a victim of a patriarchal society that valued hairless front sides over hairy ones? I decided that I didn't care what Gloria thought. I loved it. I did. It was beautiful.

I took a shower and scrubbed off the remaining wax. I could feel the shower water running down me, tickling and teasing me. Suddenly, the elusive friend, desire, was calling to me. "The Martini is here to stay," I told myself. "It's definitely here to stay."

If you're on a budget, you can shave instead of wax. Trim yourself down and shape yourself up with a small, electric razor first. Then use shaving cream and a three bladed razor (the expensive kind that men use on their faces). Then shave every day to prevent re-growth itch.

Two days before the big day, I noticed a pimple on the side of my nose. Then I noticed another one on my forehead. I felt as if someone had sucked the gray matter out of my head and replaced it with cotton. Loud noises and people in general were more irritating. I looked on the calendar.

I was more than due for the monthly visitor.

And more than a little depressed. I hadn't had sex with my husband in months, and it just figured that I was going to have my period on the one day that I planned to finally start having sex again.

Just. Figured.

Tuesday came and went, and still no period. I went to bed Tuesday night with high hopes. "It's not going to come," I told myself.

Wednesday morning, I had my period.

I was crushed.

As Mark left for work, I told him.

"I'm sorry, Momma," he said. "We're still going to have a good time."

He was right. We were indeed. Until that moment, I'd been thinking of New York as a one-night stand rather than the first sexual experience that would define the new us. As a one-nighter, the desire for everything to be perfect was excruciating. "This isn't the only time I will ever get to have sex with my husband again," I reminded myself. Hopefully, New York would be the first of countless wonderful experiences. It didn't have to be perfect. It only had to happen.

The morning before we left, my thoughts were on The Martini. I'd imagined Mark unwrapping me, taking off my clothes and lingerie, and finding this gift with surprise and curiosity. Because I was having my period, however, I'd scrapped that plan. My period made me self-conscious. After eight years of marriage, it was about the only thing that did. I didn't care if he saw me on the toilet. I didn't care how much of a close-up view he got of any area of my body, but I didn't want him around anything that involved feminine hygiene.

So I ruined the surprise. "I got a bikini wax," I said. He turned to face me, his eyebrows raised. "I got my pubic hair waxed into little lines with an upside down triangle on top. It's called the Martini Glass."

"That sounds like something I'd like to see. When did you do that?"

"Friday."

"Last Friday?"

"Yes."

"Did it hurt?"

"Yes, but not so much that I wouldn't do it again."

"You're not going to grow it out?"

"No, I'm going to keep it, or maybe I'll have her do other pictures. She seems to know others."

"What do you think of a landing strip?" he asked.

"It's a possibility," I said, "but you might want to see the Martini first."

We were quiet for a while, and then I asked him if he'd come up with his answer to, "What I'd like more of in our love-making."

"No, I don't know," he said.

"When did you become so uncomfortable talking about sex?" I asked.

"What do you mean?"

"We used to talk about it. Many years ago, when we were dating, I would tell you racy sexual fantasies that involved me and other women. You didn't mind it then."

"You used to do that?"

"You don't remember?"

'No," he said, but he looked expectant, as if he not only wanted to revisit the memory, but also wanted me to come up with a new lesbian sex fantasy as we rode on the bus.

"Why are you uncomfortable now? Did it happen when I became a mom?"

"Yes, maybe." He paused. "We're parents now. It's different."

"It doesn't have to be. There's nothing wrong with sex. If you don't tell me what you like, I have to guess."

Once at the hotel, we waited for the elevator to take us to the fifth floor.

We waited.

And waited.

And waited.

"Do you want to take the stairs?" I asked.

"Not with the bag," he said.

I was sweating. The hallways were not air-conditioned.

Finally, the elevator came. A German guy with luggage stepped out. As we exchanged places with him, he said, "Good luck." Was that sarcasm? And, if so, what exactly were we in for?

Before the doors closed, a big maintenance guy got on. He held the door. Two more guys crowded in. The elevator was about as large as the seat of Mark's La-Z-Boy. One or more of the maintenance guys smelled.

I watched the floors. Couldn't the thing get to the fifth floor any faster?

Finally, the fifth floor came.

We walked down the narrow hallway in single file and found our room. It was all bed, surrounded on two sides by wall and one side by a dresser and end table. The only floor space was a small area of carpeting at the foot of the bed.

The bed had no headboard, just a strip of wood with screws poking out where the headboard had once hung.

This room? It was not remotely what I had imagined.

In my fantasy, we'd walked into the hotel room, dropped our bags, and had gotten it on. We'd lounged in bed, ordered room service and stayed in bed until it was time to go home.

This fantasy was going to remain just that, a fantasy. After all, the hotel didn't have room service.

"I can't believe we're paying $300 a night for this dump. Do you want to get a snack and a drink somewhere?" I asked him.

"Sounds like a plan," he said.

At an outdoor café, we were seated between a man who was eating alone and a very young, very in love couple. The man was eating fresh mozzarella with a big sliced tomato. The in love couple was leaning toward one another, staring into each other's eyes, and talking fast and animatedly.

Mark and I were leaning away from each other, our backs resting against our chairs. We were having about as much conversation as the man who was eating alone. I wanted to be like the young couple. Could I ever get lost in Mark's eyes again? Could that experience ever be recaptured?

Mark mentioned the mozzarella on the man's plate. We'd both noticed it, perhaps at the same moment. I ordered what the man had. Mark ordered something that resembled deep fried ravioli with thin slices of gourmet salami on top. We shared. We did this automatically. At some point, he finished his ravioli. I gave him more cheese.

I pulled the love letters from my purse. I handed my three pages of typing to him.

"I'm not a writer," he said as I looked at the pad of paper with his all caps handwriting.

"I don't expect you to be," I said. "I only want to know why you love me, and I want you to know why I love you."

We read our letters. His said:

*Why I Love You*
*You're my best friend.*
*You have a great smile.*
*You're smart.*
*You care a lot.*
*You're patient with everyone.*
*You don't like cats.*[12]
*You did and are doing a great, fantastic, over-the-top job of raising Kaari and Rhodes.*
*You're beautiful.*
*You're an athlete.*
*You've run marathons.*
*You run meetings well.*
*You gave birth to a beautiful, smart daughter.*
*You have a great butt.*
*You're a good listener.*
*You're not a Republican.*
*You don't care about church (that much).*
*You read a lot of books.*
*You take care of Bowman Household, Inc. (bills, investing, etc.).*
*You eat healthy.*

---

[12] For the record, it's not true that I don't like cats. I'm allergic to them. My husband, on the other hand, just hates them because he hates them.

*You're a good business woman.*
*You're a wildly successful author.*
*You're not materialistic.*

I was smiling when he looked up. He was smiling, too.

"That was nice," he said.

"I didn't know you liked my smile."

"I didn't know you liked how I look with facial stubble."

"Why did you write the part about church? I was teaching Bible study when we met."

"That's why I put 'that much.'"

"Is it that you love that I don't force you to go to church?"

"I don't have a lot of time off, and church seems like a big waste of a perfectly good Sunday morning. I'd rather be on my bike."

"I know."

We talked some more about what we loved about one another. We leaned in. We weren't chattering as much as the young couple, but we said more in our silences.

We paid the bill and stood to leave. I put my hand on the back of his neck, cradling it with my fingers, directing his head toward mine. I kissed him gently on the lips. "We still need to do this," I told him. "I would like you to touch me and kiss me out of the blue, for no reason."

He pinched my butt.

"That's good. Just like that," I said, laughing.

As we walked back to the hotel, I asked, "When do you want to fool around? That's what we're here for."

"In the morning. You're always better in the morning, right?"

"Yes, I think so," I said.

Write each other love letters at least once a year, exchanging them on Valentine's Day, your anniversary, or another symbolic date.

After a quick stop at the hotel, we walked, hand in hand, down to 57th street, to a store called Eve's Garden, a sex toy and erotica shop for women. A tall, very thin woman with long jet-black hair and big eyes greeted us. She was wearing a billowy skirt and top that made her look like a cross between the St. Pauli beer girl and Morticia Addams.

The small, one-room store sold erotica DVDs, a wide assortment of vibrators and dildos, many books about sexual technique, whips, paddles, warming oils, ticklers, and other assorted fare. I looked at the books. I saw titles to the effect of *The Complete Guide to Masturbation, The Complete Guide to Anal Sex, The Complete Guide to Vibrators, The Complete Guide to the Clitoris,* and so on. How could someone find enough words to fill an entire book on masturbation?

I noticed a familiar book. I'd written a few chapters for it when I'd worked as a staff writer at the publishing company in Emmaus. I pulled the book off the shelf, thumbed through to the acknowledgements page and showed Mark my name. I was proud of myself. I actually had a book on display at a sex shop!

We purchased an erotica DVD, a book of erotica, some warming oil, and a book called *How to Give Her Absolute Pleasure.* As I checked out, the saleslady said, "After he reads this book, he is going to make you *very* happy." I wanted her to be very right.

At the hotel, we readied for dinner. I showered and slipped into the new dress, new shoes and new lingerie I'd purchased for the trip. I rubbed lotion onto my legs. And then I relaxed on the bed as I waited for him to shower. There wasn't a part of my body that hadn't been primped in some way for this night. I should have felt fantastic but, instead, I felt tired and frumpy. If I had been at home, I would have put on a T-shirt and sweat pants and taken a nap.

Mark emerged from the bathroom.

"You look beautiful," he said.

"Thanks," I said, feeling a hint of that butterfly feeling I used to get many years ago when we'd first met. I knew he thought I was beautiful, but I didn't *always* know it, and sometimes, like that night, I really needed to hear him say it.

We hailed a cab and headed to the restaurant. Unlike so many times before, when we'd gone out to dinner and stared into space, we were now chattering away. We talked about the restaurant décor. We talked about the menu choices. We talked about the other people. We talked about the white pants all of the waiters seemed to be wearing. We talked and talked and talked.

I woke in the middle of the night with an intense headache, cotton-mouth, and the sensation that I was going to lose my dinner. I got myself to the bathroom, chugged some water, and crawled back into bed. I woke again a few hours later, feeling only slightly better. I was mad at myself for ruining our morning of sex by drinking too much the night before.

Around 8AM, I woke to the sound of various hotel doors opening and slamming. Mark was hungry. I still felt stuffed from the night before, but I knew he could get scary grumpy when he was hungry. This hunger-induced grumpiness was so scary that we even had a term for it: the Hunger Emergency. I asked no questions. We dressed and walked around. We found something to eat and then walked the streets for a while. I kept looking at my watch. We needed to take the 12:30 bus home.

"Are we going to have enough time?" I asked.

"We have plenty of time," he said.

When we got back to the hotel, I didn't feel anywhere near as dreadful as I had when I'd woken. We showered and readied ourselves for our second first time. As he showered, I changed into the lingerie I'd purchased in Cape May and started reading *The Merry XXXmas Book of Erotica* that I had purchased the day before at the sex shop in midtown. The story was about a woman who has sex with Santa Claus. It was full of descriptions like, "I'm dreaming he's sliding down my chimney with a big red cock." My intelligent mind thought the story was beneath me. My brain was making fun of the fact that I was wasting my time reading this trash. My womanly bits, however, apparently liked it quite a bit.

"What the?" I muttered as I felt myself getting warm and wet. "It works."

I put the book down and lay back on the pillows. That's when I noticed the mirror. It was on the bathroom door. It was full length, and it was fully visible from the left side of the bed.

"That makes up for everything," I thought.

I piled the pillows onto the left side of the bed and waited. I was feeling sexy. I was happy. I was expectant.

He opened the bathroom door. He was naked. His hair was wet and sticking up every which way. I asked him to sit on the bed with his back against the wall. I straddled him and kissed him gently. I whispered in his ear, "I asked you to tell me what you wanted. You didn't tell me, so I'm going to try something different. I want you to sit here. I am going to pleasure you. This is all about you."

I kissed him on the lips. I bit his lower lip. I kissed and bit his neck. I kissed his forehead. I kissed his chest. I hadn't done this for him in a very long time. In the past, I'd only gone down on him as foreplay. It had always felt like work for me. I'd struggled to build the endurance to do it long enough to get him highly aroused. My jaw had always hurt. I'd tried to ignore the pain, but eventually the pain had always overwhelmed my desire to excite him, and I'd had to stop before finishing.

When I'd asked for pointers, my husband had told me that I'd been doing everything perfectly. He'd sworn on the health of his fleet of bicycles that my technique was as good as any woman's. He even once claimed that he had enormous staying power, thanks to the deep breathing, relaxation skills, and tantric liberation he'd learned in a yoga class.

I didn't buy it, which was why, in the weeks leading up to New York, I'd read up on the matter.

"That's good, Momma," he said. "That's really good."

A few minutes later, he was done. I couldn't believe it. I'd done it! I was so ridiculously proud of myself that I almost did a victory dance around the bed. I let him rest and enjoy the afterglow. Then I asked, "Good?"

"Uh *huh*," he said, his voice sleepy. "You've been studying your technique, right?'

"I got a few ideas from one of the books I read. You wouldn't tell me what you wanted, so I did the best I could."

"You did a great job."

"Are you ready to switch?"

"Yes."

"Sit just as you are sitting. I'm going to sit with my back to you, and I'm going to show you how to pleasure me with your hands." I slid off my panties. I placed my right hand over his right palm and I guided him where I wanted him. I used my fingers to direct his pressure and direction. We had a great view of the Martini.

Within just a few minutes I was done, too.

"That was great," I said. "I wish I had thought to do that a long time ago."

"Me, too," he said.

On the bus, we talked about Kaarina's birthday, which was just a few weeks away. He said, "The Wednesday after Kaari's birthday I'll be in Jersey for a business trip."

I said, "The Wednesday after Kaari's birthday is my birthday."

He was silent for a while and so was I. I'd wanted to do something romantic for my birthday, something that would make up for the lack of romance on my birthday the year Kaari was born. We were building such good momentum. My birthday, to me, seemed like a symbolic event. Three years ago it was the symbol of our marriage falling apart. This year, I'd wanted it to be the symbol of our marriage coming back together. I hadn't thought to mention this, however, because I'd been so consumed with planning New York. Until that moment, my birthday had seemed months away.

"I'm sorry," he said. "We can celebrate your birthday on Friday?"

"I want to celebrate my birthday on my birthday. Can't you stay home?"

"I really need to be there."

"We need to talk about this more. I don't have a solution right now," I said.

Just weeks before, after such a conversation, I would have sat back against my seat and turned him into Mr. Ex. I would have killed him off and become preoccupied with planning his funeral. I did none of that on the bus. Yes, I certainly was disappointed. I also knew we would work it out. I did not want him dead. I loved him. I really did.

Just because he forgets your birthday and anniversary does not mean he doesn't love you. It only means that he has a really bad memory. Help the guy out. Write your birthday and anniversary and any other date you want him to remember on his calendar.

We pledged to do something like New York regularly. Maybe next time we'd stay in Philadelphia. Another time we might go to D.C.

I wasn't kidding myself, though. We couldn't go out of town every time we wanted to have sex. I had to find a way to turn off my amygdala at home. Otherwise, we'd continue with our miserable track record of having sex just once or twice a year—or only when we were in another city—and we both wanted to improve that record to once a week or, at the very least, once a month.

Yet again, I turned to *The Female Brain*. I read a section about attraction. It claimed that women were usually attracted to men who earned a lot of money, and that this was wired into our brains. We might think we were above such things, but we really weren't, said Dr. Brizendine.

"Did I fall out of love with him when he lost his job? Did I lose my attraction when he lost his income?"

My role as breadwinner put enormous pressure on me. I worried nearly constantly about whether I'd be able to make enough money to pay the mortgage, put money in the college savings account, and be able to afford our current standard of living. Did this worry keep my amygdala on? We could have an untraditional relationship, couldn't we? Couldn't a woman earn more than a man and still feel attracted to him?

I thought about other amygdala issues. From the moment I woke to the moment I fell into bed, I was cooking, cleaning, working, grocery shopping, sorting mail, taking out trash, paying bills, paying taxes, scooping dog poop, clipping the dog's nails, wiping Kaarina's bottom, reading Kaarina books, helping Kaarina paint and then cleaning up the mess afterwards, and much more.

I didn't sleep well at night.

I almost never relaxed and, when I did, I felt guilty.

Was this ruining my sex life?

I needed to learn how to do less, but I didn't know how. I worked and lived and slept in our mess. When the house was dirty, my brain felt disorganized. I needed to learn how to be okay with paying the bills late, with leaving dishes in the sink, and with uncertainty. At the same time, I needed Mark to do more. I needed Mark to do more of the parenting, cleaning, and other tasks.

"Hey sweetie, can I talk to you about something?" I asked. At this point he was getting used to this question, and he knew that, "Can I talk to you about something?" involved a major commitment of his time and brain activity. "Can I talk to you about something?" was never as simple as, "You always buy Earl Grey tea at the grocery store. Could you get English Breakfast instead?" No, it was never that simple.

He looked at me warily out of the corner of his eye.

"What's up?"

"I've been reading this book called *The Female Brain*."

"Oh, boy," he said with a sigh.

"It's a really good book. It's really interesting," I said quickly, trying to reel him back into the conversation, trying to keep his index finger from pressing "power" on the remote. "While I was reading it, I realized why we stopped having sex."

Now, I had his full attention.

"This author did a lot of research into the evolution of the female brain. She found that females are naturally attracted to men who earn more money than they do. At first, I didn't want to believe it. I thought I was better than that, but after thinking about it for a while, it started to make sense to me. Her argument was pretty convincing."

"What do you want me to do? Do you want me to get a second job?" he asked in that voice of his.

"No, that's not what I'm saying," I said. This wasn't where I'd planned for this conversation to go. Perhaps I had not summarized the book well. I wasn't sure where I'd gone wrong. I tried to remember what I'd said and how it had affected him. "I don't know the answer," I continued. "But it helps to understand the problem, or at least a part of the problem."

I'd lost him. He was staring at the wall, and he was waiting for me to give up on the conversation.

"I'm just saying that I need your help," I said.

"Well, how am I supposed to help you with that?" he asked sarcastically.

"I don't know," I said, defeated.

He turned on the TV. The conversation was over.

"Why does he always have to be so difficult," I thought. "Why can't he contribute to this process?"

I got up, grabbed a novel, and walked to the bedroom to read. I stared at the same lines over and over. I put down the book and stared at the ceiling. At times, the work we'd completed on our marriage had felt too easy. Other times, like tonight, the work felt impossible. Would I just have to accept this about my marriage? Would there always be a lack of sexual desire? Would I always feel a little disappointed with the quality of our sex life?

He got into bed. I rolled to one side, away from him. I didn't want to end it this way. If he fell asleep—which he would do in about three minutes if I didn't say something—I'd end up sleeping downstairs in the guest room. I couldn't sleep next to him when I was angry.

"Honey, I'm sorry if I offended you earlier," I said. "I didn't mean to offend you. I didn't say it the way I'd planned to say it. I just want to have sex more often. I want to have better sex. I need to relax and reduce the stress in my life, and I don't think I can do that without your help."

He got on all fours and crawled to my side of the bed. He straddled me, lowering his 180 pounds over me.

"I'll help you," he said, kissing me gently on the lips. "Just tell me what to do."

Over time, I told him what to do, and he did it. While Kaarina was napping one Sunday, for instance, he abandoned his usual spot in the La-Z-

Boy so he could wash and vacuum my car, scoop the dog poop from the yard, straighten up the sunroom, and do the laundry. Another night, he took her to the Velodrome, suggesting that I stay home and work on my novel. They returned happy and calm, and with him teasing me, "How'd you kill me this time?"

He did this because I gave him the clues. The clues said that I was tired and overwhelmed, and that I would appreciate him getting her out of the house more often so that I could have some time to myself.

He listened. He delivered and, as a result, I already felt closer to him. I was looking at him differently. One day I caught myself having the first hint of a sexual fantasy that actually involved *him*. He wasn't yet my Dove Bar, but he was approaching the flavor of a chocolate-covered Brussels Sprout.

# 8

## And Feel Adored by Him

**"Some people claim that marriage interferes with romance. There's no doubt about it. Anytime you have a romance, your wife is bound to interfere."**

—Groucho Marx, *The Groucho Phile*

I grew up reading and watching fairy tales about beautiful heroines who were rescued from lifetimes of poverty, boredom, or imprisonment by strong, charming men. As a pre-teen, I frittered away many of my weekends dreaming about my own Prince Charming. He would come home from work each day and hug and kiss me. He would shower me with affection and allow me to live happily ever after.

And then, roughly fifteen years later, I got married.

And then, not long after that, I got disillusioned.

And then I cursed the authors of all of those fairy tales. Why had they purposely set me up for such disappointment? Why had they encouraged me to believe that such men existed? Such men did not exist!

Or did they?

Could I turn Mark into my Prince Charming? Could I teach him how to romance me? If so, then how? And assuming it was possible to turn Mark into Prince Charming, what exactly would Prince Charming do?

What did I really want? Did I want chivalry? Flowers? For him to open doors for me? To take my arm and tell me I was beautiful?

Remember my birthday?

Yes, I wanted him to remember my birthday. But what else?

To define romance, I turned to the dictionary. I read a number of definitions. The same words kept appearing: adventurous, heroic, and mysterious. I could see how an adventure, say, us sailing the Canary Islands, could be wildly romantic. I could even see how an act of heroism, say, him pushing me out of the way of an oncoming car, could be romantic. I could also see how a mystery, say, Mark giving me a key and me having to find the lock that it opened, could be romantic.

I needed more, though, so I found myself reminiscing about real-life romantic stories.

I thought about how my older brother Andy had proposed to his wife, Pam. He'd hired a limousine to transport the two of them to a romantic restaurant for dinner. While they'd dined, one of Pam's friends had placed flowers, the engagement ring, and a sheet cake with the words, "Will you marry me?" written in the icing at Pam's house. When Andy and Pam had returned to her house, he'd knelt by the cake. I loved hearing this engagement story because my older brother had tormented me as a child. The romantic way he'd proposed seemed so opposite of his personality. It made me realize how much he loved her.

I thought about my friend, Jennifer, and how her husband had proposed in Italy. It had been their first night there. They'd been jet-lagged and awoke just before dawn. Bob had walked her to the Via de Dante Alighieri, near the church where Dante had first seen his true love, Beatrice. Bob had read her some lines from Dante, dropped to one knee, held her hand and, in Italian, had asked her to marry him. When she returned from Italy and told me this story, I thought she was the luckiest woman alive to be marrying a man like Bob, especially considering that Bob was not Italian and had learned the Italian needed to recite Dante and propose just for the trip. I'd also thought that my husband would never in a million years do the same for me, even if Bob had handed him a script and how-to manual.

I couldn't expect Mark to be a Bob, though. Mark wouldn't read me Dante or discuss my latest book club read with me, but he would easily wax my car and change my brake pads. Something told me that Bob didn't know brake pads.

Romance can't be copied. Every man does it a little differently, and every woman falls in love with a different romantic man.

I fell in love with the kind of man who has grease under his fingernails, permanent scars on his knees and shoulder blades, and *Cycle Sport* in his bathroom. I fell in love with a man who occasionally walked out to the yard with a pair of scissors, cut a few random flowers and then presented them to me in a hasty bouquet. I fell in love with a man who took up running, even though it made his knees hurt, so he could keep me company during my marathon training runs.

This, I thought, was progress.

To further define romance, I turned yet again to Dr. Love. She told me that romance "is the way you demonstrate your love and respect for your partner on an ongoing basis." Yes, I did yearn for my husband to find a way to tell me that he loved me without saying the actual words. I wanted him to show me, say, by looking at me as if I were the most expensive bicycle he'd ever laid eyes on. I craved it. I wanted it because I regularly suffered from doubt. On those late nights when I was irritated because he was out with his friends and on those long weekends when I was annoyed that he was at work or on his bike, I worried that a man who preferred his bike or his friends to his wife must not really love his wife in the first place.

If he could convince me—especially the most vulnerable part of me—that I rocked his world in every way, my jealously and fear just might ebb.

Think about how you want your spouse to say, "I love you." Then share your discoveries with him.

That Mark planned to spend my birthday in New Jersey didn't make me feel like the most important being in his universe. That he didn't even realize it was my birthday made me feel so far down on his list of important people and things that I was barely on the list at all.

My three most recent birthdays had also been forgotten. My thirty-fourth marked the birth saga. I spent my thirty-fifth birthday in Newfoundland, Canada while vacationing with my parents. Mark had been too busy to join us. On my thirty-sixth birthday, I asked Mark to watch Kaarina all day so I could spend the day napping and reading. He'd entertained her for an hour, and then he'd given up.

I didn't want my thirty-seventh to be a repeat of the past. I just didn't.

Then one night as I was reading David Schnarch's *Passionate Marriage,* I learned that truly happy couples did not argue over "what I want for myself versus what you want for yourself." Truly happy couples stepped into one another's shoes and tried to find a common solution. In other words, when facing conflict, my need to be happy should be as strong as my need for my husband to be happy, and vice versa. I put the book in my lap, sat back in the chair, and thought about how this advice applied to my birthday. "Well, David, if I just let my husband go to Jersey so he can be happy, then I'm not happy. That's one of our problems. The happiness balance is in my husband's favor. He's the one who needs to learn this piece of advice, not me. Right?"

I thought about the situation a little longer. "Let's say he really needs to be there. Let's say it's vitally important for his business. Then what? Then I'll hire a sitter and do something else. Maybe I'll invite the girls to have dinner with me."

We settled Kaarina in bed. I asked Mark if we could talk.

"What do we need to talk about?"

"My birthday," I said.

"What about it?"

"My birthday the year Kaarina was born was about as bad as a birthday can get. It's the symbol of everything that is wrong with our marriage. I want this birthday to be the symbol of everything that's right."

"I don't have to go to New Jersey. I can stay home."

"Are you sure?" I asked. His face was soft. His eyes were kind. He was sure. He wanted this to work. He wanted me to be happy.

"Thanks David," I thought. "Thanks for this marital moment."

Tell him what you want, but be okay with not always getting what you want. You'll feel more loved if he understands your needs—even if he doesn't necessarily agree with them—than if he doesn't understand you at all but does your bidding because he's too exhausted to stand up for himself.

I considered David Schnarch a brilliant man, not only for helping to resurrect my birthday plans, but also because in his book he found a way to compare marital intimacy to quantum physics. It was way over my head so I won't even attempt to paraphrase it, but it gave me lots of hope that the man could help us.

Schnarch suggested that Mark and I should try a technique he called "the relaxed hug." He said it would transform our relationship. If I could fix our problems just by hugging my husband a little differently, I was all for it. From Mr. Schnarch I learned that, in every relationship, one person releases first from any embrace, and the other clings. The interplay between the releaser and the clinger was usually so subtle that neither marital partner knew who was who.

I wondered which one of us clung and which one of us released, but I mostly wondered why Mark and I no longer hugged at all. We used to hug and say, "I love you" when one of us was leaving the house. I remembered Mom one time joking, as she saw us embracing by the front door, "It's not like he's going on a two-week-long business trip." The hugs, in part, stemmed from a mild fear that it might be the last time I saw him. As a newspaper reporter, I'd interviewed enough grieving spouses who'd said things like, "I didn't kiss him or hug him or say good bye this morning when he left." I didn't want that on my conscience if Mark happened to get hit by a tractor-trailer while on his way to the mailbox. These hugs, of course, were about more than "This might be our last good-bye." They were warm and lingering. Everything about them said, "I love you more than my own life." I missed them.

I tried to remember the last hug, and I just couldn't. It had pre-dated the last sexual experience. We'd probably stopped hugging and kissing years ago. Could Schnarch teach us how to hug again?

"Hey sweetie," I said, interrupting Mark as he watched car racing. "I'm reading a chapter about hugging. I'd like to try something with you."

"What do you want to try?"

"Could you stand up? I'd like to hug you."

"Is that it?"

"Yes," I said, looking at his pale gray eyes, hoping that he wouldn't beg off until after the car race.

"I can handle that," he said.

He stood. We hugged. He leaned into me. I took a step back with my right leg so I could support his body weight. Schnarch had mentioned that one person generally leans in and the other either leans in, too, or leans out.

The leaning was symbolic of neediness, of feeling as if you couldn't stand on your own two feet. I wasn't sure I believed it, but I was trying to have an open mind. I was also incredibly uncomfortable. My leg was starting to tremble, and my upper body felt crushed under his weight. Had he always hugged me this way? I didn't remember feeling uncomfortable before.

"Honey, can you stand up more? The guy who wrote the book says leaning in is a symbol of neediness. Do you feel needy?"

"No, I just like hugging you this way."

"I'm going to fall over backward if you keep it up."

He shifted his weight. I wrapped my arms around his waist. He rested his head on my shoulder.

I was definitely the releaser. Every molecule of my being was saying, "I've had enough." I also saw the painful symbolism. I was the one who'd almost left the marriage. I was the one who'd almost given up on us. He was leaning in. He wanted me. He needed me. He might not have been able to communicate this need in words, but he was showing it in the hug.

Mr. Schnarch had informed me, however, that I could get past my urge to flee. If I waited long enough, Mr. Schnarch had written, I would relax into the hug. I would feel "profoundly calm." According to Schnarch, I'd feel my connection to my husband through my connection to myself. (See, I told you he was deep.)

So we hugged, and I waited.

I was so uncomfortable with my desire to release, however, that I chattered endlessly, repeating just about every word I'd read in Schnarch's book. "There's supposed to be a moment when you start to feel uncomfortable and want to release. We need to get past that moment, and relax," I said, as if he was the one who wanted to let go.

He wrapped his arms around me more tightly. He could have stood there all night, even if car racing hadn't been on the TV.

I tried to relax. I focused on my breathing.

I transcended discomfort and entered a state of profound boredom. Was this another ominous symbol about how I felt about our entire marriage?

We continued to hug. I continued to feel bored.

I waited.

And waited.

And waited.

"I'm sure that was long enough," I said. We released.

Had we just failed Hugging 101? If I couldn't feel comfortable hugging my husband, how could our marriage possibly survive?

The next night, I decided to try again.

"Honey, can we practice The Hug again?"

"Sure, Shortcake," he said.

He stood. He wrapped his arms around me. He leaned into me and said, "I'm going to outlast you."

"Is it a competition?" I asked.

He didn't answer.

He leaned more.

"I can't hold you up. You're heavier than me. This isn't fair," I said, laughing.

He laughed too, but he leaned even more.

I pushed all of my 120 pounds against his 180 pounds. I felt as if I were trying to push a linebacker down a football field. I wasn't bored. I wasn't uncomfortable. I did not feel profoundly calm, but I was having a great time.

He leaned toward me a bit more. I took a couple steps back.

His chest was right in front of my nose. I leaned my face toward his chest. I opened my mouth and I gently, yet firmly, pinched some of the skin on his chest between my incisors.

"Hey, ouch!" He released.

"You released first. I won," I said, doing a victory dance.

"That wasn't fair!" he grinned.

"You played dirty first. I just played dirtier," I said, kissing him gently on the lips.

I didn't think it was what Schnarch had in mind, but I liked our version much better.

There is only one wrong way to hug someone. You do it without touching them.

My birthday only comes once a year. Between birthdays were 364 days that were in desperate need of romantic attention. I knew "Could you try to be more romantic more often?" wasn't specific enough. Mark needed an instruction manual.

To figure out what to put in the manual, I emailed a few friends, asking them how their husbands romanced them. I emailed Jennifer, of Jennifer and Bob, Deb, from the dinner in New York, and Eileen, my running partner. They represented a good cross-section of the married female population. Jennifer was in her early thirties, Deb was in her mid-forties, and Eileen was approaching sixty.

Deb wrote back first. She'd been married and madly in love with Keith for seventeen years. Keith was her opposite in many ways, just as Mark was mine. I'd never seen Keith with a tense face. One of his most romantic features was his ability to gently coax Deb away from her computer so that she didn't miss out on the finer things in life, such as a dinner that he'd prepared. I should also mention that he's Scottish. The way he pronounced his every word was enough to make any reasonable woman think that Deb was the luckiest woman on the planet, but there was more. He had a way of looking at Deb that communicated, "You've made me the happiest man alive."

I read what Deb had to say.

*He brings me coffee every morning when he comes in to wake me up, and fixes it just as I like.*

*He does the laundry and knows which kid gets which clothes, something I can't even seem to get right.*

*He listens to me obsess and worry over stupid things, and never calls me stupid.*

*He teases me (lovingly) over my propensity to spill water no matter where or what I'm doing; my ability to bruise with the slightest bump; and my workaholism.*

*He understands my need for a nap every afternoon.*

*He comes up behind me when I'm working and kisses the back of my neck.*

*He signs all his emails with love, and all his little notes to me (i.e., gone fishing with the boys) with a heart.*

*Personally, I find the fact that he's trying to get into shape, biking around the neighborhood and going to the gym with me, romantic.*

*He often walks with me. We don't hold hands, because I walk so fast I'm often a few feet ahead of him, but at least we're together for an hour without a computer, TV or other distraction.*

*Honestly, simply being able to sit and talk is romantic at this stage in life.*

*We also eat dinner every night by candlelight.*

Jennifer, the friend who'd turned me onto The Martini, emailed next. I'd known Jennifer for about seven years. She was well read. I was sure she could recite lines from Shakespeare. She was a trained concert violinist. She was a gourmet cook, and, like her partner Bob, she'd had a fascination with vampire films long before vampire films were cool. Bob and Jennifer had been married just two years. Arguably, they were still in the honeymoon stage, but I could still learn from what they are doing right.

*Bob and I are always touching each other. We're not like teens hopped up on hormones. We're just touching an elbow, brushing a cheek.*

*We say "love you" a lot. Even if we're just sitting watching television or driving somewhere, he'll just say, "I love you, Jennifer," out of the blue.*

*He takes the dog out in the morning so I can sleep in.*

*He ate vegetarian with me.*

*He cooked South Beach for me.*

*He tells me I'm sexy and beautiful.*

*If I've had a bad day, I'm likely to come home to candles and flowers. Sometimes he'll have cleaned the tub so that I can take a bath, and he'll have a pot of water heating on the stove for spaghetti.*

*He listens to me.*

*He puts me first.*

*He tells me to go ahead and order dessert.*

Her email reminded me of what Mark and I used to do when our relationship was stronger. I used to rub his back every morning. Whenever one of us left the house, we would hug and kiss good-bye. We used to hold hands. We used to walk together, run together, and ride a tandem bike together. We used to watch action movies together. We used to travel and explore new places and try new cuisines together.

After he'd opened his store and we'd had a baby, the togetherness turned into separateness. We stopped seeing movies. We stopped exercising together. We stopped riding the tandem. I stopped rubbing his back. We stopped hugging. We stopped touching.

Eileen wrote back next. She'd been married twenty-one years. I'd known Eileen since I worked at *Runner's World* magazine. She was the happiest person I knew. Eileen could run twenty miles on a hot, humid summer day and never lose her smile. She and her partner, also named Bob,[13] had vacationed with us in Maui many years ago. There, they acted like newlyweds. They gently caressed one another, a soft stroke of the arm here, a touch on the neck there. Occasionally they'd look at one another and I could feel the world drop away from them. They became each other's universe.

One day many years ago, Bob had been stung by a bee and gone into anaphylactic shock. By the time the ambulance had arrived, he'd stopped breathing. A friend had called every extension at *Runner's World* in search of Eileen who, at that moment, had been out running. He'd eventually rung my extension. I waited in the hallway for Eileen. When she walked in the

---

[13] Yes, Jennifer is married to a Bob and Eileen is married to a Bob, but they are not married to the same Bob.

door, her face still red from exertion, she could tell something was wrong by the expression on my face.

"Something's happened to Bob," I told her.

She collapsed to her knees, saying, "My Bob? What's wrong with my Bob? Not my Bob!"

I put her arm around my shoulder. Another friend took her other arm and we carried her to the car and drove her to the ER. When we arrived, we found Bob fully conscious, his life saved by a shot of epinephrine. I wondered, "Would I collapse to my knees if I learned something was wrong with Mark? Does she love Bob more than I love Mark?"

The answer to that question may very well have been yes. Eileen and Bob were in their senior years, but they behaved like love-struck teens. Mark and I had a lot to learn from them.

Her email was written like an instruction manual:

*Every day, tell her you love her in a sweet, sincere way. Out of the blue, look at her, touch her face, or kiss her neck and appreciate her beauty, inside and out.*

*Do special things for her that she really appreciates. For instance, I like my toenails painted, especially in the summer. He'll do them for me without any hint of not liking it. He does a nice job, too.*

*Take a walk together and hold hands. Every so often stop and kiss and say, 'I love you.'*

*Be a team, work together, encourage each other. It just makes for a better marriage and overall relationship. Example: We always cook dinner together, drink a glass of wine and talk. It's a very romantic time for us. We start with a toast of the day.*

*And last but not least is the sex. Take the time for it. That's the true test to whether you have a great relationship.*

Her email helped me to see that I was not necessarily yearning for romance. I was yearning for togetherness.

........................................................................................

If you want him to romance you in a specific way, create a Romance Instruction manual for him to follow.

I picked up *Hot Monogamy* yet again and paged through to find the romance chapter. Dr. Love had listed 45 romantic gestures and recommended rating them on a scale of 0 (not romantic at all) to 4 (highly romantic). I copied the list, making one copy for Mark and another for myself. As I rated my list, I realized that there were a lot of so-called romantic gestures that I would prefer my husband never do.

Bathe me, for instance. I didn't want him to do that unless I was paralyzed. I was also not interested in showering together. We'd done that a few times early in our relationship. It hadn't done much for me. I'd rather wash my hair, shave my legs, and get clean without the problem of sharing the stream of hot water with another human being. I didn't want him to ever plan a surprise birthday party. I did like surprises, and I would have found certain types of surprises incredibly romantic. A surprise birthday party, however, was not one of them.

I didn't want him to write me a poem. I didn't understand poetry; I never had. The only course I ever drop failed in college was a poetry class.

I was not big on expensive gifts, either. All of our money was in the same joint accounts. When either of us wanted something big, we talked about it and made a decision together. If he bought me a $1000 necklace, I'd probably get mad that he didn't consult me about the purchase, and then I'd return it.

Other suggestions on Dr. Love's list filled me with lust. Telling me, "I love you," got a top rating. So did "giving me a thoughtful, inexpensive gift." Kaarina gave me those kinds of gifts all the time. She brought me shells she'd found on the beach, rocks she'd found by the stream, and scribbles she'd made on scrap pieces of paper. I also gave "going away for a weekend together," "staying home together with no interruptions," "sleeping in together," and "sitting by the fireplace together" 4s.

I handed my rankings to him and he handed his to me. I found his answers illuminating.

I learned that he was very interested in me giving him backrubs, praising him in front of others, taking him to cultural events, giving him thoughtful but inexpensive gifts, taking him out to eat, planning a surprise vacation, going on a picnic together, going away for a weekend together, and sleeping in together.

I was flabbergasted that he wanted me to accompany him to a cultural event, though. This was my grease under the fingernails guy. He wanted to see the ballet and opera?

"What kind of cultural events do you want see?"

"Baseball and football games."

"Those aren't cultural events. Those are sporting events."

"They're cultural."

I gently said, "There's another line on her list about sporting events. Do you want me to take you to a sporting event or a cultural event?"

"Both."

We talked about our lists, about what we'd found surprising about one another's answers, and about what we didn't. I was inspired. I knew what I wanted. I knew what I needed. I was ready to write Mark's Romance Instruction Manual.

*Touch me, not because you want to have sex, but because you love me. Touch the back of my arm. Touch my neck. Hold my hand. Place your palm against my upper back.*

*Kiss me. Kiss my cheek. Kiss my forehead. Kiss the back of my neck. Walk up to me in front of other people and kiss me on the lips, and say, "That's just what I needed."*

*Court me. Show me amazing things. Remind me to see the sunset. Marvel at the stars with me. Sit and listen to the crickets with me.*

*Be with me. Walk with me. Ride the tandem bike with me. Watch James Bond with me.*

*Tell me that I'm beautiful. Tell me in the morning, when my hair is a mess. Tell me when I'm dressed up. Tell me when I come into the shop. Tell me just because.*

*Say, 'I love you.' Say it when you leave for work in the morning. Say it when you come home. Say it as we are falling asleep at night.*

*Surprise me. Send me small gifts, even if it's not my birthday or Mother's Day. Pick flowers for me. Take me somewhere unusual. Send me a card for no reason. Hide a note in my purse. Send me a text message.*

*Help me. When I seem tired, harried or overwhelmed, do more. Ask to help and, when I don't suggest a way to help, help anyway.*

*Excite me. Encourage me to face my fears. Rekindle my sense of adventure. Help me to loosen up. Push me beyond my limits. Make me ride a roller coaster with you. Blindfold me and feed me.*

*Bring me on adventures. Take me to new places. Enjoy new cuisines with me. Explore the world with me.*

*Listen.*

After printing it out, I handed it to him. He read it. "This is helpful," he said.

I was out of clean underwear. But if I did a load of laundry, I knew Mark would complain about something. He'd tell me that the water had been too hot or too cold, that I'd used too much soap or too little, that I'd put too many clothes in the machine or too few.

Oh, he could be a true pain in the ass about the laundry. That's why I rarely, if ever, did it.

But I was in the midst of a panty emergency. I was either going to do a load of laundry or go commando. I choose the former.

And it got me into clean underwear.

As well as into a dirty fight with my husband.

The fight started hours later, when my husband walked into the room where I was sitting, rolled his eyes and, and in that sarcastic voice of his, said, "Alisa, you almost flooded the entire basement. I had towels bleaching in the sink and when the machine emptied into the sink, the sink couldn't drain. I know I've asked you not to do the laundry before and this is why."

Really? My quest for clean panties had almost flooded the basement? This was my fault?

"It's your fault for leaving the towels in the sink. I don't know how many times you've asked me not to leave anything in the sink for that very reason," I shot back.

"No, this is your fault. I'm the one who does the laundry. If you hadn't started the washer, it wouldn't have happened."

I had been doing him a favor by doing a load, hadn't I? If he'd emptied the dishwasher, even if he'd put the dishes in the wrong cabinets, I would have been ecstatic.

He was standing there with that tense look of his, waiting for me to tell him that he was right and I was wrong, but I couldn't do it. I was not wrong! He was!

Wasn't he?

I'd read that anger surfaced only when we swallowed our most important words. "I must not be telling him something," I thought to myself. But what was it? Why did we keep getting locked in this stupid power struggle? The only unsaid thought that seemed to be running through my mind involved two curse words that are not considered ladylike to say in public—or ever, really.

I didn't think saying those words would reduce my anger or his.

Instead, I asked, "Does it have to be someone's fault? Do you have to blame someone?"

"I'm not blaming."

"Yes, you are. You're talking to me in a sarcastic tone of voice. I hate when you talk to me like that. It hurts."

"It does?"

"Yes, it does."

"How did I say it?"

"You said it as if you think I'm stupid."

"I don't think you're stupid. You're probably much smarter than I am. How should I have said it?"

"You should have said it as I'm talking to you right now. I'm just telling you how I feel and laying out the specifics of why I feel that way."

"No, show me. Here, I'll pretend I'm you."

He moved his fingers as if he was typing on an imaginary keyboard. He glanced down and then up, as if he was looking at the keyboard and then the imaginary computer screen and then back at the keyboard again.

I sighed audibly.

"Oh, all right," I said, dragging out the all right part with yet another sigh. Yes, dear reader, that was sarcasm. And, yes, you would be absolutely correct if you told me that I was the pot calling the kettle black.

Established.

I said, "Honey, I was just downstairs doing the laundry. You had no way of knowing this, but I had towels soaking in the sink and, when the washer emptied, it almost flooded the basement. Because I soak the towels there a lot and because I'll probably never remember to tell you that they are there, it might be best if I did the laundry. You were trying to be helpful and I appreciate it."

His mouth formed an open O for a few seconds. Then, quickly, without a break between the words he said, "*I'llSayItLikeThatNextTime.*"

"Thanks," I said.

He held out his arms. I placed my cheek against his chest. He wrapped his arms around me.

"I'm sorry. I don't think you're stupid," he whispered.

Never assume you know what your spouse is thinking. Stop trying to interpret tone of voice and body language. Instead just ask, "Do you think I'm stupid?"

For my birthday, I asked for a simple, inexpensive gift. I wanted Mark to find my G-spot. Until I'd read *Hot Monogomy*, I'd believed that the G-spot was a hoax. Not one of my girlfriends had ever mentioned her husband or boyfriend finding her G-spot. Of course, they hadn't mentioned any details about what went on in their bedrooms, so there was that, too. Still, like the idea of multiple orgasms, I was convinced that the G-spot was just a cruel rumor members of the porn industry had perpetuated to make moms like me feel even more inadequate.

Then I read Dr. Love's chapter about the spot. She told me that this elusive G-spot was located on the upper front surface of the vagina. It was supposedly right behind my pubic bone and, if my husband was ever able to find it, he would not only be able to give me the most intense orgasm of my entire living experience, but he might even be able to give me one orgasm after another for hours on end until I was so exhausted I had to beg him to stop. I was keen on him finding it, so I dog-eared the chapter in *Hot Monogamy*, asked him to read it, and suggested he schedule some time on my birthday for a G-spot hunt. He agreed.

On my birthday morning, I met Mark at home for an early morning "nooner." I found *Hot Monogamy*. Mark had not read the G-spot chapter. I knew this without asking. I opened the book, handed it to him, and asked him to read it while I showered.

I stepped out of the shower and wrapped a towel around myself. I lay on the bed and waited for him to join me. I felt incredible. My body was changing. Our relationship was changing. Everything was changing.

He walked to the bed. He kissed every part of my body. I was filled with so much desire that I worried I might have an orgasm before he finished kissing my inner thighs. I managed to hold off, but once he got to the Martini, I was beside myself. I thought about telling him to start the G-spot search before it was too late, but, before I could say anything, it was too late.

"That was fantastic," I said, breathless.

"Thanks," he said.

We lay together for a while. I asked him if he changed his technique with the oral. I mentioned that I didn't remember getting that aroused in the past. He said he had not.

"It's the Martini," he said.

It doesn't matter how he gives you an orgasm—by a clitoral hand job, oral, G-spot stimulation, or something else. What does matter is that he thinks it's important to do everything in his power to please you in bed.

I spent the rest of the day at a spa getting a hot stone massage, manicure and pedicure. In the late afternoon, I gathered Kaarina from preschool. She wanted to use her inflatable water slide that Daddy had given her for her birthday. I suited her up and got the hose. I listened to her laughter as she slid into the blow-up baby pool. Twenty or so different-colored butterflies were on our nearby butterfly bush. The spray from the hose arched into the air, catching bits of the sunlight. The sun was low, casting yellow stripes in the grass. My skin felt cool from the spray.

Kaarina wrestled the hose out of my hands and chased me around the yard, spraying me. I was fully dressed. She soaked me, but I was laughing. I probably hadn't had so much fun since I was her age.

After the soaking, we got dressed. Kaarina was hungry and progressing into a full-blown Hunger Emergency. I couldn't get her to put on her shorts or shoes. Every time I walked near her with the shorts, she crossed her arms over her chest, stomped her foot, and said, "I don't want them!" I weighed my options. I could wrestle her into them. I could threaten to put various toys in toy jail until she got dressed. I could let her wear her panties and bare feet.

I put the shorts and shoes in my purse, got my keys, and told her I was leaving, with or without her. In her shirt, panties, and "happy feet," she raced to the car.

We drove to the store to pick up Daddy, and then to a nearby restaurant. I asked Mark to wrestle her into the shorts and shoes. When he stood afterward, he looked as if he'd survived Spain's Running of the Bulls.

We sat on the outdoor patio. It was decorated with white Christmas lights, surrounded by trees, and featured a large Japanese-style water fountain with a few koi. I sipped my wine. I relaxed. I let Mark deal with Kaarina's grouchiness. When she wanted to use the potty, I sat still. He took her. The food arrived. Kaarina's mood improved as she ate her pasta. She sang, "Happy Birfday to you. Haaaaaapy Birfday tooo you. Happy birfday dear Mooommeee. Happy birfday to you." The women at a nearby table applauded her efforts.

We drove home. Mark got her ready for bed. We read books. She drifted off to sleep.

We watched *CSI: New York*. We hadn't watched TV together in months. In the show, a couple bungee jumped off the Brooklyn bridge, somehow managing to have sex during the fall. If this naked couple tied themselves together, and jumped off the bridge, copulated on the way down, and sprung up and down for a while, did they eventually have to cut themselves lose, dive into the East River and swim to shore? If so, wouldn't the swim in the polluted river have extinguished any fireworks they had experienced on the way down?

"Seems far-fetched," he said.

"I agree," I said.

We went to bed. I placed my hand on his chest. I could feel the heat of his body. I closed my eyes, and I felt thankful.

......................................................................................................................

If you are exhausted because you can't get your kid dressed, ask for help and ask for it out loud. Your husband can't hear the words inside your head. Only you can hear those! Be as specific as possible. "I need help," is good, but "Can you please get her dressed because I'm about to throttle her" is even better.

......................................................................................................................

When I started the chapter on romance, I was hoping to recreate the sensation of the very first moment in our relationship when we realized we were attracted to one another. That's not what we created, but I was okay with that. Romance may be about giddiness, eye gazing, and lusty attraction in the beginning, but I learned that after eight years of marriage, romance becomes an exercise in:

**Touch.** A month or so before my wedding, my mother gathered her closest friends and colleagues for a pre-marital send off. One by one, these married women offered their advice for a long and happy marriage. I've forgotten a lot of the advice over the years, but one woman's advice has stuck with me. She told me, "Make love to your husband from the moment you wake to the moment you go to sleep." She was talking about committing random acts of affection all day long. She was talking about eye contact, smiling, and touching. She suggested I make an effort to remember to do those things because, at some point, after I'd been married for a long time, I would forget. Once I forgot, the touching would stop. When the touching stopped, so would the desire. When the desire stopped, so would the sex.

In Barton Goldsmith's *Emotional Fitness for Couples*, I'd read that married Puerto Ricans touched 180 times a day. The French touched 110 times daily. Married Americans touched just twice. When I mentioned this statistic to a few married friends, they told me, "I don't think we even touch that often."

Mark and I had been touching more, a lot more. We'd been hugging at night, before bed. When he came home early from work and I was at the computer, he rubbed my shoulders. When we were in the car and I was lost in thought, he grabbed my hand, holding it gently until I returned to the present moment. When I called him at work, he answered with his most enthusiastic voice, no matter how many customers were lined up to buy coffee. When we went to parties, he lingered near me rather than always hanging out with the other guys and, as he lingered, he gently touched my arm or back, and he smiled a smile that said, "I'm happy I married you. You are the best thing that ever happened to me."

I reciprocated by brushing against him or fondling him in public. One day, for example, I walked up behind him while he was at his cash register. I wrapped my arms around his shoulders, kissed him on the neck, and purred, "Did you remember to pay your payroll taxes today?"

**Adoration**. Romance was about saying thank you for the big things and the little things, and everything in between. It was about giving compliments. It was about me telling my husband, "You look great in those sunglasses, and that shirt really shows of your chest," as I rubbed my hands over his chest. It was about my husband asking me when we left a party whether he did a good job touching me in front of other people, and me, without hesitation, saying, "You did a wonderful job."

My husband needed to feel appreciated for the small stuff. I'd rebelled against this need for years. For instance, one day a few months before, he emptied the dishwasher and declared, "Look, I emptied the dishwasher!" He had been looking for praise, but I responded, "I empty the dishwasher every single day. I don't see you giving me a happy face sticker." I now understood that such snotty comebacks hurt both of us. They not only made him feel bad, they also ensured that he'd never empty the dishwasher, feed the dog, or do some other mundane task that would make my life a lot easier. It was easy to satisfy my husband's need for appreciation, and it felt a lot better than saying something snotty. When he let the dog out one morning, I said with love, "Thanks for letting the dog out." I let the dog out every morning, and he never thanked me, but that didn't mean I needed to say something snotty on the rare occasion when he did it. The snotty comebacks got me nowhere. The compliments got me folded laundry, a more attentive parent, and lots of little favors that made my life so much easier.

**Listening.** Romance was about making the time to talk to one another about what was going on in our lives. It was about listening to one another talk, without interrupting and without solving each other's problems.

**Togetherness.** Rather than doing things separately, it was about doing things together. We planned a family trip to the beach in September and a romantic getaway to Philadelphia in October. We planned a date night every other Friday.

**Creativity.** Romance was in the small surprises, in me texting him "your lips are like sugar" and in him texting me, "I love you," even though he was sitting on the other side of the room.

**Adventure.** Romance was about Mark driving his new car home and asking me whether I wanted to go for a ride. "We can't. Kaari's asleep," I'd said.

"Come on, she won't wake up. Nothing's going to happen to her," he said. Within a nanosecond of him saying, "Nothing is going to happen," my mind had obsessed over every news story I'd ever written or read that detailed the story of a toddler or young child who had been left in a house or apartment without supervision. Mark saw the look on my face and read my mind.

"Where's your cell?"

"Why? Here." I handed it to him. He dialed my phone with his, answered mine, and set it by Kaarina's door. He handed me his phone. "It's just like a portable baby monitor. You can hear everything that happens."

With his phone in hand, I walked outside to the car. We circled the neighborhood once, with him chattering on about various features of the car. It had been exciting. It had been verboten. I loved him for it.

**Growth.** Romance was about me learning how to ask for help and him learning how to give whenever I asked, and even when I didn't. It was about him allowing me to feel worthy and me allowing him to feel competent.

Most important, romance was an exercise in dedication. It was easy to become household partners who never touched, never gazed into one another's eyes, and who never, through words or actions, said "I love you." We had so many dishes in the sink, bills to pay, paychecks to earn, bottoms to wipe, parties to plan, thank you notes to write, and messes to clean to distract us from noticing each other. Yet, I would rather I remembered to hug my husband than write the thank you notes.

Even at the close of the chapter on romance, despite the fact that we'd been working diligently on our marriage, we got distracted. Kaarina spent one evening at "Parent's Night Out" at her school. We had the night off. Mark had been out with his friends. I'd been at home working. Around mid-afternoon, it occurred to me that the plan lacked something really important: togetherness.

I grabbed my cell and sent my husband a text message: "My martini misses u. Meet me @ The Farmhouse @ 9:30?"

At 6PM the phone rang. "Hi, hot stuff," he said.

"How are you?" I purred back.

"My phone was dead. I just got your message. I would love to meet you," he said.

We ordered appetizers. I had a glass of wine. He had a beer. I rubbed his thigh. He kissed my cheek. I gazed into his eyes. It felt as if we'd just met, but it also felt as if we'd met eleven years ago. Unlike the day eleven years ago when we met for the first time in that very bar, on those very bar stools, we finally knew one another. I might not have had giddy falling in love chemicals lusting up my brain that evening, but what I had now was so much better.

# 9

## Poof! He Turned Back into a Prince ... or Did He?

### MID-AUGUST 2007

**"When a woman says, 'let's talk,' guys go to this place in their heads where they start to think, 'Oh my God, what did I do now?'"**

—Barton Goldsmith, PhD, *Emotional Fitness for Couples*

It had been just over two months since the start of the Marriage Project. We'd resurrected our sex life, started joking and laughing again, and solved a lot of problems. Mark helped with bedtime and bath duty, and he occasionally emptied the dishwasher without me asking him to do it. When he picked Kaarina up from preschool, he no longer asked me to pack supplies. He filled a sippy cup with juice and put together a small snack all by himself.

Had we not just kicked some ultra-fine almost-divorced booty? I certainly thought so.

Our relationship had improved so quickly that I found myself doubting that we'd ever had problems in the first place. Had my marriage really been that bad? Had I really been serious about getting a divorce?

I was super proud of myself, of him, and of us.

I was also super sick of working on my marriage. For two months I'd spent nearly every night reading relationship books or websites. I'd read twelve books. Twelve!

Don't you think that, after reading twelve self-help books, you might just never ever for the rest of your life want to read, see, or hear about another self-help book ever again? Because if that's something you can imagine, you know precisely how I felt just two months into our marriage project.

Novels? I wanted to read those things again. Magazines? I wanted to flip through them. Mindless TV shows? Bring the diversion on.

I wanted my life back.

When I started the project, I planned on including two more months and two more issues. After romance, I assumed we'd work on our communication skills and then on intimacy. But we were talking more than ever. We'd solved so many problems in the past few months, and we'd done it through good communication—right? I was tempted to declare the project complete.

Maybe we didn't need to work on communication. Maybe the intimacy issue would fix itself over time.

Maybe we were done?

# 10

## They Learned a Common Language

### MID-AUGUST 2007, CONTINUED

**If people who do not understand each other at least
understand that they do not understand each other,
then they understand each other better than when,
not understanding each other, they do not even
understand that they do not understand each other."**

—Gustav Ischheiser, *Appearances and Realities*

We weren't done.

I've always felt as if there were two voices inside of me. One was the voice of a scientist. The other, the voice of a wizardess. The scientist looked only at the facts and figures. The wizardess cast opinions based on gut feelings. The scientist relied on proof. The wizardess thrived on intuition. The scientist lived in my head. The wizardess lived in my heart and in my stomach. I valued input from both, even when they provided conflicting information.

Which was exactly the kind of information these voices gave me when I decided that we were done. The scientist fed me a lot of data, listing the facts about everything we'd tried and everything we'd accomplished. All the while, the wizardess had been giving me that sinking gut feeling. This feeling was her way of saying, "Don't buy it. You two have plenty of issues. I may not be able to list them all for you as Ms. Scientist can, but you're not done."

The sinking feeling continued for a week or so, but I did my best to ignore it.

I moved the pile of self-help books off my desk, inserting them neatly one by one into the bookshelf. I emailed a couple of close friends and told them that my marriage was healed. When one emailed back asking, "Can you really fix a marriage in two months?" I thought, "What does he know? He's not married."

We celebrated The Project's end by going out to dinner. During dinner, Mark took Kaarina to the bathroom, rather than suggesting that I do it, even though he still had a slice of pizza on his plate. The scientist whispered, "See, he's such a good husband now." When Mark encouraged her to sit on his lap most of the meal so I could have my hands free to slice up the chicken on my salad, the scientist said, "You go girl! Look at how far this man has come." All the way home in the car, she teased the wizardess, "See, he's a complete doll. He's fixed. I declare this marriage cured."

Then we arrived home. Mark walked to the computer and got lost in the Internet. I walked to the kitchen to unload the dishwasher. Kaarina followed me.

"Mama, can I watch a movie?" she asked.

Every bit of my being wanted to crawl into bed. I looked at her round brown eyes and her pink porcelain skin. Either I could either find the energy to help her put together jigsaw puzzles, paint pictures, or play hide and seek, or I could let her watch a movie. I was well aware of the research on kids and TV. I knew the more they watched, the higher their risk of developing behavior and attention problems. She had already reached the day's TV quota.

But I was so tired.

But I didn't want to give her attention deficit disorder.

But I was so tired.

"One day of too much TV isn't going to ruin this child for life," I thought. That was the scientist speaking. Or was it the wizardess? Sometimes I wasn't sure who was who.

It was definitely the wizardess who spoke next. She spoke with a tense feeling in my gut and hardness in my heart. She said, "If your husband wasn't lost on the Internet, he could play with her, and she wouldn't want to be in front of the TV." I ignored the wizardess. After all, I'd sided with the scientist regarding my marriage. It was cured. I had no issues with my husband. We were swimming in wedded bliss.

I couldn't shake her, though. "Don't you feel resentful?" the wizardess persisted.

"Let it go already," I told her.

I could have tapped Mark on the shoulder. I could have explained how god-awful tired I felt. I could have asked him to pull himself away from the sounds of BMW exhaust systems that were, for some reason, broadcasting their way out of the computer. I could have suggested he entertain our daughter for a while.

It seemed so much easier to just let her watch TV.

"What do you want to watch, honey?" I asked.

She chose a movie on a VCR tape. To get the VCR to work, I needed to unplug a few cables from the DVD player and insert them into the VCR. I crawled behind the TV and attempted to do just that. I'm somewhat technologically challenged. I'll admit that. Unplugging one color-coded cable from the DVD player and inserting it into the same colored spot on the VCR probably isn't difficult for most people, but it is for me. As soon as I'd unplugged the cable, I ran into problems. Was red for "video out"? Was yellow for "audio in"? Did I need to plug something into audio in or audio out or both?

Mark asked, "Do you need some help?"

I said, "Yes."

I handed him the cords.

"Where did you get these?"

"From the DVD player."

"I know, but where? What holes did you unplug them from?"

"I don't remember; that's the problem."

He spoke slowly, as if I was a kindergartener who was learning to tie her shoes. "Do you want me to show you how to do it?"

"No, I really don't. I want you to do it."

Did I say I was tired? He could give me the world's best lesson on how to switch cables from the VCR to the DVD player, and I'd forget it as soon as I walked into the next room. Why bother? I mean, seriously. He could teach me how to switch the cables about as easily as he could get me to memorize the Periodic Table. It was a complete waste of his time. Perhaps I should have told him this, though, so he would understand why I didn't want the lesson.

The phone was blinking. Someone had called while we were at dinner. I dialed into voice mail. I heard my mother's voice asking about Kaarina's well-being. Kaarina had been sick with one ailment or another for the past few weeks, and Mom had been threatening to drive to Emmaus and take the girl to the doctor. I sighed. I dialed Mom's number. She answered. I explained that Kaarina's health had dramatically improved. As I convinced her that our daughter didn't need to go to the emergency room, I could hear sounds of discontent coming from just a few feet away. Kaarina was repeatedly saying, "I want to watch my video," and Mark was repeatedly saying, "I'm trying to fix the VCR so you can watch your video." Both were saying the same line over and over, progressively louder. I heard, "If you don't stop asking me about your video, I'm going to put it in toy jail and you're going to go to your room."

I hung up. I'd cracked enough times to know that Mark was close.

"Hey sweet pea, you want to help me make popcorn?" I purred.

"Yeah!" she said.

"Well, let's go."

She ran into the kitchen. She stood on a chair, and I handed her the popcorn bag. She put it in the microwave. When it finished, I put the popcorn in a small bowl, made her a juice, and walked back to the room. I settled her into the La-Z-Boy with the popcorn and juice.

"I don't know what you did to this, but now it doesn't work," Mark said in that that condescending voice of his.

Did he really think that I'd sabotaged the VCR just to torment him? Really?

The scientist was chattering away, "This is an anomaly. He hardly talks to you like this anymore. He's just frustrated. He doesn't mean anything by it. Plus, if you were in his situation, back there behind the TV, you'd be saying much worse." She had a point. If I were still back there behind the TV, our daughter would have just learned at least three new words that would get her into trouble when she repeated them at preschool.

A few minutes later, Mark pulled out a tape that Kaarina had inserted backwards while I'd been behind the TV trying to plug in the right cables. Mark turned the tape around, reinserted it, and the movie started. Kaarina became mesmerized with the tape, and we walked into the kitchen.

I asked, smiling, "Do you understand what just happened?"

"What happened?"

"You blamed me. Do you remember when we talked about how that bothers me?"

"No, I don't. While we're talking about what happened in there, it needs to be said that you left me hanging," he said, flatly.

"I left *you* hanging?" My muscles were tense, my face hot, and my throat tight.

"Yes, you did. If you hadn't unplugged the cables, I would have been able to figure out what to do with them."

I thought, "Why does he have to be so difficult?" (Actually, my true thought was much, much worse, but my editor asked me to keep the real one to myself.) But I said, "If *you* hadn't been at *my* computer, I wouldn't have unplugged the cables because *you* would have done it." I said this a bit more loudly than I probably needed for him to actually hear the words, considering the fact that he was standing right in front of me.

"Can we just establish that you should not have been on the phone?" His words were slow, his voice monotone, his gaze that of a snarling pit-bull.

"Can we establish that if you had not been on the Internet, she would not have put the tape in backwards because someone would have been able to pay attention to what she was doing!"

And so it continued. Me saying, "But you did this," and him shooting back, "And you did this." Me saying, "If you hadn't have done this" and him saying, "If you had only done this."

Me blaming. Him blaming. Me blaming. Him blaming.

I wanted to put an end to the blaming and I wanted to start talking like the grown-ups that we were, but a voice inside was whining, "Why do I always have to be the big person? Why can't he break us out of this cycle for once? I hate him. Our marriage is over. Why did I ever marry him in the first place?"

We stood, arms crossed, facing off. I stared at him. He stared at me. Then we parted. He walked down the steps to the basement. I finished unloading the dishwasher. I threw the flatware into the drawer. I mixed the knives in with spoons and spoons in with forks. The noise was therapeutic. It was better to make a lot of noise than to stab my husband with a butcher's knife.

I grabbed the dog's leash and, at 7:30PM in the dark and rainy drizzle, I went for a walk. During the first five or ten minutes, only one thought ran through my mind and that thought included the two unladylike curse words. I spent the next ten minutes talking to myself, reminding myself how far we'd come, reminding myself that my husband wasn't Mr. Ex, and reminding myself that he really did love me although it may not always seem like it. I promised myself that I would read up on communication techniques and that he and I would do the exercises together.

All of these thoughts, however, were continually interrupted by the curse words. Part of me wanted to calm down. The other part of me clung to the anger as if it were a life jacket.

I was still fuming when I walked by a preteen neighbor. He had carried a container of recyclables outside and dumped them onto the front lawn. He set up the recycling bins by his parents' expensive SUV and, one by one, he picked up a bottle or can, wound up his arm, and threw his fastest pitch toward the side of the SUV. Each bottle or can bounced off the side of the car before landing in the container below. I waved. He waved back. He looked as if he felt a lot better. I knew he would regret this therapy technique later, however, when his parents discovered the dinged up SUV and grounded him for the rest of his young life.

When I got home, Mark was at the computer. I sat down and tried to explain my feelings calmly. We hugged, but the tension lingered for the rest of the evening. It was there as he gave Kaarina a bath. It was there as he washed the dog. It was there as he asked me in a strained voice whether I felt like folding the clothes that were in the dryer.

Later I followed them into Kaarina's bedroom. I listened as Mark read the first book. I closed my eyes. I tried to relax, and then, finally, my wall crumbled. I touched Mark's back with the palm of my hand, and I felt a connection. Tears slid down my cheeks, washing away my anger. I did love him. I did, even if I wanted to kill him sometimes.

Later we talked about the VCR incident like normal adults. We said our sorries and we promised to work on our communication skills.

I turned to Barton Goldsmith's *Emotional Fitness for Couples*. Goldsmith told me that, despite the previous night's blowup, Mark and I were amazing communicators, at least when you compared us to the married couples he usually counseled. For instance, Goldsmith mentioned that couples that were in conflict more than 20 percent of the time usually did not stay together. There was no way we fought that much. Right?

Goldsmith also said that big arguments were a normal part of married life. He said that some arguments happened for no other rational reason than one or both partners were tired, hungry, or sick. I thought back to our argument over the stupid VCR tape. We hadn't been arguing about the VCR; we argued because we were grumpy. We'd lost a considerable amount of sleep during the previous week when Kaarina was sick. She kept us up most of one night coughing. She kept us up another night because of the stomach flu. She kept us up a third night, complaining of incessant itching from a rash.

Share the privilege of sleeping in on the weekends. He gets up early with the kids one day so you can catch up on sleep. You do it the next, so he can. That way you'll both be more rested and less likely to fight about stupid stuff.

Goldsmith even said that walking away from each other, as we did when Mark went to the basement and I went to the dishwasher, was normal and healthy. He said that it was impossible to talk rationally when we were mired in anger and blame. A cooling off period was important.

As long as we eventually calmed down, solved the problem, and apologized for anything hurtful we'd said, we could stay happily married. Solving problems was how we learned, he said, so that the next time Kaarina stuck a tape backwards into the VCR, the fight might not go on for quite so long. One of us might stop and say, "It's not the cables. The tape is in backwards, and it's no one's fault after all."

Goldsmith worried about the couples that didn't fight more than he worried about the couples that did. Backing away from difficulties—the clichéd sweeping problems under the rug—was what really caused problems, he said. That's what had happened to us when we became parents. We ignored one problem after another, hoping time would make them go away. I'd told myself, "Things will be easier when Kaarina is older. Things will be easier when the store is more established. Things will be easier when my career is more established." Things hadn't gotten easier. They'd gotten harder. Our problems had piled on top of each other until we had the problem of figuring out how to recycle our trashed marriage into something worth saving.

........................................................................................................

When in doubt, talk. It's better to say something badly than to not say anything at all.

........................................................................................................

Still, we needed to learn how to talk to one another without getting defensive. We needed to learn how to not use any of the unfair fighting styles that Goldsmith mentioned. These included the silent treatment (*I'm mad at you, but I'm not going to tell you about it. I'm going to make you guess by slamming doors and being mean to the flatware, and don't even think about trying to have sex with me right now! At the rate you're going, you'll be lucky if you manage to get laid this month. Make that this year. And when you ask me if something is wrong, I will say, "No, everything is fine."*); the heated retort (*You want me to fold the laundry? That's your job, remember?*); and bullying (*You're such a numbnut. I don't know how anyone in her right mind could be married to you. I'm packing my bags right now*).

Neither one of us bullied, but we both occasionally inflicted the silent treatment. My silences weren't so much about me saying, "I'm pissed and want you to prove you love me by guessing that I'm pissed," as much as they were about fear, about me worrying that Mark would dismiss my concerns as unimportant.

Don't let fear stop you from speaking your voice. If you stay mum, nothing will ever change. You are sick of nothing changing. That's why you are reading this book. Make something change. Ask for the change you need.

..............................................................................................................

I wasn't sure what Mark's silences were about, but he had them, too. He kept telling me that he had no issues with me and that everything about our marriage was perfect. He couldn't possibly feel that way. He just couldn't.

Our biggest communication problem, however, was the blame game. One of us blamed the other, the other person felt threatened, and the person who felt threatened blamed the original blamer right back. These arguments were generally over something pretty mundane, and they went something like this:

"You ate the last ice cream bar."

"So? You ate all of the waffles."

"At least I go to the grocery store to buy food every once in a while."

"I grocery shop."

"I do it more."

"Hurumph."

"Hurumph."

In retrospect, the blame game was comical. In the heat of the moment, it was hurtfully serious.

To break out of the blame game, Goldsmith suggested we ask ourselves questions such as, "What am I after? Am I part of the problem? Am I trying to cast blame? Is there old stuff I'm using to fuel this fire? How did this all get started? Am I just trying to win?" Those questions? I wasn't all that convinced that they were going to help us. Don't get me wrong. I would have *loved* to find a way remind myself of those questions in the middle of an argument. I had a notion, however, that, come the middle of an argument, I was much more likely to be thinking my favorite two curse words than those questions.

Just being honest here.

So I kept reading. I picked up Howard Markman's *12 Hours to a Great Marriage*. (12 Hours? I know, right? To think I thought four months might be overly optimistic.) Markman wrote about "I statements" and the "speaker-listener" technique. These were the communication tactics my parents had learned in marital therapy more than twenty years ago. The techniques seemed to make sense. I could see how my husband would feel less threatened if I said, "I feel hurt when you blame me" rather than, "You hurt me." I could see how he'd have an easier time with, "Wow, I was really in the mood for an ice cream bar, but there aren't any left" than he would with, "You ate the last ice cream bar. You're so thoughtless."

The speaker-listener technique seemed to make sense, too. One of us was supposed to speak about an issue as the other listened. When the speaker ran out of words, the listener paraphrased what the speaker had said. Then the speaker and listener switched roles. I could see how the speaker-listener technique might have circumvented the fight about the VCR. Had I been able to step back and listen to my husband, rather than ignoring his every word as I formulated my comebacks, we might have actually solved the issue in just a minute or two. It might have prevented the need to ding up the flatware altogether.

It couldn't hurt to practice.

That night I explained the idea behind using "I statements" and the speaker-listener technique. I said, "For example, instead of saying 'you broke the VCR' you would say "I am frustrated because. . . ."

He finished my sentence, "You broke the VCR."

We laughed. "That's not how it works," I said smiling. "You would say, "I'm frustrated because I can't fix the VCR."

We joked about I statements for a while, and then I asked, "Do you have any issues you want to talk about? We could try out the technique."

"No, I don't think so," he said.

If your first attempt at polite communication turns into a knock-down, drag-out curse-word-flying fight, try again. You don't evolve from a bad communicator to a good one overnight. It takes practice. The more you practice communicating your needs, the better you will get at it.

I didn't believe Mark about not having any issues. For instance, he seemed uneasy with me being anywhere near the washing machine. Wasn't that an issue? My wizardess voice kept prodding me. "There's something here," she kept saying. "You need to explore this."

So I turned yet again to the books and read about power struggles. Most couples had them. The Friels even listed all of the typical power struggles:

| | |
|---|---|
| We spend too much time together. | We spend too much time apart. |
| You are always late. | You always want to be on time. |
| This doesn't belong in the cabinet; it belongs in the garage. | This doesn't belong in the garage; it belongs in the cabinet. |
| The dishes should go in the washer as soon as we use them. | The dishes can wait until the morning. |
| We should talk about our feelings. | I don't do feelings. |
| I want to eat at X. | I want to eat at Y. |
| I want to watch X on TV. | I want to watch Y on TV. |
| It's okay to leave the toilet seat up. | It's not okay to leave the toilet seat up. |
| The clothes should get folded as soon as the dryer stops. | It's okay to leave clothes in the dryer until I need to use the dryer again. |

I added the last one.

According to the books, power struggles were not about power. They were about identity. If I always gave in, I lost my identity. If Mark always gave in, he lost his. If neither of us gave in, we'd fight endlessly and saying, "I gave in last time so it's your turn to give in this time" wouldn't cut it.

In our case, however, I also thought the power struggles were about power. The most common power struggle—the laundry—was Mark's issue and, for the most part, Mark had less power than I did. I was the boss of our marriage and our household. He admitted as much, and even joked about it, calling me, "El Presidente" in front of his friends and teaching our daughter that, "Mommy is number one, Daddy is number two, Kaari is number three, and Rhodes is number four." Translation: everyone must listen to Mommy. Kaari and Rhodes must listen to Daddy. Rhodes must listen to everyone.

I didn't ask for the power, and I didn't necessarily want it. The power, however, came attached to my roles as breadwinner, family financial guru, family budget maven, and family organizer. Mark should have been arguing with me about money and decision-making but, instead, he was fighting with me about the laundry.

One morning I decided to push him a little, to see if I could dig to the bottom of the dirty clothes pile.

"Could you explain why you don't want me to do the laundry?"

"You can do laundry if you want."

Was he not the same husband who, just weeks before, had requested that I never do laundry again for the rest of my living days?

"I thought you didn't want me to do laundry."

"You can do laundry if you want. Knock yourself out."

"I thought I didn't do it right. Would you like to show me how you would like me to do the laundry?"

"No, knock yourself out."

I'd learned from Goldsmith that men, more so than women, shied away from conflict. By shutting down and saying nothing, they assumed the fight wouldn't take place. This perplexed me because my husband was so good at conflict with others. Why was it so hard for him to be assertive with me?

I was stuck. I didn't know how to get past the laundry issue, and I was not confident there was something to move past. What if he was telling the truth? What if he had a change of heart and now truly didn't care whether or not I did the laundry? What if he really was okay with everything? How could I know unless he told me?

# 11

## And They Revealed Their Souls

### LATE AUGUST 2007–SEPTEMBER 2007

**"We are afraid that if people really knew us they wouldn't love us. . . .**

**And although we are afraid to reveal ourselves because of the possibility of rejection, it is only by revealing ourselves that we will ever open the possibility of truly being loved."**

—Matthew Kelly, *The Seven Levels of Intimacy*

We needed something to communicate about so we could practice our new skills. I decided to practice our new techniques as we built our intimacy.

The time had come for me to turn to Matthew Kelly and his *The Seven Levels of Intimacy*. In this book I read that that all humans craved to be known, yet also feared it. Without being known, life was an incredibly lonely experience. On the other hand, allowing people to know us involved vulnerability. To be known we must reveal our opinions, our feelings, our dreams, our values, and our deepest desires. We must have the courage to be transparent and real.

In Markman's book, I found a set of questions that were designed to encourage us to share those opinions, feelings, dreams and values that Kelly said were all so important.

I copied them down on a pad of paper, and then I asked Mark if he had some time to answer some questions.

"Sure, but I was planning on meeting Dave at The Farmhouse. Will it take long?"

"No, I don't think so."

"Okay, shoot."

"What is the purpose of life?" I asked.

"Beer," he said.

"Come on," I said, "Give me a real answer."

"That is a real answer," he said.

"You're joking and you know it," I said.

"Then I change my answer to, 'I don't know.'"

I moved onto another question.

"Do you feel marriage is forever? Is it until death do us part?"

"Yes," he said.

"Is there anything I could do that would cause you to give up on me?"

"You could have an affair."

"That's fair," I said.

"I don't know, maybe I wouldn't give up on you."

"Do you want to know what I think?"

"Sure," he said.

"If you had an affair, our marriage would be over."

He scooted closer to the edge of his chair. His hands were on his thighs. He was drumming his fingers.

"Are you in a hurry?" I asked.

"No," he said.

"You look as if you are."

"I wasn't prepared to talk about this tonight," he said. "You're interrogating me."

"I'm just trying to get to know you better. I want to feel closer to you."

"You're interrogating me."

"I didn't know you wanted to go out tonight."

"I didn't know you wanted to interrogate me tonight."

"I just want to work on our marriage," I said. "I want things to be better."

"So do I," he said.

"Why aren't you trying?" I asked.

"I am trying. I wasn't prepared to try tonight, though," he said.

I saw Kaarina standing in the doorway between the kitchen and the sunroom.

"Mommy, will you tuck me in again?" she asked.

"Yes, honey," I said, and I led her back to her room. I snuggled her into her bed. I spread her blanket over her. I kissed her on the head, and I walked into the hallway. I stood there, motionless, thinking. I didn't know where to go with our conversation. I was frustrated. I was disappointed. I thought about the "I messages" and the speaker listener technique. Weren't all of these techniques pointless? No wonder marital therapy failed for so many couples. Were "I statements" the best thing these therapists could come up with?

Mark was obviously tired of working on our marriage. He was tired of the role-playing, the technique practicing, and the deep, heartfelt conversations. Truth be told, so was I. I'd wanted to have tonight's conversation only because one of the books had suggested it. I wasn't sure it would bring us closer. If I didn't believe in it, how could I convince him that it was vitally important to talk about these questions? I didn't want him here if he didn't want to be here. I was also thinking about something the Friels had talked about: "Healthy adults know that they can't make someone else have a relationship at a deeper level than the other person is capable of having."

"Maybe this is as good as it's going to get," I thought.

I walked to the sunroom. Apparently he'd been thinking, too.

"Do you still want to talk?" he asked tenderly.

"Not if you don't want to be here," I said.

"Can we do it another night?" he asked.

"Yes," I said. "But I want you to answer the questions thoughtfully. This isn't a joke."

"I will. How about Monday night?" he asked.

"Monday sounds great," I said.

He hugged me. I hugged him back. It was a long and gentle hug. We stood motionless for a while and then he wrapped his arms more tightly around me, lifting me off the ground. He brought his face to mine and kissed me.

"I love you," he said.

"I love you, too," I said.

---

When you tell your husband, "I'm fine," he thinks you're fine. When you say, "We need to talk," he thinks, "Crap, I'm in the doghouse," even if you really just want to talk.

---

On Monday evening we sat in the sunroom for the official intimacy discussion.

"Are you ready?" I asked.

"Yes," he said.

I asked, "What's the purpose of life?"

"To have fun."

"Are you serious, or are you joking?"

"No, I'm serious. Life is about having fun."

"Do you want to know what I think about my life purpose?" I asked.

"Yes."

"It's about achieving my potential. It's about being the best mom, the best wife, and the best writer I can be. It's about pushing myself to be more than I would normally be if I didn't push myself."

Silence.

His facial expression offered not one hint as to whether or not he had been listening. In fact, I was fairly certain he was giving me his church face.

"Are you paying attention?"

"Yes, of course."

"What did I just say?"

"That you want to be the best that you can be."

"What do you think of what I said?" I asked.

"It sounds good. I would agree with that purpose," he said.

We talked about what it meant to be responsible. We talked about what it meant to be respectful.

"What do you think happens when we die?" I asked.

"Nothing," he said.

"You think we decompose, get eaten by maggots, and turn back into carbon?" I asked.

"Yes," he said.

"Do you want to know what I think?" I asked.

"Yes," he said.

"I don't believe in hell, and it's hard to believe in a heaven up in the clouds where angels are playing harps, but I do believe something happens. I don't believe our time on Earth is the only time we have. We all have more in us than just a physical body. When we die, I think our collective energy melds together. The Hindus believe something like that, that everyone's soul joins into one huge soul. Maybe we're all a part of the same cosmic energy. We're separate physically during life, but we join back together after death."

We continued to talk. We talked about the household tasks, about who did what, and about whether one of us did more than the other. We talked about how I probably did more, but that, if he did more, he'd spend less time with Kaarina.

We talked about feelings.

"Are you uncomfortable talking about your feelings?"

"Yes," he said.

"Why?" I asked.

"I don't know. I just am," he said. "Guys don't do feelings."

Months ago, I would have given him a list of reasons why he should talk about his feelings. I'd changed. I'd changed because I now knew that he might actually be telling the truth. In Dr. Goldsmith's book, I'd read, "Emotions are scary to men. Much of the time, many men don't even know what or how they are feeling." I'd read that women's brains could think and feel simultaneously. Men, on the other hand, couldn't multi-task thinking with feeling. They could do one or the other, but not both at the same time.

I didn't think these generalizations were true for all men and all women. I was sure there were men who were great about communicating their feelings, and women who weren't. I did, however, think that the generalizations were true for us, which was why I believed my husband when he said, "Guys don't do feelings."

"Is it because you worry I'll reject you if you tell me about them?" I asked.

"No," he said. "I just don't like talking about them. I'm a Finn, remember?"

"That's no excuse," I said, smiling.

"Finns don't have emotions or feelings," he said. "Finns aren't big on talking about anything. Google 'Finland and feelings.' You'll find studies that show that Finns don't have feelings."[14]

---

[14] I did, in fact, Google "Finns and feelings." I found a site about Finnish customs that quoted the following Finnish proverb, "Take a man by his words and a bull by its horns." Because Finns take all words seriously and literally—with "we must have lunch some time" literally meaning "let's schedule a lunch date"—Finns generally refrain from small talk. I also learned that Finns make better listeners than talkers, and that silence is considered a part of communication. I could find nothing, however, about Finns not talking about their feelings. This is what I think of my husband's theory about his heritage being the cause of his inability to talk about his feelings: hogwash.

"Okay, you win," I said, laughing.

We talked about dedication. We talked about the difference between being dedicated to one another because we *wanted* to be rather than because we *had* to be. We talked about the importance of continuing to work on our marriage, so that we would continue to want to be together, rather than relying on the legal document that held us together.

I read him some passages from *The Seven Levels of Intimacy*.

I read the sentence, "Our essential purpose is to become the best version of ourselves. "

"That's what I meant when I talked about life purpose. What do you think?"

"I like it," he said.

I read another passage: "The purpose of marriage is for two people to challenge and encourage each other to become the best version of themselves. "

"What do you think?" I asked.

"I agree with that," he said.

"So do I," I said.

We talked some about our goals and dreams, and about our "best versions."

I read, "We are afraid to be ourselves. We are afraid that if people really knew us, they wouldn't love us."

"Read that again," he said. I did.

"What do you think?" I asked.

"I don't know. What do you think?"

"Life isn't worth living unless you let people know you. Friends are not really friends unless they know you."

"Yes, that's true," he said.

"Do you really know me?" I asked.

"I think so," he said.

"Do you really know me?" he asked.

"I think so," I said.

"Now here's where it gets interesting," I said.

I kept reading: "Once we fool ourselves into believing we know a person, we stop discovering that person."

"Do you like that?" I asked.

"I think so," he said. "What do you think?"

"We are constantly growing and changing. If you allow your view of a person to get stuck in the past, you eventually are disappointed in the future when your expectation of someone is different from your belief of who they are."

"Yes," he said.

"Will you promise me that you will continually work on knowing me? Promise that you will never stop trying, that you will never decide that there is nothing left to know."

"I promise," he said.

"I promise, too," I said.

"I don't know where to go from here," I said. "I've read all of the books. There's nothing else to do. Do you think we're done?"

"Yes," he said.

"On a scale of 1 to 10, where you would put our marriage?" I asked.

"An eight," he said.

"Four months ago, where would you have put it?" I asked.

"A six," he said. "What about you?"

"I agree with the eight. I don't agree with a six for four months ago. I would say we were a two."

"Things were that bad?"

"Yes," I said. "But they are so much better."

"Yes," he said.

"Will you promise me that you will keep working on it? Will you promise that you will take the initiative, that it won't always just be me reading the books and trying to figure out how to make things better?"

"Yes," he said.

"I'd like to do something symbolic to celebrate. What do you think about renewing our vows?" I asked.

"That's a great idea," he said.

The vows were already in my head. I just needed to type them.

*I will strive to continue to get to know you better.*

*I will strive to challenge, support, and nurture you to become the best version of yourself, whatever your definition of that is.*

*I will strive to help you become the person you wish to become.*

*When you act inconsistently with your beliefs, dreams, or values, I will strive to point it out, but I will not stop loving you.*

*When I feel hurt by your actions or inactions, I will tell you, and then I will forgive you.*

*When my actions or inactions hurt you, I will own up to my shortcomings, apologize, and strive not to do it again.*

*I will strive to see you as a mystery to be accepted and experienced, rather than a problem to be solved.*

*I will strive to love and accept you for the person you are, and the person you want to become.*

*I will strive to be your partner when you need companionship and to step back when you need solitude.*

*I will strive to sacrifice my time and energy, especially when it means that those sacrifices will move us closer to common life goals and dreams.*

*I will strive to accept every part of you that is different from me.*

*I will strive to enjoy your opinions, even when I don't share them.*

*I will strive to give selflessly.*

*I will strive to receive guiltlessly.*

*When you need to talk, I will strive to listen to you with rapt attention.*

*When you need to reveal your feelings or deepest darkest secrets, I will strive to make you feel safe, loved, and accepted.*

*I will strive to have the courage to share every part of my self with you that is worth sharing.*

*I will strive to have the vulnerability to allow you to see me for the person I am, even if that person is far from perfect.*

*When we argue, I will strive to give up my urge to win or get even, and instead focus on listening to your view and solving the problem.*

*I will strive, on a daily basis, to do what it takes to enrich our marriage.*

*I will strive to stay committed, no matter how bad things may get.*

I printed the vows and asked Mark to read them. "Let me know if you want to delete, change, or add any," I said, as I handed him the print-out and a pen. He read.

"These are good, Momma. Did you come up with them all by yourself?"

"I got a few ideas from the marriage books. They didn't suggest them as vows. They suggested them as advice," I said.

"They're good," he said again.

"Do you want to renew them next Friday at The Farmhouse?" I asked. "Next Friday Kaarina is at Parents Night Out, so we have a night to ourselves."

"Let's do it."

A week later I was waiting for Mark to get home from work. His business partner, who usually closed on Friday nights, had somewhere important to be. I wondered if it was as important as Mark renewing his marriage vows. I somehow doubted it. I also somehow doubted that Mark had mentioned that he would be renewing his vows. If Mark would have only explained the situation, I was sure his business partner would have closed the store. I was sure of it.

But I knew Mark. He would rather sit through another Lilith Fair with me than tell his business partner that he was renewing his vows. Talking about vows fell into the same territory as talking about feelings, and talking about feelings with another guy was even worse than talking about them with your wife. I got that.

So I was puttering around the house, trying very hard not to become annoyed with my husband on the night I promised to marry him all over again. Our reservation was at 7:30PM. I looked at my watch. It was 7:20.

I was dressed. I was made up. My hair was done. I printed out the vows. I put them in my purse along with a miniature flashlight and headlamp. It was apparent to me that Mark would be late enough that we would be reading our vows outdoors in the dark. I sat on the patio and waited.

I closed my eyes. I listened to the cicadas. I felt the warm breeze over my face. I breathed. I focused on the sensations of breathing.

I looked at my watch.

"Stop it," I told myself. I closed my eyes and returned to calm.

I looked at my watch.

"Stop it," I told myself.

I spent the next three minutes alternating between calm breathing and checking my watch.

7:30PM

7:35PM

7:40PM

Why had he ridden his bike to work rather than take a car? Why hadn't he brought a nice outfit to work with him so he could change and have me pick him up? Why hadn't he planned ahead?

"It's not in his nature," I told myself. "I'm the one who plans ahead. I'm the one with the flashlight in my handbag."

I finally relaxed and, as I did so, I thought about how far we'd come in four short months. I thought about an outdoor party we'd attended recently, one during which Mark endlessly played games with Kaarina. He'd never once asked me to take over the job of parenting. After I apologized for not sharing the parenting, he said, "You've been the parent all day long. You don't need to do it at night, too." Four months ago? I would have chased Kaarina around all night and, when I'd finally become too exhausted to do it any longer, I wouldn't have been able to find him to suggest we might think about going home.

Recently when he was out of town on business, he called from the airport to explain that he'd been bumped and would not arrive at his destination until after bedtime. "I'll call as soon as I get there to tell Kaarina good night," he said. He called every night at 8:30PM during that business trip just to wish his daughter a good night. Four months ago? He wouldn't have called once.

I thought about the day I suffered an allergic reaction to something I'd eaten. I called him, and he immediately left work, drove home, gathered me and Kaarina, and chauffeured us to the ER. After he dropped Kaarina off at school, he'd driven back to the ER. He sat with me during the long boring hours that I was under "observation." When I downplayed my symptoms to the ER physician, saying, "The swelling is already going away. I'm not sure I need to be here," he calmly told the doctor, "Her lips and eyes are a lot more swollen than usual." He found me magazines to read. He turned on the TV and found the remote for me. He searched the ER for blankets when I'd complained of feeling cold. When I mentioned that I was fine and that he should go back to work, he said nothing. He'd stayed. Four months ago? He would have dropped me off at the ER door and asked me to call when I was ready for him to pick me up.

I thought about a party we'd attended a few weeks before. A friend had commented, "He's so good with her," as she watched Mark play with Kaarina in the pool. The thought, "Are you talking about *my* husband?" had floated through my brain, but I managed not to say it out loud. He'd changed so much in such a short period of time that it was hard for me to get used to the new him.

I really did love him, even if he was an always-late slacker.

At 7:45PM I saw him. He was riding fast. He turned the corner and rode up the driveway.

We got to The Farmhouse shortly before 8. Mark gave me his arm. He opened the door. We were greeted by Chef Michael who showed us to our table in the bar, just a few feet away from where we first met.

We savored heirloom tomato salads, lamb (for Mark), salmon (for me), and cobbler (for both of us.) During dessert, the man sitting behind us answered his cell with a loud, "Yell-low!" I gathered from his conversation that his kids were acting up and the sitter had had enough. As the man talked, my husband's body stiffened. His eyes rolled, and he sighed loudly. I rubbed his arm with my fingertips and said, "I love that I know what you are thinking, even when you don't say anything." He was thinking that the guy was a rude jerk for sitting at the table and talking on his phone, rather than excusing himself and having the conversation outside.

Eight years of marriage was worth something. We could, at times, read one another's minds.

We finished our meal, paid the bill, said our good-byes, and walked outside toward the adjacent golf course. We climbed a small hill and sat in the dewy grass. I pulled the vows and the small flashlight from my purse.

"I'll read a line and then you read it," I said.

I read, "I will strive to continue to get to know you better."

I waited for him to read the same line. He didn't.

"It's your turn," I said.

"I thought you would read them all, and then I would read them all," he said.

"I thought I would read one vow, and then you would read the same vow, and then we'd move onto the next one."

"You should read them all, and then I'll read them all," he said.

"No, one at a time," I said.

Were we seriously locked in a power struggle about the best way to read our vows? Was this really happening?

"How about we read them together," he said.

"Yes, let's do that," I said.

We came to the last vow, "I will strive to stay committed, no matter how bad things may get."

"Maybe we should have ended on a more positive one," he said.

"Maybe," I said, "But isn't that what it's all about? Things could get horrifically bad. I could be diagnosed with something like Huntington's Disease and get so crotchety that I throw my food at you and call you all of the bad names I've ever learned. That's the 'worse' part of for better or worse."

"Let's not go there," he said.

We stood. We hugged. He squeezed me.

"You are squeezing the stuffing out of me," I said.

"I know," he said.

I brushed my lips against his shirt and I whispered, "I can get you to release if I want." He released. We kissed.

We held hands as we walked to the car, walking with the belief that our marriage would endure. It would do so even after we'd lost our hair, our teeth, our looks, our tight, young bodies, and even our short-term memories. It would do so because, no matter what, we'd keep trying. The Project had forced us to try everything, and I now knew that it was in the trying that we'd found the happiness.

# 12

## As a Result, They Lived Happily Ever After (Most of the Time, Anyway)

### SEPTEMBER 2007–SEPTEMBER 2008

**"You come to love not by finding the perfect person, but by seeing an imperfect person perfectly."**

—Sam Keen

If I'd ended this book at the vows, I would probably have left you thinking, "Fat chance that marriage is gonna last." That's precisely what one of my very close friends told me after she'd read an early draft of the book that ended right there.

So, thanks to her, you still have more to read. Thanks to her? You're not only going to read about what took place during the year after The Project (this chapter), you'll also get the chance to find out what transpired the year after (the Epilogue).

Truth be told, my friend was probably not the only person who doubted the effectiveness of The Project. Had I asked people to take bets on the longevity of my marriage in September 2007, I'm not sure anyone would have put money on us staying together.

Together we stayed, and we accomplished this feat because we never stopped working on our marriage. The official Project might have ended in September 2007, but an unofficial one continued on indefinitely.

It continued with me speaking up for myself over and over again. I asked a lot from Mark in 2007 and beyond. I asked him to cut back his work hours and to stay home on nights he would have preferred to go out. I asked him to eat at home with Kaarina and me, rather than at the local pizza place he preferred, regardless of whether he was in the mood for left-overs. I asked him to leave parties earlier than he wanted. I asked and I asked and I asked, and every time I did so, the asking got a little easier. I didn't feel as guilty, and he didn't seem as threatened.

He didn't always provide me with an immediate loving response and I didn't always use the best communication tactics, but we somehow managed to continually bring our marriage to a better place. One late spring afternoon in 2008, for example, I found myself glancing at my watch repeatedly, counting down the minutes and seconds until he arrived home from work. I'd exhausted my reservoir of creative and physical energy. What else could I possibly do to entertain my kid? I was tapped. I was bored. I was exhausted.

When he arrived home, he found me lying on my back in the grass, my forearm over my eyes. Kaarina was sitting on my belly.

"Can I go for a mountain bike ride?" he asked.

I moved my arm, opened my eyes and searched his face for a hint. He had to be joking.

"No," I said. I thought of telling him all of the reasons why I didn't want him to go mountain biking. I thought of explaining that Sunday after-noon was not his scheduled time away from family. I considered explaining that I'd been lying in the grass for the past fifteen minutes, waiting for him to arrive home. I left it at no, and he walked away.

Later, I sat in a chair on the patio, closed my eyes, and felt a hint of relaxation creep into my body. "What, do you want to take a nap or something?" he asked, in that voice he knew I hated to hear.

I opened my eyes. "What's your problem? You don't need to talk to me like that."

"I gave up my ride because you didn't want me to go and now you're just sitting there doing nothing. I worked hard all day. I just wanted to come home and ride my bike and you wouldn't let me, and I don't understand why."

Images raced through my mind of him very happily doing nothing. While I cooked dinner and entertained Kaarina, I saw him watching TV, reading the newspaper, and surfing the Internet. Was it a crime for a mother to simply relax in a chair out on her patio for a few moments and enjoy the last warmth of sunshine? Was I so wrong to tell him that he couldn't go on his ride? Should I reconsider? Guilt and anger wrestled inside me.

The anger prevailed. "What do you think I've been doing all day? You think it's so easy entertaining a three-year-old for hours and hours? Do you think I have endless amounts of energy? Did it ever occur to you that I might need a break? Did it even enter your mind that I might want to go for a walk or run, read a book, or just have five minutes to myself? Have you even noticed that I've been so busy with mothering and work that I haven't showered in two days? You're irritated that you don't have four spare hours to ride your bike, and here I don't have ten spare minutes to take a fucking shower."[15]

"Alisa," he said sternly, tilting his head toward Kaarina.

I walked into the house, away from him. My anger intensified. In my mind, I asked him to leave and never come back. In my mind, I moved to Delaware to live with my parents. In my mind, I heard a voice asking, "Are

---

[15] My editor is not a fan of that word. I'm guessing you might not be either. Most people aren't. That's why, on my editor's advice, I've written around it several times in this book. In this one instance, though, I thought it helped to show just how angry I was in that moment. I also could not find a way to write around it. I apologize if I've just made you incredibly uncomfortable.

you really going to divorce him over a snippy comment? He's just in a bad mood, and this is how he is. He's a grumpy human being. You know this. Just the other day you were thinking about how happy you were. You were thinking of how wonderful he was. This is just one fight. Talk to him."

"No, this is it," I told that voice of reason. "I hate him. I can't do this anymore. It's over. I'm sick of him talking to me like this. We've been working on our marriage for almost a year. There's a limit."

I walked back outside.

"Go," I said. He was in his bathing suit, water dripping down his body. He'd just run through the sprinkler. Kaarina was laughing as she ran through after him.

"Go where?"

"Leave." Inside, I heard a little voice whisper, "Never leave and never ask him to leave. You're not fighting fair." I told the voice, "Shut up. I'm sick of you. I don't care."

"You're mad," he said.

"I don't want you here. Leave."

"I'm not leaving," he said, crossing his arms over his chest. "I'm not going anywhere."

He walked toward me, his arms out. "Come here," he said. He wrapped his arms around me. I sobbed into his wet shoulder.

"Why do you talk to me like that? You know I hate it. You see what it does to me. Why?"

"I don't know. It just comes out sometimes. I forget how tired you are. I forget how hard this is."

I stared at him. He didn't know how tired I felt? Really? Could that possibly be? Then it occurred to me that he could not possibly understand it. He had not stayed up all night long with our infant. I had. He had not lost sleep on countless nights for the past four years. Despite how much progress we'd made in our marriage, night duty was still my duty. Our daughter still could not be placated by Daddy if Mommy was an option.

And he'd rarely spent an entire day with our daughter. I'd nearly always been around to help him.

"You know how you feel after you've been riding your bike all day long, how you just want to sit on the couch and never get back up?"

"Yeah," he said.

"That's how I feel, and I feel like that all the time."

About a week later, he went for his usual ride on a Thursday afternoon. About 10 minutes after leaving, he called me. "Hey Momma," he said, "I forgot to ask you if it would be okay for me to go on a ride. I'm sorry. I should have thought to ask you. Do you need me to come home? Do you need me tonight?"

I was stunned.

"Mark, this is when you always ride. This is your scheduled night off."

"I know, but I worked late Tuesday night and it occurred to me that maybe you might want me to stick around tonight. I should have asked. Are you sure you're not mad? I can come home."

"No, go ride. Everything's fine here," and it was. Fine really meant fine. It wasn't code for, "I wish you would drop dead."

Another time on one icy winter Sunday, I drove the hour and a half to my parent's house to retrieve Kaarina, who had spent the weekend there. After visiting with them for a couple hours, I packed Kaarina's stuff and drove the two of us back home. I called Mark when I left, telling him I'd be home in a couple hours. As I drove north, I thought about my eventual arrival. I thought about my sciatica, and that by the time I got home, my right leg would be numb from sitting for so long. I thought about the ice storm we'd just had, and how our walkway would be slick. It would be past Kaarina's bedtime. She'd fall asleep in the car. I'd have to carry her over ice with a numb leg. He was at a holiday party. "I should call him and ask him to be home," I thought. I thought about reaching for my cell phone, but ice blew off the trees and onto the car, obliterating my view for a few seconds. I wanted to keep both hands on the wheel.

"He'll be there," I told myself. "He hasn't seen her in two days. He'll want to see her. He knows about my leg. He'll be there."

When I got home, the house was dark. My heart sank. I slowly carried her in. I grabbed the phone on my way to her bedroom. I called Mark and asked him to come home. Kaarina sleepily asked me to read her a book. I did. "Where's Daddy?" she asked. "He'll be home soon," I told her.

It took him thirty minutes to ride his bike home. In that thirty minutes, as I lugged bags and blankets from the car and into the house, I lost control of my emotions. By the time he walked in the door, I can't say I provided him with the happiest of greetings. I told him I would have appreciated him being home, but my words were as hard as steel, and his "I'm sorry" didn't penetrate my armor. Later that evening, I found myself in the laundry room, with my back to the washing machine and my knees pulled into my chest. Tears slid down my cheeks. "It hurts. It hurts so bad," I sobbed. Now that I've allowed myself to love him again, the misunderstandings and disagreements are excruciating.

A couple days after that argument, I was talking to my friend Larry. He could tell I was sad.

"What's wrong?" he asked.

"Mark and I got in an argument the other night. We made up, but the sadness from it is lingering."

"What was it about?"

I told him.

"Did you tell him that you wanted him to be home?"

"No," I said, "It didn't occur to me. I assumed he knew."

"Why would he know? I wouldn't have known," Larry said.

"You really wouldn't? If you really loved a woman, you don't think you'd think to yourself while you were at that holiday party, 'She's going to be home soon. The walkway is really icy. She'll need help carrying in all of the bags. I haven't seen my daughter in a couple days. I'll leave now so I'm home when they get there.'"

"Nope," he said.

He asked, "He said he was sorry?"

"Yes," I answered.

"You're still sad?"

"Yes," I said.

"Women are so complicated."

I'm complicated. Mark's clueless. This will never change, which is why we will always fight. I've learned to accept the occasional arguments as necessary rather than fear them as an omen. Each fight shows him a vulnerable part of me. Each fight tells him, "I am not indestructible. I need you." Each fight allows us to get to know one another on a deeper, more authentic level. Each fight shows me that he is willing to do whatever I want and need. He just needs me to ask. Each fight does this even when we don't fight fair, even when we don't use some or all of our new techniques, and even when our emotions overpower our reasoned intentions. Goldsmith was right. It's better to fight than to be silent. It was the not fighting that almost ended our marriage.

We started The Project with forgiveness, with me forgiving Mark for neglecting me during early motherhood. In the months afterward, I forgave myself. I forgave myself for being an imperfect mother. It wasn't until December, a full three months after ending The Project and three and a half years after becoming a mom, that I realized that I'd suffered from post partum depression. The realization came as I was writing this book. I picked up *The Female Brain* to refresh my memory of its contents. I read a paragraph I hadn't paid much attention to during the official months of The Project.

It said, "A vulnerable woman's brain ends up hyperactive to stress and she makes too much of the stress hormone cortisol. Her startle reflex will be up, she'll be jumpy, small things will seem like enormous problems. She'll be hyper-vigilant over the baby, hyperactive, and unable to get back to sleep after feeding the baby at night. She'll be walking around all day and night jittery, as though her finger is in a light socket even though she is exhausted."

It was as if Dr. Brizendine had watched me unplug the phones from their jacks. She'd heard me tell friends that I didn't need help, that I was doing just fine. She'd felt my startle reflex, the one that fired up over and over again. She'd seen me continually slam on the brakes to avoid rear-ending cars that didn't really exist. She understood me, and that understanding allowed me to understand myself, and to forgive myself, especially for that night, that dreadful night when I'd almost shaken our baby.

The sleep deprivation, the high-pitched cries, the absolute fatigue, the pressure, the lack of support, the lack of quiet time, and the lack of appreciation had been overwhelming. The part of my brain that had stored common sense and the part of my heart that had stored compassion had been replaced with rage. The anger had lingered for years.

Mark had forgiven me as soon as I'd told him about that night. It took me more than three years to forgive myself. Some mothers could entertain a young child for an entire day without losing their minds or wearing themselves into exhaustion. I wasn't one of them. Some mothers could make it through a weekend of parenting without a break. I wasn't one of them. Some mothers liked to stay home with their children instead of work. I wasn't one of them. I have to work so I can earn money to pay the bills, but even if I had no bills to pay, I'd still work. My writing is a part of who I am, just as my husband's bike is a part of who he is. If I gave up writing to become a stay-at-home mom, a part of me would die. That I allow myself to work, have a night out, and hire babysitters as needed does not mean I do not love my daughter. It means that I love myself. I love her, but I love me more. That's not just normal. It's healthy.

After forgiveness, The Project forced us to deal with our nonexistent sex life. A year after The Project, our stats were closer to once or twice a month rather than once or twice a week, but I learned to focus on the quality and not so much on the quantity. I continued to buy and wear lingerie. I kept reading about new techniques. I even went back to Carmen and asked for the full Brazilian. I highly recommend it.

And one morning—with Kaarina at her grandparents for the weekend—Mark found my G spot. Yes, indeed, it really and truly does exist.

After sex came romance. One winter morning of that first year after The Project, I walked Kaarina out to my car to take her to preschool. I discovered that Mark had scraped the ice off my windows at 6:30AM. before riding his bike to work. Another morning, as I walked to my car, I remembered that Mark had borrowed it the night before. "It's probably completely empty. I bet it didn't occur to him to fill it up," I muttered to myself. I sat down, turned on the engine, and looked at the gas gauge. It was full.

Communication? We learned how to talk about the laundry without blame and without tension. When I bought a pair of expensive pants that required a cold, gentle cycle and to be hung dry, I asked Mark whether I should put them in with the rest of the clothes or whether I should wash them myself.

"What do they look like?" he asked. "Show them to me." I did. "I can remember," he told me. "I'll wash them."

A couple days later, as we ate dinner, he said, "Your pants are on the drying rack."

"Thanks sweetie," I told him.

One day, I asked, "Why didn't you help me when Kaarina was an infant?" His body stiffened. "I'm not trying to start a fight, sweetie. I just want to understand."

"I don't know," he said.

"Is it because I'd always been so independent? Did you think I could handle it on my own?"

"Yes, that might have been part of it," he said.

"Is it because, in the same situation, you wouldn't have needed help?" I asked.

"Maybe," he said. "Yes, I think it's both."

These explanations were probably as close to the truth as I would ever get. I also realized that it didn't matter. He was helping me now.

We ended The Project with intimacy. For Mother's Day, Kaarina spent the night with my parents and Mark and I spent the night in Philadelphia. Mark booked the hotel and made the restaurant reservations. He took me to a beer, wine, and cheese restaurant and then to a brewery and then to a bar. I yawned around 10PM. "I don't think I'm going to make it. How many places did you say you wanted to take me tonight?"

"You'll make it," he said. "Pace yourself. I'm saving the best for last."

"Which one is that?"

"It's a surprise."

Around 11PM. we were on our way to the surprise. He turned down a narrow alley.

"You see that awning down there?"

"Yes," I said.

"That's McGillin's Olde Ale House. It's the oldest bar in Philadelphia. It's been here since 1860. It's really hard to find. You have to know what you're looking for."

I heard the pride in his voice. I understood that he was showing me one of his man places and that he was giving me a rare glimpse of the Mark outside of marriage.

We walked in the door. He grabbed my hand.

"It's too loud and crowded for you, isn't it?" he asked.

"No, it's okay. I'll sit here and have a beer with you. I know you really wanted to come to this place. You've been looking forward to this."

He tugged on my hand. "Let's go. It's getting late, and you're tired," he said. In that moment, I felt as if he knew me inside and out.

It wasn't until we visited his parents in Florida in early March, though, that I knew without a doubt that I no longer wanted him dead.

One night while there, I was getting dressed for dinner at a restaurant when Mark said, "I don't feel right. Do you think I should see a doctor?"

"You never go to the doctor. You want to go to the doctor? You must feel really bad. What's wrong? You want to see a doctor? It's a Sunday."

"I feel funny. I feel like I'm going to throw up."

"Like you have a virus?"

"I'm kind of faint. I just broke out in a sweat for no reason, and I have pain behind my left shoulder blade."

His face was pale, and I saw something in his eyes that I'd only seen once before. It was fear. I thought the pain behind his shoulder probably stemmed from muscle soreness induced from riding his bike everyday during our vacation. I also thought that his nausea and dizziness were caused by the virus I'd had just a few days before. I figured the fear came from the fact that his high school friend had dropped dead just a week before of a sudden and massive heart attack.

But I didn't want to tell him to ignore it all and then have him die in the middle of dinner.

"If you think you need to see a doctor," I said, "I think you probably need to see a doctor."

"Okay," he said, "I'm going to go to the hospital. Sorry for missing dinner."

"Wait, I'll go with you," I said.

"No, stay with Kaarina. I want you to be with her. She needs you more than I do right now."

He hugged me, told me he loved me, and walked away.

I stood, my mouth open, processing what he'd just told me. By the time I snapped to and came to my senses, he was already on his way to the hospital.

During the next few hours, I called him repeatedly, always asking the same questions, "Are you okay? What's going on?"

"Yes, I'm still in the waiting room," he said the first time I called.

"Yes, they are running some tests," he said the second time I called.

"Yes, I'm waiting for test results," he said the third time I called.

Each time I asked, "What can I do for you? Do you want me to ask your mom to drive me over there?"

Each time he said, "No, I'm fine. Stay with Kaarina."

When I wasn't on the phone with him, I self-obsessed, "Is he going to be okay? Is he going to be okay? Is he going to be okay?"

Instead of the death fantasy that had pacified me just a year before, I saw a much different reality. I saw myself too distraught to write. I saw our daughter asking, "Where's Daddy? When is Daddy coming home?" and myself trying to answer that question. I couldn't bring myself to think of the funeral, but I could clearly see the lonely, empty life afterward.

Hours later, he got his test results. He was not having a heart attack. He had an electrolyte imbalance, possibly from riding his bike so much in the unfamiliar Florida heat. The hospital kept him overnight for observation.

The following morning, Kaarina and I visited him. He was wearing a blue hospital gown. His skin looked sticky, sweaty, and pale. I hugged him. "I so glad you are alright," I said. I really was.

Kaarina hugged and kissed him, and then sat on his lap.

I stroked his arm and then held his hand. I stared into his eyes. I'd never felt so happy to have him alive and in my life.

I never finished the novel. It lost its allure once I stopped wanting my husband to drop dead. Now that I wanted him alive, it just felt wrong, you know?

We finally went on our long postponed second honeymoon in August 2008. My parents agreed to watch Kaarina for a week. On my thirty-eighth birthday, we flew to St. Kitts in the Caribbean where we snorkeled, hiked, walked on the beach, relaxed, and made love five days out of seven. Toward the end of the trip I looked at him and saw a person I had not seen in a long time. I no longer saw a selfish, neglectful, blockhead[16] of a man. I saw a man who adored me. I saw a man who surreptitiously snapped photos of me. (I found them later on the digital camera). I saw the man I'd married. I saw the man I'd once dated. I saw the man with whom I'd fallen in love.

You might still wonder: What if The Project had failed? What if I had tried everything for four months and still had gotten a divorce anyway? Wouldn't it have been a colossal waste of time?

Not in the least.

I needed The Project just as much as I needed a healthier marriage. The Project taught me how to validate my feelings, how to ask for what I need, and how not to take no for an answer on the few occasions when no is truly unacceptable.

The Project helped me to become a stronger, happier, and more authentic person. If I had not learned these lessons with Mark, I would have learned them later with someone else. If I never took the time to learn them, my life would be that much less fulfilling as a result. As a friend once said, "You can work on your stuff with Mark, or you can work on

---

[16] Well, perhaps I still saw a blockhead, but now I saw an endearing blockhead, one that I loved rather than hated.

your stuff without him, but you're still going to have to work on your stuff." Yes, indeed.

We don't have a perfect marriage. We fight. There are times when we'd rather be doing anything alone than anything with each other. We have many differences. I'm a morning person. He so isn't. I'm a runner. He's a cyclist. He's a fun-loving, relaxed, live-in-the-moment person. I'm a serious, anxious, let's-save-all-we-need-for-retirement-before-we-turn-forty person.

We will always be different. He will always sleep deeply, wake up grumpy, and take life at a slow pace. That's who he is. I can't change who he is, but I can change how he acts, especially the actions that wound me deeply. Changing his behavior was much easier than I would have ever predicted. Deb was right. All men may not be clueless, but my man definitely was and still is.

# 13

## The End

SEPTEMBER 2008

**"All she had needed was the certainty of his love, and his reassurance that there was no hurry when a lifetime lay ahead of them."**

—Ian McEwan, *On Chesil Beach*

If he died tomorrow, I would write this eulogy. This is what I would say to help Kaarina, our daughter, remember her father in years to come.

*Your father was a difficult man. I do not say this out of nastiness. I tell you this because it's true. I can't think of a friend of his who would not agree. Even his mother thinks he's difficult. I'm convinced he, at times, disagreed with me for the sport of it. He did it because he was as stubborn as he was competitive.*

*But, when he really was wrong, he tended to secretly right himself. He even started folding the laundry correctly, the way I suggested. He just couldn't bring himself to tell me that he was doing it, and I didn't call attention to it, either.*

*Your father had a prickly exterior at times. I'm convinced a harsh word from him would have been enough to make a serial killer do an about-face. He never raised his voice, but he had a way of talking that could bring the biggest, strongest man to his knees.*

*Despite this, he really was a softie. He's the one who wanted the dog to sleep on* our bed instead of on the floor. He's the one who would buy you nearly anything you wanted. At night, he always covered you with the blanket that you always kicked right back off.

And he had a kind heart. He visited some of his customers because they lived alone, and he knew they were lonely. If someone was new in town, he helped them find friends and feel welcome. If anyone needed help with pretty much anything, he was always the first to volunteer. But he never wanted to be thanked, and he never wanted others to know what he'd done.

He'd hate that I told anyone, but he loved to point out the first flowers that bloomed in the spring. He would stand by the magnolia tree when it was covered with flowers, and he'd say, "Look at our tree. Do you see all of the flowers? Can you smell them?" He also didn't know a tulip from a daffodil, but he knew you and I smiled when we looked at either, especially if it was the first burst of yellow, red, or purple of the year.

Your father was a class clown. Do you know, at our wedding, he pretended to pull a pair of panties out from under my dress when he was supposed to be getting the garter? Yes, your father did that. My grandparents were watching! One April Fool's Day, when you were four, he tried to get you to tell me that you'd accidentally pooped in your bed. You didn't do it, though. I thank you for that.

Your father was so competitive. He sulked for weeks when a friend of his made an offhand comment about him being a slow bicyclist. He wasn't slow, though. Your father was proficient at every physical pursuit he tried. He was good at rock climbing. He was good at wind surfing. He was even a pretty good runner. He was a natural when it came to athletic talent.

That was a good thing, because he hated to lose. If I congratulated him for second place, he would say, "Second is the first loser." Many parents let their kids win at board games and other things. Not your father. He won at Chutes and Ladders, foot races, and air hockey. He had a winning affliction!

I thought it served him right when, after one bike race when he came in second, you looked him in the eye and asked, "Daddy, why did you lose? I wanted you to win!"

I had to sit him down, though, and explain to him that he had to let you win *every once in a while. It was only fair! It was one of the hardest lessons he ever learned. That he let you win, well, let's just say that allowed me to know that he would have done anything for you.*

*Your father made the best BBQ chicken I've ever tasted, and he knew it. He despised vinegar and any food that tasted remotely like it. I could always count on him to give me his pickles and olives.*

*He had a secret love of junk food. He let you eat foods I never would. You and your Daddy savored Cheetos, potato chips, and other junk foods whenever I turned my back, but I loved that you shared those loving moments together, even if you end up with heart disease later in life.*

*Your father loved apple strudel. He loved lamb. He loved sour beer, and he loved a good espresso.*

*He also loved his bike. If he didn't get in a ride, he was the grouchiest human being on the planet. He loved speed. He loved driving fast. He loved riding his motorcycles. He loved fear and danger. If you could get killed doing it, he loved it.*

*Most of all, though, he loved you and he loved me. He loved us more than his own life, and more than his bike. That he did.*

# Epilogue

## SEPTEMBER 2008–DECEMBER 2009

It was more than two years since The Project's end, and I was at a Buddhist meditation class. We'd just done a meditation about compassion, one that involved bringing difficult people to mind and wishing them happiness.

Afterward, someone said, "I think it's hardest to do this with our spouses. They are the most difficult people to see compassionately." Everyone nodded and said, "Ain't that the truth."

Except for me. I was thinking, "Next to my daughter, my husband is the easiest person for me to wish happiness for. The easiest. Hands down."

And then I thought, "I can't believe I just thought that. Me? I'm the person who once planned her husband's funeral. I'm the one who used to snicker that anyone who claimed to love their spouse must really be lying."

Me?

Yes, me.

Yes, my husband was once the guy who blew our Babymoon savings on a ski trip. He was once the guy who went to a work party rather than celebrate my birthday with me at home with our newborn. He was once the guy who couldn't bother himself with greeting me when I walked into his store.

But now? Now he's the guy who doesn't make a single complaint about me blogging about our marriage and sex life. Not a one. He's the same guy who agreed to visit a sex therapist with me, and then accompany me on set on FOX News to talk about that experience. He's the guy who read every word of this book and only asked me to change a few sentences.

Yes, him.

He's also the guy who, when I told him I'd had a bad day and was on the verge of tears, took his fingertips and gently used them to rub my face and head—which was the perfect gesture for that moment.

Another time, after I'd announced that I might have to go on house-duty strike for a week because of an upcoming book deadline—he went to the grocery store, cleaned the house, and made a pot of chili—all while playing the role of dad, too. And for the rest of the week? Whenever I put a dish in the sink, it magically ended up in the dishwasher.

Yes, he's that guy.

He's also the guy who, after our daughter's holiday pageant, crumbled under the pressure of her fake tears and told her that, yes, she could spend the rest of the day with him instead of in school where she belonged.

That guy.

One of my friends even went so far as to say this recently, "The world needs more husbands like yours." Can you believe that?

I know. It's mind blowing. It's crazy. It's almost unbelievable.

But you can believe it because it's true. He loves me. He'd do anything for me. He loves his daughter. He'd do anything for her.

He's the best person who ever walked into my life.

Now, two years after The Project, I can more easily look back over those dark days of my marriage, and I can clearly see how things went wrong and why. I once felt jealous of that bike. I once referred to it as "the other woman." Now? I understand it. He loves riding. It's a part of his soul. For him, a life without cycling would not be a life worth living.

Just as a life without words would not be worth living for me. That's why he doesn't complain when I write about our marriage and sex life. He understands that the writing is a part of me.

I used to feel jealous of his store, too, referring to it as "the illegitimate child." Now? I finally understand why he spent so many hours there rather than at home with me and our baby. So many people had told him that the store would never work. So many people had cautioned him not to do it.

And after nearly being fired from one job and laid off from another, he could not allow that store to fail. He could not allow the naysayers to be right. He had to prove them wrong. He had to make that store a success. The stubborn competitor that he is had to win.

But he couldn't possibly balance what it took to make that store a success with what it took to be a good father and a supportive husband. There were not enough hours in the day for that. So he deluded himself into believing that everything would work out—that our love was strong enough to last through hard times and that he would never have to choose between his marriage and his store.

Sometimes I wonder if the man I once saw was merely a projection of my deluded mind. Had I been searching for his missteps, his failures, and his weaknesses? Had I interpreted his tense, stern expressions and tone of voice the wrong way? Was he really just terrified that the woman he loved had fallen out of love with him? Maybe the sincere, loving guy had always been there. Maybe he was just hidden behind my anger, my disappointment, and my depression.

I'll never know for sure. What I do know is this: I would never have been able to predict just two short years ago that my marriage could ever have gotten this good. I would never have expected to feel such a deep, unwavering, strong love for my husband. Now, whenever I allow myself to think about that funeral, tears come to my eyes and an ache comes to my heart. No, he's not allowed to die. No, not my man. No, not the one person in the world who understands me and loves me anyway.

No, not him. He's here to stay.

# SPECIAL BONUS SECTION

I don't know about you, but when I get to the end of a really good book, I'm sad. I don't want it to be over, so I end up reading every single word that's left. I even read the copyright page.

It's probably a bit presumptuous of me to assume you might feel the same way about *my* book. For all I know, you never got past the introduction. For all I know, you just left a scathing review on Amazon.com about how this was the worst book you didn't really read.[17]

On the off chance that you loved reading this book almost as much as you thought you loved your spouse on your wedding day, then I wrote this Special Bonus Section for you. I wanted you to have much more than the copyright page to savor during your final moments with *Project: Happily Ever After.*

It's my sincere hope that, by the time you come to the end of this section, every stray "How do I save my marriage like you saved yours?" question of yours will be answered. It's also my hope that you will agree that the $19.95 you spent on this book was the best $19.95 you ever spent. And, finally, it's my hope that you will feel pleasantly sated, so you can close this book and start a Project of your own.

---

[17] If you are even thinking of doing that, just know that I am the type of person who will read my Amazon book reviews and who will cry big fat girly tears at every negative statement.

# 10 Steps to Happily Ever After

Finding your Happily Ever After is a lot like tending a garden. You plant seeds. You water them. You pull out the weeds. You strain your back. You scrape up your knees. You worry about whether there's been too much sun, too much rain, or too much sun and rain. You curse when the deer eat your strawberries.

You rejoice whenever anything manages to grow.

Then you do it all over again. You do it because the one strawberry that made it is worth all of the hard work you put into growing the strawberries that didn't.

That's marriage. You work. You work harder. You work even harder. Some of your work pays off. Some of it doesn't. If you persevere, you will find that something does indeed grow. You will savor the sweetest of strawberries. Those strawberries will grow in the shape of a new and better sex life, a closer relationship, and the knowledge that you are loved, treasured, and understood.

And even if none of that happens, even if, in the end, you divorce—it will still be worth it. Your marriage project will teach you many important lessons about yourself, and it will help you to grow into a stronger and better person.

In the following pages, you'll find my best advice for making marriage work. Note this: I am not a marriage counselor or psychologist. I did not go to school for this. As a matter of fact, if you must know, I was a journalism major.

Yet, my friends and the thousands of people who visit my blog seem to think I have a gift when it comes to counseling people about their relationships. It's your prerogative whether or not you decide to take my advice. I offer it here, in the following pages, with just one desire: to share what I learned the hard way, so that others like you can learn it the easy way.

## Step 1: Find Yourself

It's easy to blame your spouse for your unhappiness, but the truth is that unhappiness is self-inflicted. It comes from within. You are in charge of your mood, your bliss, and your well-being. It's not your spouse's job to take care of you. It's your job to take care of yourself. Your spouse is here to support you in that quest.

### Use these tips to find happiness:

- Nurture yourself. Fill yourself with energy so you have energy to give to your family and friends.
- Do what you need to do to get and stay healthy. Exercise. Relax. Get enough sleep. Eat good foods. Have regular sex. Do something you love, often. Give yourself "me time" on a regular basis.
- Discover that one thing you love and do it often.
- Examine your friendships. Stay friends with people who get you and support you. Walk away from dysfunctional friendships that are based on cattiness, shallowness, and competitiveness. Forge new friendships if needed.
- Stop feeling guilty. It's impossible to be a good spouse and a good parent if you are not a good you. You come first. Marriage comes second. Kids come third. If you mix up that balance, no one is happy.
- Smile. It makes you look happy, and people are attracted to happy people. When people are attracted to you, it makes you feel good.
- Laugh. See "smile" above.
- Be okay with the times when you are unhappy. Sadness doesn't kill you. It won't last forever, either. Once you release the fear, the negative emotion won't feel nearly as uncomfortable.
- Pass it forward. Help others feel good about themselves and suddenly, you will feel good about yourself, too.
- Face your fears. Fear of failure is worse than failure itself. Have the courage to live the life of your dreams. The more you chase your

dreams, the happier you will become. The more you hide from your dreams, the sadder you will become.

- Practice the art of speaking up for yourself and asking for what you need.
- Don't stop finding yourself until you know—without a doubt—that you can be just as happy alone as you can be married. It's the knowledge that you can stand on your own two feet that will give you the courage you need to face and solve your marital problems.

**Use this reading list for more advice:**

*The Way of the Peaceful Warrior* by Dan Millman

*Finding Your Own North Star: Claiming the Life You Were Meant to Live* by Martha Beck

*Your Erroneous Zones* by Wayne W. Dyer

*168 Hours* by Laura Vanderkam

*Queen of Your Own Life* by Kathy Kinney and Cindy Ratzlaff

## Step 2: Define Your Problem

What parts of your marriage work? What parts don't? Envision your future. Imagine a perfect day in a perfect marriage. What does your spouse do? How do you interact with each other? See the sex. See the love. See the happiness. Envision it all.

Then create a plan that will take you from Point A (wanting your spouse to drop dead) to Point B (your perfect marriage).

Use these tips to start your own Marriage Project:

- When you find yourself wishing your spouse dead, don't waste mental energy feeling guilty about the thought, fantasy or emotion. Rather, spend your energy on doing something about the problem.
- Break big problems down into small ones. Take small, doable steps toward your goal.

- Embrace failure. You can't ever know whether a solution will work until you try it. When it doesn't work, learn from the journey, and change course.
- Take a leap of faith. Your mind will come up with all sorts of excuses for why you shouldn't try marital counseling, speaking up for yourself, or some other solution. Ignore those excuses. If you're already at rock bottom, how much worse could a new strategy make things? Stop doing nothing. Try something—anything.
- Believe in your future together. Without faith in your future together, you won't be able to persevere when the going gets tough, and the going will get tough many, many times.
- Be patient. It takes a lot more than a peck on the cheek to grow a frog into Prince Charming.
- Every day during your project, wake up and tell yourself, "I have chosen to stay married. Today I choose to be married." Marriage is a choice—your choice. You have the control.
- Whenever you are tempted to just give up, visit your Happily Ever After. Spend as much time as you need with the fantasy you've created. Eventually it will not be a fantasy. Eventually it will be a reality.

## Step 3: Get Your Spouse On Board

Tell your spouse how you feel. Explain what you'd like to do and why. If your spouse resists, be firm. Deliver an ultimatum if needed. Use this advice:

- Visualize the experience before doing it.
- Stay positive. Your mind will come up with all sorts of possible negative scenarios. Make sure you balance these with the more realistic, more positive scenarios.
- If you worry that you might become too emotional, write down what you want to say. Then either read from your script or ask your spouse

to read it.

- Talk to your spouse about your death fantasies. Say something like, "I am so mad at you that I gave you pancreatic cancer." From there, you can talk about your anger and disappointment and move on to what you will both do about it.
- Only give him an ultimatum if you are truly willing to end it. Don't make empty promises.
- Deliver your ultimatum when you are calm. Keep your voice even the entire time. Smile if you can.
- State why you are unhappy. Try not to blame your partner for your misery.
- Suggest a plan for change. Ask for his help.
- Designate one night a week as a "problem solving" night. Each week, talk about one problem that you'd like to solve, and invite your partner to talk about one he'd like to solve. Work together to come up with viable solutions that you can both live with. You won't need this night forever, but you will need it in the beginning. Without a designated night, it's much too easy to ignore your problems and delude yourself into thinking that they will go away by themselves.

## Step 4: Stop Fighting About Old Stuff

It feels really good to stockpile. If it didn't, none of us would do it. Every time we scratch open an old wound during a new fight, it's our way of saying, "I am better than you. It's all your fault. See? See? See!?"

But it's not all your spouse's fault. It's partly your fault, too. More important, holding onto past grudges prevents you from improving your marriage. If you stay stuck in the past, you'll never be able to create a better future.

Still, forgiveness is hard. It's really hard. I've so been there, okay? Here's how I released my grudges. I hope this will work for you, too.

- Remind yourself that you're part of the problem. Your spouse hasn't been perfect, but neither have you. When you see yourself as a person who deserves forgiveness, it's easier to see your spouse as the same type of person.
- Think of everything that has ever made you mad. Write it down. Recount it with your partner. Ask him to say, "I'm sorry."
- Meditate on it.
- Be patient. It takes time to see your spouse for who he is today and not who he was yesterday.
- Make a mental note of all of the things he is doing right, so you can remind yourself just how far he's come.
- Remember why you fell in love. If you can't remember why, keep thinking about it until you do.
- Write and exchange love letters.

## Step 5: Get Busy

If you don't want to have sex with your spouse, something is wrong. You might have a health problem that makes sex painful. In that case, see a doctor. Since you are reading this section of the book, however, I'm guessing you don't want to have sex because

1) you are no longer attracted to your spouse or

2) you can't stand your spouse. Do something about this.

Work on your marriage. You can't want to have sex with a man you don't want in your presence. Talk about what's wrong. Give it some time. Then, set a date to rekindle your sex life. As that date approaches:

- Do everything possible to feel sexy on this day. Get a bikini wax. Buy lingerie. Purchase a sexy little dress and shoes. Definitely get shoes.
- Keep working on your marriage.
- Learn how to relax. Tension is another form of horniness. If you feel corked up—like you are about to explode—learn to read that for what

it is. You need to get laid, sister.

• Have sex regularly. The more you connect with your spouse sexually, the more sexually attractive your spouse will become.

Once you've rekindled your sex life, do everything possible to keep it hot. Keep educating yourself. I highly recommend Ian Kerner's books *She Comes First* and *He Comes Next*, both of which I discovered about a year after the project ended. If you are like me and your spouse does not like to read, though, consider educational DVDs. The Sinclair Institute has a number of great ones.

Also, remember that attraction is a lot like a fire. You need to continually add fuel to keep the fire burning. In this case, fuel comes in the form of experimentation. You're used to your spouse by now. The thrill and newness has worn off. But you can recreate that thrill by experimenting in the bedroom (and outside of it, too!). Try new positions. Try new lingerie. Try new locations. Explore the world of sex toys, role-playing, and erotica. Share your sexual fantasies. If appropriate, act out your sexual fantasies. Be open-minded. Have some fun.

## Step 6: Learn How to Romance Each Other

Keep dating. Keep touching. Keep hugging. Keep saying "I love you" in your words and actions. Use this advice:

• Think back to the early days of your relationship. What did he do then that he no longer does now? Think about your friends' husbands, particularly those who are naturally romantic. How do they romance their wives? Think about the romantic men in movies and books. What do they do?

• Write it all down in a Romance Instruction Manual.

• Give this manual to your spouse. Ask him to read it.

• Whenever your husband performs an act from the manual, reward him with sex.

• Act more romantic, too. Look at him. I mean, really look at him. Have you noticed what he looks like lately? See the new haircut. Notice how he looks in certain outfits. See him. Compliment him. Touch him. Smile. Tell him, "Thank you."

## Step 7: Learn How to Talk Out Loud... But Not Too Loud

Stop asking him to read your mind. He doesn't have ESP. He never did, and he never will. Use this advice:

• Address problems sooner, not later. If you leave them unaddressed for too long, it's like trying to scrape old food remnants off dishes that have been sitting in your sink for a week.

• Don't wait for things to get easier all by themselves. That's like trying to win the lottery without buying a ticket.

• Before you confront your spouse, calm down. Go for a long run or walk. Call a friend and rant. Break a wine glass that you got as a wedding gift in the sink.

• Once you've calmed down, calmly address the issue. Tell your spouse how you feel and why you feel that way. Talk about how to prevent this problem in the future. Would you appreciate a change in behavior? For instance, do you want your spouse to not talk to you in a certain tone of voice, not make fun of you in front of your friends, or not ignore the kids?

• Talk one at a time. If needed, flip a coin to see who goes first. While one person is talking, the other is listening. Take notes if needed. Repeat back to your partner what he just said. This will force you to listen.

• Focus on solving the problem and not on making your spouse feel oh so very sorry.

• Whenever you feel the tension rising, remind yourself that your objective is not to win. This isn't a chess match. It's your marriage. Your objective is to come to a common understanding.

• If the tension is still rising, repeat this phrase over and over to yourself, "Accept defeat. Hand over the victory." And really do it. You gain more

power by surrendering than you do by conquering, but you won't
believe me until you try it and experience this power for yourself.

- When you screw up and start hurling curse words at your spouse, forgive yourself. You are a good communicator in training. Just like playing
an instrument or a sport, good communication is a skill that requires
lots of practice. Keep practicing and you'll get better at it.

## Step 8: Feel Understood

Make it your goal to know your spouse better than anyone else, and to
allow him to know you better than anyone else, too. Use this advice:

- If he doesn't want to talk about the meaning of life, let it go. You did-
n't marry Yoda. You married a man. Be thankful.
- Instead of the meaning of life, find out what he cares most about. What
are his hobbies? What are his values? What does he most fear? What
does he most love? What is his idea of a perfect day? What are his
favorite books and movies? Where does he go on the Internet? What is
his favorite food? Where in the world has he always wanted to travel?
What life dream has he always wanted to accomplish? The answers to
those questions will deepen your relationship.
- Don't make eye contact. He'll have an easier time accessing his feelings
if you are not looking at him. Talk while in the car. It's a lot less threatening for him than if you are face to face.

## Step 9: Write Your Spouse's Eulogy

As I look back on those dark days of our marriage, I can clearly see that
my funeral fantasy helped to save us. It helped me to fess up to the fact
that my marriage was in big trouble. The funeral fantasy forced me to come
up with a eulogy, and the eulogy forced me to see that my husband was
not 100 percent bad. I encourage you to write a eulogy, too. It will help
you to remember to appreciate your spouse.

- Work on it a little at a time. Your spouse probably has many years left to live. It doesn't have to be perfect until the day of the funeral.

- Try to notice what your spouse does right. He feeds the cat every day because the smell of cat food makes you want to hurl? Put it in the eulogy.

- Imagine how other people might eulogize your spouse. What positive things might they have to say?

- Finish the sentence, "If someone really knew my husband, they would know that he. . . "

- Think back over the years you've known this man. When did he make you laugh? When did he make you cry tears of joy? When did he surprise you? When did he do things that seemed counter to his personality? Put it in the eulogy.

## Step 10: Repeat as Needed

You will be tempted to stop trying. You will become complacent. You will curse the heavens, asking, "Does it really have to be this hard?" Yes, it does.

A marriage is never cured. It's a lifelong project. Get over it.

## ₂ading

, the books I read during my Marriage Project. Perhaps they
wɪ     ou, too.

- *Tn* 7 *Best Things (Happy) Couples Do* by John and Linda Friel
- *Hot Monogamy: Essential Steps to More Passionate, Intimate Lovemaking* by Patricia Love
- *Passionate Marriage: Keeping Love and Intimacy Alive in Committed Relationships* by David Schnarch
- *The Female Brain* by Louann Brizendine
- *How to Give Her Absolute Pleasure: Totally Explicit Techniques Every Woman Wants Her Man to Know* by Lou Paget
- *1001 Ways to Be Romantic* by Gregory J. P. Godek
- *The Seven Principles for Making Marriage Work* by John Gottman
- *12 Hours to a Great Marriage: A Step-by-Step Guide for Making Love Last* by Howard J. Markman et al.
- *The Great Marriage Tune-Up Book: A Proven Program for Evaluating and Renewing Your Relationship* by Jeffry H. Larson
- *The Seven Levels of Intimacy* by Matthew Kelly
- *Emotional Fitness for Couples: 10 Minutes a Day to a Better Relationship* by Barton Goldsmith
- *The New Rules of Marriage: What You Need to Know to Make Love Work* by Terrence Real

## Discussion Questions for Couples

1. On a scale of 1 (I wish my spouse would drop dead) to 10 (My spouse rocks my world), how would you rate your marriage and why?

2. Why did you fall in love with your partner?

3. What do you still love about your partner?

4. Do you have old wounds from the past that you still tend to bring up? If so, why have you not forgiven your spouse for these hurtful actions?

5. When your spouse confronts you and you are obviously in the wrong, do you apologize or do you tend to try to convince your spouse that she or he should not be mad? Why or why not?

6. How often do you think you should have sex? Is there a way to compromise so you are both sexually fulfilled?

7. What are some ways you can help each other get in the mood for sex? Talk about what turns you on in bed and what turns you off.

8. How do you define romance?

9. How would you like your partner to romance you?

Talk about what types of gifts you both prefer to receive for birthdays, anniversaries, and holidays. Talk about how you want to celebrate birthdays, anniversaries, and holidays. Talk about how to help each other remember these special occasions.

10. Are you a good listener? How can you be a better listener?

11. Do you tend to speak up when you are annoyed or do you try to get your partner to read your mind? How can your partner help you feel more comfortable voicing your feelings?

12. In what ways can you get to know each other better? Name one thing that your spouse does not know about you. Why have you kept it a secret?

13. Is there anything you are too scared to tell your partner? Why does it scare you?

14. List three things you wish your spouse did more often. Explain why each is important to you.

15. What are three things you could do every day that would allow your spouse to feel loved?

16. What are three things you need from your spouse?

17. List three ways you could enrich your marriage.

18. If you died, how would you like your spouse to memorialize you? How do you want to be remembered? How do you want your spouse to help your children to remember you?

## Discussion Questions for Book Clubs

1. The author opens with her death fantasy, one that is very elaborate and detailed. Have you ever imagined your spouse dropping dead? If so, what were the circumstances and did it make you feel guilty?

2. When the author started her marriage project, did you think it would work? Why or why not?

3. Did you think the book could possibly have a happy ending? Why or why not?

4. Do you think this story offers hope for other unhappily married couples? Why or why not?

5. Do you think all marriages can be saved? Why or why not?

6. Should unhappily married people stay together for the kids, even if their marriage is hopeless?

7. What illusions did you have about marriage years ago that you no longer have now?

8. What is your definition of "marriage"?

9. How have fairy tales, romantic comedies and other media distorted our ideas about what it takes to have a happy marriage?

10. Do you believe in the idea of soulmates?

11. Do you ever wish your partner could just read your mind?

12. Do you ever say you are "fine" when you are really pissed as all get out?

13. What is your definition of "Happily Ever After"?

14. The author writes a short fairy tale in the chapter titles. What did you think of this technique?

15. The author talks directly to the reader in a number of places. Did you find this engaging and effective or tiresome and overdone?

16. Would this book have had the same impact if the marriage had not been saved and had instead ended in divorce?

17. The author used self-help to heal her marriage rather than going to marital therapy. What do you think of this decision of hers, and is it one you think you might make for your own marriage?

## An Interview with Alisa Bowman

**Q: You planned your husband's funeral to the last detail. Why did you do this and do you feel guilty about it?**

I used to think I did it because I had a screw loose. It wasn't until I began talking about my marital problems that I realized I wasn't state hospital material. I told one friend, "I used to want my husband dead, but we've really worked on things, and I feel much better." She replied, "I've wanted to kill my husband! I have this fantasy about pushing his back up against a wall and strangling him. I just want to strangle him sometimes!"

Another friend said, "Me, too! I've just wanted to hit him so hard. What is it about husbands? Why is it that they can get us madder than anyone else? I didn't know anger until I got married."

Yet another simply said, "Been there."

These were people I'd assumed were happily married. They were women who, to the outside world, seemed to have doting husbands who were wonderful fathers. They were men who, on the surface, seemed to be madly in love with their wives. Yet they'd all had the funeral fantasy.

The funeral fantasy gave me emotional solace during a very difficult time in my life. It allowed me to see what was wrong. It allowed me to see what I wanted to change. It allowed me to yearn for more, and it allowed me to see my life without him and understand that the marriage I had was worth saving.

**Q: Your marriage was in such a dark and miserable place when you started your marital improvement project. Did you think that the project would really work?**

Truthfully? Not really. During the first few weeks of the project, I was only doing it so I could tell my friend Deb that I really had tried everything. I also wanted to give it one last-ditch effort for our daughter's sake, but I didn't have great hopes for turning things around.

I promised myself that I would continue to try as long as two things were happening:

1. My husband was trying.

2. Our marriage was improving, even if just a little bit.

Both of those things were happening throughout the marriage project, and they are still happening to this day.

## Q: When did you know that you were going to write a book about the story of your marriage?

As I was working on my marriage, I was sending very long and somewhat humorous emails to Deb, the friend who convinced me to work on my marriage. One of these emails, for instance, was about The Martini wax. Another was about the New York trip. Another was about the Relaxed Hug.

She kept emailing back telling me that she laughed until she cried. She encouraged me to send my emails—as is—to Slate.com and Salon.com. I didn't have the courage to do that at the time, though, so I continued to focus on *Fall From Grace*, the unfinished novel depicted in this book.

During the midst of the marriage project, I signed up for an essay writing class. At first I had no idea what I was going to write about. I kept thinking, "Why am I taking an essay class? My life is so boring. I don't have any interesting stories to tell."

Then I thought about those emails that Deb had encouraged me to turn into essays. I started with The Martini email. My teacher loved it. So did everyone in the class.

One day, not much later, I was walking my dog. I started thinking about how I had my husband's funeral completely planned out. I wondered, "Do other people do this?" And just like that, this line came to me, "I knew something was terribly wrong with my marriage when I planned my husband's funeral." You never saw a woman walk back to her house so fast. I sat at my computer and started typing. Before I got up from the desk, I had an entire first chapter.

## Q: You also have a marriage blog. When did that come about?

Other writers had been telling me to start a blog for a while. Nowadays, nearly every freelance writer has one. I'd resisted starting one, though, because I didn't know what I would blog about. Most freelancers write about writing, and I didn't want to do that. Then one day I had one of those "Duh, you silly person" moments and realized my blog should be about marriage. I launched ProjectHappilyEverAfter.com in October 2008.

## Q: What does your husband think about all of this?

When I told him that I wanted to write a book about our marriage project, he said, "Sure, why not?" At the time, I assumed he thought I'd never finish it. He probably figured it would just end up being one more half-written project, like the novel.

When I finished it, I asked him to read it. I was just terrified. I tried not to stare at him as he turned the pages. I thought for sure he was going to come to the end and say, "I'm sorry. I just don't feel comfortable with you doing this."

He never said that. He got to the last page and he said, "This is really good. I can see you talking about this on Oprah." I hugged him. I cried and I thanked the gods that I'd married him in the first place.

He was just as supportive about the blog. I think he could see that writing the book and the blog made me happy. They both allowed me to express myself with writing in a way that I had not been able to do before. I also felt as if I was having a direct impact on other people's lives. Not a day went by that I didn't get an email or a comment from someone who wanted to let me know how much my advice had helped. It was so gratifying and heartwarming to know that I was making a difference.

He might be clueless in some ways, but I'm sure he knew that a happier wife was more likely to want to have sex and be less likely to nag him. A happier wife was more likely to make him happy.

## Q: Are you against divorce? Do you think all couples should work on improving their marriages?

I'm not against divorce. I'm against misery. Many people stay mired in bad marriages for years, mainly because they don't have the courage to either work on their marriage or end it.

I think most couples should try to work out their differences before ending it, though. If you don't try everything, then you'll always have that nagging fear in the back of your mind, "What if my marriage could have been saved? What if I didn't try hard enough? What if I've just made the biggest mistake of my life? What if he/she really was my soulmate?" If you try marital counseling or something else, at least you'll know you gave it your all.

Not every marriage can be saved, though. Some people are not meant to stay together. There are two ways to know if you should give up on your marriage. They are:

1. Your spouse refuses to try.

2. You both try, but you make no progress. After four months, you are just as miserable as when you started.

If either or both are true, I think divorce is the best option. I don't think anyone is obligated to stay in a bad marriage, even if kids are involved. You deserve to be happy. If you need a divorce to be happy, get one.

## Q: You write about some very intimate, personal stuff. How do you approach the issue of transparency?

Many years ago, I was a very secretive person. I was also very depressed. I've since learned that I'm much happier when I keep no secrets. I have nothing to be ashamed of and nothing to be embarrassed about. I'd rather people know the real me. If they know everything about me and still like me, I know they are true friends. If I hide parts of myself from people, how will I ever truly know what they think of me? I used to worry about the effects my writing would have on my daughter, especially the sex column I write for *Sex Is* magazine. She's only five now, so I'm not sure what the future holds. I like to believe that I'm a better parent because I can talk and write about these issues openly. When she's older and it's time for that birds and the bees discussion, I know I'm not going to have any problems. For me, talking about sex is no different than talking about eating. It's something we all do.

I'm sure she'll hate that I write about my sex life when she's thirteen, but she's going to hate something about me during that time in her life anyway. Teenagers are universally embarrassed about their parents, even parents who don't write about blowjobs and bikini waxes.

My general rule about the transparency is that it has to have a point. I don't write about my sex life just to be graphic. I always make sure I have a point or that I'm trying to be helpful. It's my hope that someone can benefit from every word I write. I write to help others—to help them feel normal, to give them courage, to inspire them, to offer solutions to their problems, and yes, to make them laugh.

## The Best Marriage Advice You'll Ever Get

Not long ago, I asked the readers at ProjectHappilyEverAfter.com to send me their favorite marriage tips. What follows is the sage advice from many different married men and women—some of them long married and others newlyweds. I hope it helps.

"My grandparents help each other around the house, they talk about issues, they show genuine care for each other, they joke with each other, they love their family and make that a priority. They appear to make being married effortless, and it's for all those reasons." —Courtney Herceg

"In one of my two breakdowns during wedding planning, I was sobbing on the couch. I was just plain scared, and I said, 'What happens if we fight and get divorced?' My fiancé just looked at me like I was being silly and said, 'If we fight, we get through it and move on.' It was then that I realized that it was just as possible for people to stay together as it was to divorce. Every once in a while something silly will set my mind off and I'll get nervous about where we'll be in 20 or 30 years. I just repeat the words he's said to me since then: 'We have no idea what can happen 20 years from now. All we can do is deal with what we have today, fix what's wrong today, and hope that takes us into the future.' He's right. What's the point of worrying about the future? We can only do the best with what we're given today." —Jodie Brook

"You are two individuals, living two very individual lives, lives that your marriage is going to combine and blend. Neither of you needs to change nor give up your friends, etc. Both of you need to compromise and communicate. I have seen too many marriages split up because one person expected the other to change, or give up his or her friends, or stop doing things. I also knew none of them had been friends first, and I knew that wasn't a good foundation. I wanted the foundation of my marriage to be solid. We have always been friends, and I truly believe that's what has held us together. We talk, we love, we keep life interesting by surprising each other now and again.

And, we celebrated 19 years together this spring." —K. Maile Ka`ai

"What has helped me the most came from my Buddhist meditation practice. You learn not to react instantly but to create a little space for reflection before doing or saying whatever your worst impulse is whispering in your ear. So if I'm angry and I want to say something mean, on my best days, I remember to say to myself, 'What's my intention in saying that?' Once the intention is made clear, there's no way I can possibly say that thing. Do I really want to hurt him and prolong the fight?" —Stephanie Golden

"Always keep your promises. Once you break a promise to your spouse, it is very hard, if not impossible, to get back to the same relationship baseline that you had before. If you were promised something in a certain time frame but it didn't come to fruition, you'd be upset, wouldn't you? Yes, you would. Promises are commitments. If you promise something to your boss, you are saying that without a doubt this is going to be done. If you promise something to your spouse, you are saying, 'I love you, and because I love you, I will most certainly do this.' If you don't follow through with that promise, it feels like a piece of love is lost, and we all need all the love we can get, don't we?" —Carla Hawkins

"My mother told me to go into a marriage accepting your partner for who he or she is (good, bad, awful, or indifferent). Do not go into it expecting that you can change him, mold him, or fix him. Doing so is a formula for failure." —Adrienne Bransky

"My mother told me two very important things. One was to remember that no one person can fulfill every need that you have and you should not expect them to. You have to have other people, interests, and so on to keep you balanced and happy. The other is that sometimes the thing that you love most about a person will be the thing that will drive you crazy. When I get frustrated at my husband's need for order (which does not match me at all), I try to remember that it is also the thing that I love him for. He is stable, responsible, and can help me find things that I lost!" —Sarah

"Remember the way you talked to one another when you were first dating. Use that tone of voice now, even though you might have issues to address. It just takes a tone of voice—the wrong tone—to turn things ugly." —Sheryl Kraft

"The one thing that is working for me this time: we know what our jobs are. We each have our duties with the house, income, how the money is spent, and so on. Also now, no matter how mad I get, I don't say I want a divorce. That's a killer. I used to say it often. But that's what I learned from my parents. When the going got rough, you ran to grandma's (my mother's mother). I've also learned to just shut my mouth when I get really, really mad. I'm in no shape to talk rationally or nicely. So, I don't talk anymore until I've had time to cool down. And when I get that mad, I stay polite and don't behave like a spoiled child having a tantrum." —Kathy

"The best advice I've gotten was from a friend, who also happens to be a counselor. She said, 'Happiness in life (and marriage) is all about perspective. Often all it takes is one tiny thing to change, and your whole outlook shifts. This could be one tiny shift in your thinking, or perspective, or one tiny action on your part (or your spouse's). So when things look bleak and hopeless, remember that that one tiny thing could even take place today, and you could find yourself feeling happy and hopeful again.' I like to hang onto this when things are feeling hopeless. I have found it to be true. Not that the tiny thing makes the problems disappear, and not that it always

lasts, but it's so good to know there are tiny bits of hope along the way."
—Holly Klaassen

"Your kids will grow up and move out, but you will be with your spouse forever. I didn't receive that advice. I discovered it myself. I didn't really receive a whole lot of advice when I got married considering I was seventeen years old and everyone was placing bets on the numbers of months it would last. I've been married almost sixteen years now and have a four-teen-year-old son and a twelve-year-old son.
"I think one huge mistake couples make is engulfing themselves so completely in parenthood that they forget to still be boyfriend and girlfriend. You can't wait until the kids move out to discover each other again. By that time, it may be too late. You have to learn to (gasp!) put your marriage ahead of the kids sometimes. You have to learn to be seventeen again sometimes. Having two teenage children isn't very conducive to me being a seventeen-year-old girl. Ipso facto, children must be compartmentalized over here in this corner of my brain for an evening, not to be released until morning. It works."
 —Aimee Davis

"You cannot change your spouse. You can change yourself, which will indirectly change your spouse. It's hard to change yourself. It's hard to look inward. It's hard to get past the ego and see the raw ugly truth about yourself. You have to be patient with yourself. But once you see it, you can do something about it. And once you do something about it, everyone else around you seems to change." —Judy Armstrong

"It's very difficult to 'never go to bed mad,' especially when you're in an argument, and it's already midnight, and you have to get up for work at 6AM the next morning. It's especially difficult when you're so mad that even if you did somehow get enough nerve to say, "I'm sorry," through gritted teeth, you'd still lay awake all night regretting that you said it, because you really aren't sorry at all, and now you resent your partner. Basically, your fight has now escalated to a whole new level. The real advice should be: always sleep in the same bed, even if you're mad. This way, when you both wake up in the morning, your partner might just roll over, put his/her arm around you and say, 'I'm sorry for being poopy last night.' Then it'll be all over and done with.

"Even if your partner isn't as apologetic as I've listed above, this advice serves many other purposes.

1. Neither one of you has to be thrown out of your own bed.

2. This reduces the opportunity for slamming the door (which always makes me more angry).

3. There will be no opportunity for last words before you or your partner storm out of the room.

"If nothing else, it gives you both the time to sleep on it." —Sarabeth Geddes

"Sometimes you have to be selfish. It used to be that everything I did, I did for my husband, from cleaning up the house to folding and putting away all the laundry. I usually did it thinking that he would be appreciative and it would make his day easier. Then we hit the biggest speed bump in the world in May, which led to not knowing the fate of our marriage. After wallowing in depression for a couple months, I picked myself back up and started thinking about what I wanted for the first time in my married life. I was selfish and did what I knew I wanted to do and not what I thought he wanted me to do. You have to focus on yourself once in a while so you can be a healthy contributing partner in the marriage." —Martyna Halsey

"My best marriage advice came from my grandparents, who were also celebrating their sixtieth wedding anniversary the year I got married. When our DJ asked the wedding guests for advice from the stage, my grandpa stood up and said, 'When you're wrong, admit it. When you're right, shut up!'" —Jamie Freedom

"My 80-year-old great-grandmother sat and listened to all the advice at my wedding shower as she sipped her coffee. She never nodded in agreement and never contradicted my guests. They went on with the standard 'Don't go to bed mad', 'Don't let yourself fall apart,' 'Be sure he is sexually satisfied or he will cheat,' 'Have your own interests and hobbies,' and so on. One of my dear friends asked Little Granny what advice she had to offer. She replied, 'When he folds towels different then you do, and he will, don't criticize or refold the towels, let it go. For God's sake, he folded the towels. The towels aren't all that important.'" —Kayle

"One of my favorite quotes comes from my father. He said, 'Marriage is like housekeeping; you gotta work at it regularly, or else you end up with a huge mess.' Marriage isn't something that should happen easily. It takes work. Sometimes it takes more work than other times, but it takes work. Going into marriage realizing this will help you to keep your expectations realistic." —Martha

## Author's Note

I've tried to tell this story as truthfully as possible. I asked most of the characters described within the pages—including Mark and Mom—to read one or more drafts of the book and comment on any part they felt was not true. Mom, for instance, took offense to an earlier version of this book that quoted her telling me, "If he can get the milk for free, he will never buy the cow." She said she'd never heard such a saying before and even if she had, she'd never say it. I deleted it.

In one place, my memory of dialogue conflicted sharply with my husband's memory of the same event. I believe him to be wrong, which is why I added his version in a footnote rather than changing the dialogue to suit his memory. You can decide for yourself which version you prefer. I've added footnotes in two other places where my memory of an event differs from his.

I've used the real names of most of the characters. My past boyfriends are exceptions. They deserve their privacy. More important, my depiction of them here is both one-sided and told through the lens of my depression. They were good to me and for me in many ways, and they also had many admirable qualities that I did not describe in this book.

I'm sure I could have added many different scenes that depicted my husband's endearing nature. For instance, I could have told you about the time he stood in the rain for two hours, cheering me on as I ran laps around a park for a marathon training run. Oh, I could have written many flattering stories about him. I didn't. They would have contradicted the point I wanted to make.

Regarding the email exchange between Mark and his former boss. We no longer have copies of those emails. When my husband read my rendition of the email exchange, however, he thought it sounded very close to dead on.

I did, however, accurately quote Mark's 1996 datebook. I happened to find it in the bottom of a file cabinet as I was finishing this book.

# Acknowledgments

If it were not for my husband, this book would not have been possible. He's the epitome of the frog prince. In a short period of time, he changed from a neglectful, clueless dolt and into a doting, loving husband, and he helped me to evolve from an insecure, passive-aggressive woman into a confident wife who isn't afraid to speak her voice. He not only gave me a great story to tell, he allowed me to tell it. That takes courage. And love. And integrity. I admire him, and I love him deeply.

Mike Harriot, my literary agent, took time away from his beach vacation one summer so he could read my first stab at what eventually became this book. He was equal parts tactful and honest, letting me know that my first draft had commercial potential, but that it needed quite a bit of work. He believed in me before I believed in myself. He cheered me up when I was morose and defeated. He calmed me when I was manic. He strategized with me when I was confused and overwhelmed. He caught and fixed so, so, so many typos. If it had not been for Mike, I would have embarrassed myself by using the phrase "find the salami" in Chapter 7. As he tactfully explained, my husband and I might play "find the salami," but the rest of the world plays something called "hide the salami" instead. He has been my confidant, friend, therapist, copy editor, career coach, marriage counselor, lawyer, negotiator, and style consultant. No writer could have a better agent. I'm honored to have him represent me.

Jennifer Kasius, Craig Herman, Nicole De Jackmo and the rest of the crew at Running Press were brave enough to take a chance on me and on this book. They embraced my voice, my story, and my blog. It was love at first sight and the publishing equivalent of a marriage made in heaven.

My parents have read so many drafts of this book that they could recite it to you without notes. They allowed me to invade their privacy so I could tell this story. They dreamed with me and never stopped believing. A big thanks to the rest of my extended family for allowing me to be myself so publicly.

With one question, Deb Gordon convinced me to start the project that eventually saved my marriage and led to this book. She encouraged me throughout the writing process, sharing an early draft of this book with a couple family members and friends and reporting back that they were so engrossed they'd stayed up all night to read it. It was the thought of what this book could become that kept me writing during the times I felt most stymied.

Jennifer Kushnier, a retired book editor, not only introduced me to The Martini (how could I ever thank her enough?), she also helped me to define what I was trying to say. She scribbled notes in the margins, drew large Xs through much of the superfluous details, and convinced me to delete the not-so-charming details about my menstrual flow that had some-how crept into the first draft. Under her guidance, I deleted close to 60,000 words, and then wrote more than 60,000 more to take their place. She is a wonderful friend and talented editor. She also bakes a mean apple pie. I'm thankful for having the pleasure of knowing her.

Mary Lengle helped me envision a dream and put the pieces in place to turn that dream into my reality. She coached me through each and every media appearance. She held my hand, offered advice, made sure my bra wasn't showing, helped me with my makeup, and always made me feel like a superstar. She allowed me to believe that anything and everything was possible. So. Be. It.

Ron Doyle used his technical, artistic, creative, and literary genius to beautify my blog, create the coolest media kit any author has ever had, and even edit my demo reel.

Melissa Cassera filled out my publicity team, helping me nab my initial TV spots and, without fail, dreaming up ever-so-brilliant pitch ideas.

Tim Brownson is a hot life coach with an English accent. It's one so easy on the ears that any middle-aged woman with even a smidgen of common sense ought to pay good money to hear him talk. In just one session, he cured my fear of public speaking and of appearing on camera. He did it by telling me that the Janet Jackson moment that I most feared would be the best thing that could ever happen for my career. He's a genius.

Bill McGowan taught me how to appear on camera without looking like a lizard with a hair primping addiction.

Mariska Van Aalst spent countless unpaid hours reading my manuscript and book proposal, offering advice, and listening to me describe every detail of the process of finding a publisher. I can't thank her enough.

Thank you John and Linda Friel, Patricia Love, David Schnarch, Louann Brizendine, Lou Paget, Gregory J.P. Godek, John Gottman, Howard Markman, Jeffrey Larson, Matthew Kelly, Barton Goldsmith, and Terrence Real. Without you, I'd be divorced. My husband thanks you, too. Without you, he might very well be dead.

Thank you to Carmen Toro. If it were not for you, I would never have fallen head over heels in love with my front side.

Jerry, the manager at FedEx Kinko's, kept me company the million and one times I stopped by to print out this manuscript. He always seemed happy to see me. Someone give that man a raise, will you?

It takes a sisterhood to prevent a writer from wallowing in the dark place. I'm blessed to have found the most wonderful of friends—friends who, without fail, continually helped me to dig down and find courage whenever the fear of just how abysmally I could embarrass myself threatened to keep me from writing this book and the related blog. A special thank you goes to Rachel Weingarten, who helped me to identify my inner superpower and who saw my potential long before anyone else did. Also to Liz Reap Carlson, Michelle Hamilton and Mariska (mentioned earlier) who prayed over me during the long week I was waiting to find out whether a publisher would take on this project. Fellow blogging sisters Julie Roads, Anne Fitten Glen, Andi Fischer, Tracy O'Connor, Alexandra Grabbe,

Melanie Haiken, Roxanne Hawn, Donna Hull, Claudine Jalajas, Debbie Koenig, Sheryl Kraft, Jennifer Margulis, Melanie McMinn, Christine Gross-loh, Meredith Resnick, Brette Sember, Sarah Henry, Nancy Monson, Ruth Pennebaker, Stephanie Auteri, Stephanie Stiavetti, Kristen Gough, Vera Marie Badertscher, Kris Bordessa, Kerry Dexter, Jane Boursaw, Susan Johnston, Jesaka Long, Peggy Bourjaily and Eve Del continually spread the word about my blog and just generally made me feel awesome. My Savor the Success sisters—especially Melissa Cassera, Deena Burgess, Lynn Colwell, Payson Cooper, Andrea Howard, and Lara Galloway—kept me focused, energized, and positive. And Beth Eck, Eileen Shovlin, and Deb Cosgrove kept me from losing my mind—on more than one occasion.

And although they technically have that icky thing known as a Y chromosome, I include Sam Greengard and Nando in the sisterhood. They may or may not understand why. All of my sisters and honorary sisters seriously rock. I'm blessed to have them rooting me on.

A huge thanks goes to fellow freelance writers from the American Society of Journalists and Authors and from Freelance Success who helped to promote me and my brand.

Finally, I'd like to thank the thousands of readers and subscribers of ProjectHappilyEverAfter.com. You taught me how to be a better writer. You laughed at my jokes. You helped me to feel normal. You kept me going.

Oh, and to the universe: thanks. You know what for.